6/03

Culture and
Customs of
the Congo

Recent Titles in
Culture and Customs of Africa

Culture and Customs of Nigeria
Toyin Falola

Culture and Customs of Somalia
Mohamed Diriye Abdullahi

Culture and Customs of the Congo

∾

Tshilemalema Mukenge

Culture and Customs of Africa
Toyin Falola, Series Editor

GREENWOOD PRESS
Westport, Connecticut • London

Library of Congress Cataloging-in-Publication Data

Mukenge, Tshilemalema.
    Culture and customs of the Congo / Tshilemalema Mukenge.
       p.   cm.—(Culture and customs of Africa, ISSN 1530–8367)
    Includes bibliographical references.
    ISBN 0–313–31485–3 (alk. paper)
    1. Congo (Democratic Republic)—Social life and customs. I. Title. II. Series.
  DT649.M85   2002
  967.51—dc21   2001033692

British Library Cataloguing in Publication Data is available.

Library of Congress Catalog Card Number: 2001033692
ISBN: 0–313–31485–3
ISSN: 1530–8367

First published in 2002

Greenwood Press, 88 Post Road West, Westport, CT 06881
An imprint of Greenwood Publishing Group, Inc.
www.greenwood.com

Printed in the United States of America

The paper used in this book complies with the
Permanent Paper Standard issued by the National
Information Standards Organization (Z39.48–1984).

10 9 8 7 6 5 4 3 2 1

Contents

Series Foreword

AFRICA is a vast continent, the second largest, after Asia. It is four times the size of the United States, excluding Alaska. It is the cradle of human civilization. A diverse continent, Africa has more than fifty countries with a population of over 700 million people who speak over 1,000 languages. Ecological and cultural differences vary from one region to another. As an old continent, Africa is one of the richest in culture and customs, and its contributions to world civilization are impressive indeed.

Africans regard culture as essential to their lives and future development. Culture embodies their philosophy, worldview, behavior patterns, arts, and institutions. The books in this series intend to capture the comprehensiveness of African culture and customs, dwelling on such important aspects as religion, worldview, literature, media, art, housing, architecture, cuisine, traditional dress, gender, marriage, family, lifestyles, social customs, music, and dance.

The uses and definitions of "culture" vary, reflecting its prestigious association with civilization and social status, its restriction to attitude and behavior, its globalization, and the debates surrounding issues of tradition, modernity, and postmodernity. The participating authors have chosen a comprehensive meaning of culture while not ignoring the alternative uses of the term.

Each volume in the series focuses on a single country, and the format is uniform. The first chapter presents a historical overview, in addition to information on geography, economy, and politics. Each volume then proceeds to examine the various aspects of culture and customs. The series highlights the mechanisms for the transmission of tradition and culture across generations: the significance of orality, traditions, kinship rites, and family property distribution; the rise of print culture; and the impact of educational institutions. The series also explores the intersections between local, regional, national, and global bases for identity and social relations. While the volumes are organized nationally, they pay attention to ethnicity and language groups and the links between Africa and the wider world.

The books in the series capture the elements of continuity and change in culture and customs. Custom is not represented as static or as a museum artifact, but as a dynamic phenomenon. Furthermore, the authors recognize the current challenges to traditional wisdom, which include gender relations; the negotiation of local identities in relation to the state; the significance of struggles for power at national and local levels and their impact on cultural traditions and community-based forms of authority; and the tensions between agrarian and industrial/manufacturing/oil-based economic modes of production.

Africa is a continent of great changes, instigated mainly by Africans but also through influences from other continents. The rise of youth culture, the penetration of the global media, and the challenges to generational stability are some of the components of modern changes explored in the series. The ways in which traditional (non-Western and nonimitative) African cultural forms continue to survive and thrive, that is, how they have taken advantage of the market system to enhance their influence and reproductions also receive attention.

Through the books in this series, readers can see their own cultures in a different perspective, understand the habits of Africans, and educate themselves about the customs and cultures of other countries and people. The hope is that the readers will come to respect the cultures of others and see them not as inferior or superior to theirs, but merely as different. Africa has always been important to Europe and the United States, essentially as a source of labor, raw materials, and markets. Blacks are in Europe and the Americas as part of the African diaspora, a migration that took place primarily due to the slave trade. Recent African migrants increasingly swell their number and visibility. It is important to understand the history of the diaspora and the newer migrants, as well as the roots of the culture and customs of the places from where they come. It is equally important to understand others in order to be able to interact successfully in a world that keeps shrinking. The accessible nature of the books in this series will contribute to this understanding and enhance the quality of human interaction in a new millennium.

Toyin Falola
The University of Texas at Austin

Acknowledgments

MANY INDIVIDUALS contributed to the completion of this work. Professors Tshiunza Mbiye of the University of Kinshasa, Congo, and Tshibangu Mashinda of Morris Brown College in Atlanta, Georgia, shared with me rare sources on Congolese media and literature, respectively, which are in French and difficult to find in the United States. Many other people, too numerous to list here, shared their knowledge on various aspects of Congolese culture through interviews or documentation. They are credited by notes in the appropriate chapters. Other individuals authorized me to use photos from their family collections. Professor Makidi Ku-Ntima of Payne College, Augusta, Georgia, wrote the section on modern Congolese popular music in Chapter 8, "Music and Dance." My wife, Professor Ida Rousseau Mukenge of Morehouse College, Atlanta, Georgia, assumed the task of editing the notes, the bibliography and parts of the text. She also owns the art objects used in the illustrations. My son, Tshimpo Mukenge, a professional photographer, processed the photos. My daughters, Ndaya, Muadi and Malongo, helped in many other ways. To all I am very grateful.

Chronology

500	Formation of the group that later founded the Kuba Kingdom.
520–845	Formation of the group that later became the Luba Empire.
1275	Estimated date of the foundation of the Kingdom of Kongo by Nimi a Lukeni Ntinu Wene.
1482	The Portuguese navigator Diego Gao reaches the mouth of the Nzadi River, which later became Congo River, also called Zaire River during the Mobutu dictatorship.
1491	First Catholic missionaries arrive in the Kingdom of Kongo. Mani Kongo (King of Kongo) Nzinga Nkuwu and his court are baptized. He becomes João I Nzinga Nkuwu. The Portuguese ship the first cargo of Enslaved Africans to America. Kongo political and social structures disintegrate.
1500s	Songye immigrants found the Luba Empire under the leadership of Nkongolo Mwamba. The Portuguese establish a protectorate over the Congo. Slave trafficking settles in the Kingdom of Kongo and Angola.

1600s	The Dutch capture the ports of São Tomé and São Paulo de Loanda at the mouth of the Congo River. Italian Capuchin missionaries intensify evangelism in the Kongo Kingdom. Nyimi Woot founds the Kuba Kingdom. The Luba Immigrant Chibinda Ilunga founds the Lunda Empire.
1800s	Zande warriors from Sudan invade the northeastern region of what later became the Congo.
1815	Nabiembali founds the Mangbetu Kingdom in the northeastern region.
1816	The British explorer Turkey penetrates into the Congo River up to Yalala Falls.
1869	Msiri founds the Kingdom of Garengaze in southeastern region.
1874–1878	Henry Morton Stanley explores the Congo River from east to west down to the mouth. Slave traffickers from Zanzibar penetrate the forest zone and settle west of Lualaba.
1876	Belgian King Leopold I organizes the International Geographic Conference in Brussels out of which the African International Association will be born with the mandate to open Africa to European domination deceitfully baptized civilization.
1878	King Leopold II concludes an agreement with Stanley for the latter to negotiate submission treaties with local chiefs on behalf of the king.
1880	Catholic missionaries open the first children's school at Boma.
1882	The Bia-Franqui-Cornet geologic expedition demonstrates the existence of mineral resources in Katanga.
1883	The Congo is renamed l'Association Internationale du Congo (AIC), Congo International Association.

1884–1885	At the Berlin Conference, the AIC turns Congo Free State. King Leopold II becomes sole proprietor of the Congo. The Congo is declared open to free international commerce. The Congo Free State is divided into administrative districts overseen by commissioners.
1888	Organization of la Force Publique, the colonial army.
1889	Leopold II declares all lands presumed vacant property of the state.
1891	Intensive exploitation of ivory, rubber and natural products from state lands.
1895	Force Publique mutiny at a Luluabourg station.
1897	Compulsory cultivation of commercial crops (cocoa, cotton) for the benefit of the colonial state and companies begins.
1898	Opening of the Matadi-Leopoldville railroad.
1903–1904	In Britain, The Reform Association denounces Leopold II's abuses against the Congolese.
1904	Creation of an Inquiry Commission to investigate Congo Free State abuses (mutilations, taking hostages) associated with rubber harvesting.
1906	Belgium annexes the Congo Free State.
1908	The Congo Free State officially becomes a Belgian colony.
1911	The railroad Katanga-South Africa is established.
1913	Beginning of industrial exploitation of copper. Discovery of diamonds in Kasai.
1916	The colonial government introduces money wages for Congolese workers—a prerequisite to money taxes.
1917	Cotton cultivation is introduced in Maniema. Exploitation of Kasai diamond begins.
1920	The minister of colonies, Louis Frank, outlines a plan for restructuring chieftaincies and traditional courts and for creating administrative entities called secteurs.
1921	Development of the Kimbanguist movement in Lower Congo.

1925	Islam develops in Maniema. The Kitawala revolt movement preaches imminent departure of the White oppressor.
1928	Inauguration of the railroad Bas-Congo-Katanga.
1931	The Bapende revolt erupts following a severe deterioration of farmers' revenues.
1933–1934	Administrative restructuring of the Congo including generalization of the secteur system and creation of new provinces (Kasai and Kivu) bringing the number of provinces to six: Congo-Kasai (later Congo Leopoldville), Equateur, Kasai, Katanga, Kivu and Province Orientale.
1935	Forced labor and compulsory cultivation officially set at sixty days per year.
1939–1945	Congolese participation in the war effort under the ministry of Paul Ryckmans.
1941	First strikes of Congolese workers in Jadotville (Likasi) and Elisabethville (Lubumbashi), severely suppressed with massacres.
1942	The duration of forced labor extended to 120 days per year.
1944	Workers' revolts in Katanga and in Kasai following massive recruitments of manpower and severe deterioration of working conditions. Mutiny of the colonial army (la Force Publique) in Luluabourg (Kananga).
1948	Recognition of the workers' right to go on strike, fixation of legal minimum wages and introduction of public transportation ("fula-fula" trucks) in Kinshasa.
1950	Creation of l'Alliance des Bakongo (ABAKO).
1951	Foundation of the group Conscience Africaine (African Consciousness).
1954	Inauguration of Lovanium University in Leopoldville (Kinshasa).

1955   King Beaudouin of Belgium visits the Congo and an-
                    nounces a thirty-year plan to unite the Congo and Bel-
                    gium into one community.
                    Minister of colonies, August Buisseret, creates three
                    schools of public administration to promote gradual
                    access of Congolese to administrative posts.

1956   La Conscience Africaine rejects the Belgo-Congolese
                    Community, supports the thirty-year plan, provided
                    that the Congolese participate in the implementation
                    of the plan.
                    ABAKO critiques the plan and demands immediate
                    granting of basic liberties to the Congolese.
                    Inauguration of the state university, l'Université Offi-
                    cielle du Congo, in Elisabethville.
                    Formation of the first national soccer selection in the
                    Congo, Les Lions, which later (1966) became Les Léo-
                    pards.

1958   First municipal elections in Leopoldville and Elisabeth-
                    ville.
                    Patrice Lumumba founds le Mouvement National Con-
                    golais (MNC), which he represents at the Pan-Africanist
                    Conference in Accra, Ghana, in the same year.

1959, January 4   Popular riot irrupts in Kinshasa in protest against last
                    minute cancellation by the colonial government of a
                    political meeting convened by Joseph Kasa-Vubu, pres-
                    ident of ABAKO.
                    King Beaudouin promises to lead the Congo to inde-
                    pendence and sets general municipal elections and for-
                    mation of city councils for December.

June 23   ABAKO demands the creation of Kongo Republic.

December   Martial law instituted in Kasai to stop hostilities be-
                    tween Luba and Luluwa.
                    A coalition of ABAKO, le Parti Solidaire Africain (An-
                    toine Gizenga wing), le Mouvement National Congo-
                    lais (Albert Kalonji and Joseph Ileo wing) request the
                    organization of a round table in Brussels to discuss the
                    transition to Congo independence.

1960, January 29	Congolese delegates to the Round Table demand Patrice Lumumba liberation and participation in the conference. Congo independence is set for June 30, 1960. Provisions are made for an economic round table to be held in February.
May	Belgian parliament enacts la Loi Fondamentale (the constitution of the future Congo state). Patrice Lumumba's political party, MNC, wins the legislative election with a relative majority.
June	Joseph Kasa-Vubu becomes president of the Congo.
June 23	Patrice Lumumba is appointed prime minister.
June 30	The Congo becomes independent. Belgian cadres begin to leave. Belgian Congo becomes Congo Leopoldville.
1960, July	Revolt of the army within a week of independence instigated by Belgian officers of the former colonial Force Publique. Katanga and South Kasai announce secession from the Congo. Colonel Joseph Mobutu, army Chief of Staff, arrests prime minister Patrice Lumumba, takes over power militarily and forms a temporary government of technicians called College of Commissioners.
1961, January 17	Patrice Lumumba is murdered victim of conspiracy between Mobutu, leaders of secessionist provinces, Belgium and other western countries. Rebellion in North-Katanga.
1963–1964	Rebellions in North-Katanga, Kwilu and Kivu.
1964	Rebellious provinces are defeated with the help of mercenaries and Belgian troops. Moise Tshiombe, leader of the secessionist Katanga Province, becomes prime minister of Congo. Congo-Leopoldville is renamed République Démocratique du Congo (Democratic Republic of Congo).

| 1965 | Mobutu takes over military again, declares himself president of the Second Republic and gradually eliminates all semblances of democracy, establishing himself supreme master of the Congo. |

1965 — Mobutu takes over military again, declares himself president of the Second Republic and gradually eliminates all semblances of democracy, establishing himself supreme master of the Congo.

1966 — At Pentecost, Mobutu orders public hanging of four politicians with no apparent criminal record: Jerome Anany, Emmanuel Bamba, Evariste Kimba and Alexandre Mahamba.

1970 — MPR, Mobutu's political party, becomes the only recognized party in the country and all Congolese are declared members.

1971 — Democratic Republic of Congo is renamed Republic of Zaire.
All citizens are forced to take on authentic Congolese names in lieu of European first names.

1973–1975 — Deterioration and gradual exacerbation of economic conditions in the aftermath of nationalization of foreign-owned small businesses to the benefit of party loyalists.

1977 — Collapse on world market of copper prices, Zaire's major source of foreign currency.
Former Katanga Gendarmes exiled in Angola invade South Shaba (Shaba I) and are expelled thanks to foreign assistance (France, Morocco).

1978 — Second invasion of South-Shaba (Shaba II) by former Katanga exiles from Zambia. Once again foreign forces come to the rescue of the Mobutu regime, this time a Pan-African peace keeping force.
Purging of army commanders and execution of same and civilians allegedly having participated in a failed military plot.

1980–1988 — The economic crisis aggravates, serious political opposition to the regime surfaces, opposition leaders are arrested and Amnesty International intensifies accusations of human rights violations.

1989   Student demonstrations in Kinshasa and Lubumbashi
                result in over thirty-seven students massacred.

1990   New demonstrations both in Kinshasa and Lubumba-
                shi are met with more brutality, over 150 students mas-
                sacred by the presidential guard reportedly carrying out
                Mobutu's orders.
                New legislation authorizing political parties and trade
                unions is enacted. Oppression continues.

1991–1993   Mobutu authorizes other political parties, provoking a
                proliferation of political parties.
                Mobutu announces a national conference to elaborate
                democratic institutions, pro-democratic debates inten-
                sify.
                The economic crisis deepens, mass protests multiply,
                government repressive measures become frequent: over
                forty-two persons killed in Mbuji-Mayi in 1991, over
                thirty victims during the Christians' March in Kinshasa
                in 1992, five persons killed during civil disobedience
                campaign, and over sixty-five during army riot in Kin-
                shasa in 1993.
                The National Conference convenes intermittently.
                Several short-lived crisis governments succeed to one
                another. Tshisekedi, Mungul Diaka, Nguz Karl-I-Bond
                and Faustin Birindwa.
                National Conference changes to Sovereign National
                Conference; the latter is changed to a 453-member
                High Council of Republic.

1994–1995   Instability goes on. High officials put thirty tons of
                counterfeited Zaire currency into circulation. Economy
                sinks deeper. Mobutu abolishes the High Council of
                the Republic.
                Mobutu appoints Kengo wa Ndondo prime minister.
                The High Council of Republic resurfaces as High
                Council of Republic-Transitional Parliament (HCR-
                PT).
                More social disturbances and more killings: nine civil-
                ians gunned down by security forces in 1995.

1996–1997	Mobutu undergoes cancer treatment in Switzerland. The Kengo government is unable to handle explosive situations: in northern Congo and Kivu Rwandan Hutu refugees attempt to rally with local Hutus and elements in the Zaire Air Force to expel long-time Tutsi residents (Banyamulenge). Banyamulenge, ordered to leave South Kivu, fight back by occupying the area militarily in union with other Tutsi and with the support of Rwandan and Ugandan armed forces. Dissident groups join the Tutsi to fight the Mobutu regime under the umbrella of l'Alliance des Forces Démocratiques pour la Libération du Congo-Zaire (AFDL), headed by Laurent-Desiré Kabila, a Mobutu opponent since the 1960s.
1997	Mobutu returns to Zaire but his forces are unable to stop rebels' advance. Tshisekedi replaces Kengo wa Ndondo at the head of the government, only to be replaced a few days later by General Likulia Bolongo.
May 16	Unable to stand the fire, Mobutu leaves the country for exile in Morocco. He dies there in September.
May 17	AFDL troops invade Kinshasa.
late 1997	Kabila proclaims himself president of the Democratic Republic of Congo and disbands preexisting political institutions with the exception of the judiciary. Mass protests against the ban on political institutions are repressed. Clashes erupt between army factions.
1998	UN reports confirm allegations of Hutu refugee massacres by AFDL and its Tutsi allies. An anti-Kabila rebellion, le Rassemblement Congolais pour la Démocratie (RCD), in alliance with Rwandan and Ugandan troops, attacks from the east and attempt to capture Matadi, the Inga hydroelectric dam and Kinshasa, the capital. They are expelled thanks to large

troops from Angola, Namibia and Zimbabwe. In the east the territory under rebel control expands. A new group, le Mouvement pour la Liberation du Congo (MLC), joins the rebellion.

War and atrocities committed by government troops, the rebels and their Rwandan, Ugandan and Burundian allies provoke massive displacements of civilian populations in war zones.

1999   Government authorizes public political activities and registration of new political parties and calls for political debate on the future of the Congo.

Kabila dissolves his unique party, l'Alliance des Forces Démocratiques pour la Libération du Congo-Zaire (AFDL), and replaces it with the People's Power Committees.

July   Meeting to develop a cease fire agreement (the Lusaka Accord) in Lusaka, Zambia. Congo, Angola, Namibia, Zimbabwe, Rwanda, and Uganda sign the Lusaka Accord.

August Rebel groups sign the Lusaka Accord.

The UN Special Envoy visits the Congo and expresses concern for human rights violations by the various factions at war.

2000–2001   All parties continue to violate the Lusaka Accord.

Laurent Kabila is assassinated January 8, 2001. His son, Joseph Kabila is named his successor.

1

Introduction

THE CONGO is impressive due to its size, immense waterway system, rich and varied populations of vegetation and animal species, and seemingly inexhaustible mineral reserves. Congolese history reflects all the forms of political and social organization known to the ancient world. More recent history reflects the challenges of modern Africa in the struggle for socioeconomic and political development.

GEOGRAPHY

The word *Congo* refers to two modern central African countries, as well as a river and an ancient African kingdom. The countries are the Republic of Congo, also called Congo Brazzaville, and the Democratic Republic of Congo (DRC), also known as Congo Kinshasa or Zaire. Congo is also the name of the river that separates the two countries. Both the countries and the river derive their name from the ancient Kongo Kingdom, which once surrounded the mouth of the Congo River, covering the adjacent portions of the two countries and northern Angola.

DRC is the last in a series of names by which this country is known. From 1885 to 1908, it was called Congo Free State. Then, it became a Belgian Congo. At independence, on June 30, 1960, it changed its name to Republic of Congo. It was also called Congo-Leopoldville to distinguish it from Congo-Brazzaville, a former French colony, also named Republic of Congo. In 1964, Congo-Leopoldville became Democratic Republic of Congo, a misnomer since the country has practically never operated as a genuine democ-

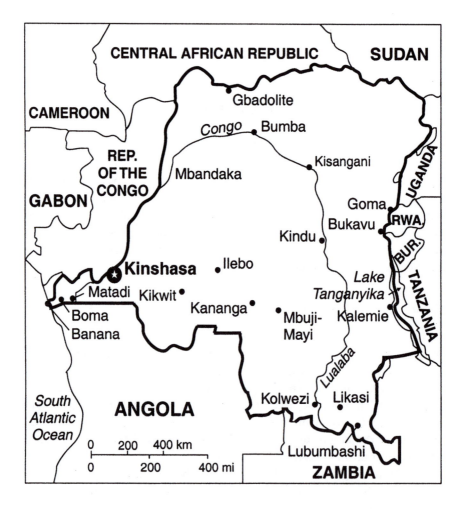

racy. In 1971 the dictator Mobutu Sese Seko renamed it Zaire. In 1997, Laurent Desire Kabila, Mobutu's successor and another dictator, reinstated the appellation Democratic Republic of Congo.

The DRC is a vast country in the center of Africa, covering an area of 905,063 square miles. It is the third largest country in Africa, following Sudan (967,247 square miles) and Algeria (915,541 square miles). Its neighbors are Congo Brazzaville (Republic of Congo) to the west; Central African Republic to the north; Sudan to the northeast; Uganda, Rwanda, Burundi and Tanzania to the east; Zambia to the southeast, and Angola to the south.

Congo River Basin Waterway Networks

Possibly the most striking physical feature of Congo's geography is the Congo River Basin waterway complex.[1] The complex includes the Congo River, its main tributaries, their own feeders, innumerable smaller rivers and several lakes.

Rivers. The Congo River Basin, with an area of 1.467 million square miles, covers practically the entire country. The Congo River, the central force of this immense waterway complex, is 2,914 miles long. It is the world's fifth longest river, after the Nile, the Amazon, the Mississippi, and the Yang-Tse. With a water volume second only to the Amazon, the Congo River crosses the entire country, running right to left. Congo River tributaries are distributed throughout the country. Some even come from the neighboring countries of Angola and Congo-Brazzaville. Uele-Ubangi, the northernmost major tributary, is perhaps the longest, second only to the Congo River itself. The Kasai River, another major tributary, which is located much farther south, is most noted for the importance and complexity of its own primary and secondary tributaries.

Lakes. Eight lakes are residuals from the recession of the ocean in prehistoric times: Tumba and Mai-Ndombe, in the western part of the country; Munkamba and Fwa in Central Congo; and Moero, Kisala, Upemba and Bangwelu in the east. The most important and better-managed lakes are mountain lakes in the Great Lakes Region: Edward (Amin), Albert (Mobutu), Kivu, and Tanganyika. The greatest of these is Lake Tanganyika, at 12,700 square miles. At 4,823 feet, Lake Tanganyika is the second deepest in the world, following Lake Baikal in Siberia. Lake Kivu is the highest lake above sea level in Africa, at 4,593 miles altitude. The Semiliki River links Lakes Edward and Albert, both of which feed into the Nile River.

River Travel and Fishing Grounds. The lakes and the large rivers are used for long-distance travel by canoe, boat or ship. The Congo and its tributaries give the country 8,783 navigable miles. However, steep rapids frequently interrupt navigation on the Congolese rivers. The Lualaba/Congo River, for example, is navigable for 397 miles from Bukama to Kongolo, 68 miles from Kasongo to Kibombo, 191 miles from Kindu to Ubundu and 455 miles from Kisangani to Kinshasa. Downstream from Kinshasa, Inga Falls further interrupts navigation.

Congolese rivers and lakes are the natural habitat of all kinds of fish. Lake Moero is celebrated for its large fish reserves. Bandundu is known for the fishing port of Salamita. The rivers and lakes also have an abundance of other species in their waters, including mammals, such as the hippopotamus, and amphibians, such as the turtle, as well as birds, reptiles, and insects. Bolenge, near Bandundu, is a well-known fishing village and has numerous other forms of water life, including large herds of hippopotamuses.

Energy Reserves. The waterways that make up the Congo River Basin complex represent more than 13 percent of the world's reserves of hydroelectric power. Inga Falls on the Congo River in Lower Congo province is one of the most powerful. It had been hoped that Inga Dam would become Africa's greatest source of energy, servicing the entire continent. Unfortunately, this has not happened, due to the lack of political will and commitment by the Congolese leadership and international financiers. Also well known on the Congo River is Boyoma Falls (formerly Stanley Falls), south of Kisangani. Shaba province is home to Lufira River Falls, site of hydroelectric stations that supply electricity to the city of Likasi. Guillaume Falls and Inzia River Falls are in Bandundu province, near the Angolan border. Mai Munene Falls (near Tshikapa, on the Kasai River), Lulua River Falls and Lubi River Falls are found in Western Kasai province. Tshiala Falls is in Eastern Kasai on the Mbuji-Mayi River.

Minerals. The Congo is known for being a geological wonder because of its many rich mineral resources. The most abundant of the Congo's minerals is probably copper, which, in times of prosperity, placed the Haut-Katanga Industrial mineral production complex among the world's largest producers. The Katanga province is also known for its cobalt and zinc, as well as manganese and malachite. However, Katanga is not the only province endowed with minerals. Kivu produces tin and gold. Eastern Kasai is known for its industrial diamond mines at Bakwanga. Western Kasai, Bandundu and Upper Congo have diamond reserves as well. Upper Congo has gold and iron ore, and Lower Congo has petroleum.

Climate, Flora and Fauna

Tropical Climate and Vegetation. Approximately 65 percent of the Congo lies south of the Equator. Its climate is entirely tropical, with perennial rains along the Equator and rainy and dry seasons alternating between the northern and the southern regions. South of the Equator, rainy seasons run from September to December and February to April; January and the period of May to August are dry.

The rainy seasons are warmer than dry seasons. The highest heats and the heaviest rains are to be found in the Equator province, the location of the Equatorial Rain Forest. Here daily temperatures vacillate between 86 and 95 degrees fahrenheit around midday and 68 degrees fahrenheit at night. Temperatures vary considerably from region to region because of influences from the Atlantic Ocean and the trade winds from the Indian Ocean and from the eastern mountainous regions. Thus, the Ruwenzori Mountain, at the borderline of DRC and Uganda, is known for its permanent cold temperatures. In the southern savannah zones, particularly in the southern part of Shaba province, the nights can be very cold during the dry season. Unstable humidity levels in the rest of the country can produce considerable temperature variations, even during the course of the same day. In Lower Congo, temperatures can range from 65 to 90 degrees centigrade in February. Kivu is in a separate category because of its temperate climate, which makes it a preferred vacation spot.

Rainfall patterns determine vegetation. The high heat and high amount of moisture found in the zone along the Equator are responsible for the heavy rains found there. The Tropical Rain Forest occupies the zone along the Equator. This is a dense forest of tall trees, lianas and numerous other plants. The intensity and frequency of rains diminish as one moves away from the Equator, whether to the north or south. In the zones adjacent to the Equator, rains are abundant but seasonal. The vegetation there consists of tropical woodland savannah, which combines tall trees and tall grass. Farther from the Equator, the intensity of rains diminishes, producing a vegetation of grass and dispersed trees known as tropical grassland savannah.

Flora and Fauna. The Tropical Rain Forest occupies almost the entire northern half of the country, from Lake Tumba to the foot of Mount Rowenzori. It is the natural habitat of innumerable vegetal species that are basic to the Congolese diet: roots, including many kinds of mushrooms and leafy vegetables. The forest houses a myriad of medicinal plants. Various palm trees grow here as well, including palm oil trees, raphia trees, copal trees.

Wood is omnipresent in all kinds, shapes and sizes. It includes many of the best species for making furniture and for construction. Lower-quality tree species are used for making paper. Other tree species can be found in dry areas near water. An example is the papyrus tree, which grows in large quantities on the shores of Lake Upemba and Lake Kisale.

Many animal species live in the forest. Some of these occupy an important place in Congolese people's diet, including game and insects. The forest is the natural habitat to monkeys and apes. The gorilla, the chimpanzee, the bonobo (or pygmy chimpanzee) and the okapi (resembling a cross between a zebra and antelope), waterbuck, buffalo, elephant, and wild pig also reside here.

Protected Parks. The forest and the animals in some parts of the Congo are protected by the Congolese Institute for the Conservation of Nature. The institute manages seven national parks, including Salonga on the Equator, which is considered the world's largest protected forest. Protected lands occupy between 12 and 15 percent of the Congolese territory, 1 percent of Africa's area. The history of legally protected lands goes way back to the times of the Congo Free State. In 1889, King Leopold II of Belgium, the first ruler of the colonized Congo, created land reserves devoted to the protection of the elephant. In 1908, Prince Albert considered expanding natural reserves in the Congo. In 1925, Albert Park, now called Virunga Park, was created, and additions were made to the park in 1929, 1934 and 1935. New parks, notably Garamba (near the Congo-Sudan border) and Upemba and Kundelungu (in Shaba province) were also established. Garamba is the home of the giraffe and the rhinoceros; Upemba and Kundelungu shelter various hoofed species; and the Epuli region, in the Ituri Forest, is famous for the okapi, which is only found in the Congo. Salonga, another forested park, is the only place in the world where the bonobo (pygmy chimpanzee) is found. It is also the home for innumerable other animal species. The Rutshuru and Rwindi Rivers flow through the Rwindi Park in the Goma area. All kinds of animals live along these rivers and in the nearby plains, including thousands of hippopotamuses, as well as elephants, lions, buffalos, antelopes and hyenas.

During the years of political turmoil that followed the independence of the Congo (June 30, 1960), the parks were constantly violated, and poachers killed many animals as well as park guards. In 1972, the government of Zaire created four new land reserves. One of these, the Kahuzi-Biega National Park (near Bukavu, in Kivu) is the natural habitat of the gorilla. In the same year, the statutes of the Zairean Institute for the Conservation of Nature were revised to include the protection of the human environment, that is, the rights of farmers, herders and hunters who live in the protected zones to draw their subsistence and prosperity from the lands incorporated in the parks without compromising the natural environment.

THE PEOPLE

The Congo is a typical African country. Its populations include hundreds of ethnic groups speaking different languages. The oldest inhabitants, now an assimilated minority, belong to the pygmoid race. Small stature is perhaps their most characteristic trait. They mostly practice hunting and gathering for a living. The largest majority of Congolese people are negroids who came to the area during the historical Bantu migration. They speak Bantu languages and practice agriculture for the most part. The newest immigrants are Hamites, who practice a combination of agriculture and cattle raising. They are concentrated in the east and northeastern parts of the country.

Traditional Economic Systems

Both the hunter-gatherers and the herders live in symbiosis with the farmers. This section elaborates on three patterns of ecological adaptation that one historian has termed the civilization of the bow (hunters-gatherers), the civilization of the granaries (farmers) and the civilization of the spear (herders).[2]

Hunters-Gatherers. The oldest inhabitants of the Congo are called Pygmies, Batwa, Mbuti, or Bushmen, depending on the region in which they live. Perhaps the best-known pygmoid populations who live in the Congolese forest are the Mbuti of Ituri, in the northeast.

Members of these groups are generally small in stature. They are hunters and gatherers who live in bands rather than large villages. The arrow and the bow are their most characteristic instruments of production. Not being food growers, they generally depend on their neighbors for their supply of agricultural products, which they obtain in exchange for meat. Once found throughout the Congo River Basin and beyond, today most of Congo's pygmoid populations live in the equatorial forest. Whether living in or outside the forest, many have integrated into nonpygmoid societies and adopted linguistic and other cultural traits of the latter. For instance, the Mbuti are culturally and linguistically differentiated into three subgroups: Efe, who speak Balese; Sua, who are Bira speakers; and Aka, whose language is Mangbetu.[3] Reportedly, the Aka were known to the Greek historian Aristotle and to the Egyptians during the era of the Pharaohs.

Farmers. The largest majority of Congolese people practice agriculture above any other production system. Farmers are present throughout the country. Traditionally, they measured their success by the quantities of food items they could store and the size of the granaries that housed them. Some examples are the Zande and the Mangbetu, who live in the basins of the Ubangi and Uele Rivers in the extreme north of the country; the Mongo of the Equator province; the various branches of the Luba people, who are scattered in the Western Kasai, Eastern Kasai and Northern Katanga provinces; the Lunda and Bemba of Southern Katanga; the Pende and the Yansi of Bandundu; and the Bakongo of Lower Congo.

The Congolese people practice agriculture in the savannah, in the forest and along river banks. The hoe is the dominant instrument of production. The machete is used to cut lianas, and the ax, to fell trees. Two natural methods of fertilizing the soil are universal. First, the grass from clearing the land is dried and burned into ashes, which in turn are mixed into the soil before planting. This is the so-called slash-and-burn technique. Second, new fields are opened periodically to allow the soil in the old fields to rest for a number of years and regenerate. This is the fallowing system.

In most part, Congolese farmers are negroids. They possess the most typical racial traits of black people: dark to brown skin, curly hair, large lips and a flat nose. The majority speak languages pertaining to the Bantu family, whose varying degrees of similarity and dissimilarity suggest a diffusion movement traceable to a common origin in the Nigeria-Benin region of West Africa. In turn, trajectories of linguistic differentiation identifiable with Bantu languages suggest gradual movements of the peoples who spoke these languages, thus constituting the base for what has become known as the Bantu migrations.[4]

Four languages nowadays dominate in four different regions as vernaculars. They are Kikongo, in Lower Congo and Bandundu; Lingala, in the capital, Kinshasa, and in the Equator province; Swahili in Upper Congo, Katanga and Kivu; and Tshiluba in the two Kasai provinces. As the language of the army, Lingala is now understood by many people in practically all provinces. These four are recognized as national languages, but French, a colonial legacy, is the official language. It is the language of education, government and expatriate business.

Herders. Many ethnic groups in Upper Congo and Kivu provinces are cattle raisers. For example, the Bira who live in the region east of Kisangani and the Bahema of Ituri are among these groups. Pastures and natural water springs are central to the pastoral lifestyle. The spear is the herder's major instrument of labor. They used it in the past to conquer and dominate the populations that had preceded them in the region and today carry it to protect the cattle and defend the conquered lands.

In the Great Lakes region, west of Lake Kivu, there are peoples who traditionally are either herders or farmers. They occupy an area extending from northern Tanzania in the south to just beyond Lake Edward in the north. Moving from north to south, the groups are the Banande, Bahutu, Bahunde, Bahavu, Bashi and Bafuriiru. These and other groups in this region are related to similar groups in Uganda, Rwanda and Burundi. They speak Bantu languages and are reported to have come to these areas in waves of immigration from the northeast during the sixteenth and seventeenth centuries. Some of these groups represent a mixture of racial types. For example, the Bahunde and the Banande are related to the Hamites through the Tutsi of Rwanda. Similarly, the Bahema are classified among the Hamites-Semites by some and among the Ethiopians-Nilotics by others.[5]

Traditional Political Systems

African societies in what later became the Congo had reached different levels of political sophistication long before colonization. They were organized, from the simplest to the most complex forms, in bands, lineages, chiefdoms, kingdoms and empires.

Levels of Political Sophistication. Band communities were composed of a limited number of nuclear families. Their cooperative arrangements were temporary and task specific. The Mbuti are a band society. Lineages are localized communities composed of extended families, whose members trace descent to a known ancestor. Lineages are often lower descent levels of a clan. The clan is a descent group whose members no longer can trace the descent lines connecting them to a common ancestor. Nonetheless, they maintain among themselves a high sense of community based on shared cultural traits such as a language, a totemic name (family emblem) and taboos, including a prohibition on intermarriage. The Ambum exemplify this model of political organization. Chiefdoms are permanent political entities based on kinship, and have a deeper hierarchical structure, incorporating several lineage levels. The highest level of common descent in a chiefdom can be a maximal lineage or a clan. The Luba of Kasai live in chiefdoms of various sizes.

Kingdoms were composed of chiefdoms united on bases other than common descent. The bases for kingdom national unity could be marriage alliances, pacts or patron-client relationships. The Kingdom of Kuba is a good example. Empires were political entities born out of conquests and composed of unrelated kingdoms. The Luba-Lunda Empire is a case in point. The forms of political organization identified here for illustration had in common a high degree of democratic participation, although the bands alone were egalitarian. At the same time, the social organization of nonegalitarian groups appears to have functioned simultaneously as an incubator of forces of unity and conflict.[6]

Mbuti Bands. The Mbuti are hunter-gatherers who live in the Ituri forest. The nuclear family was the only type of corporate group existing in Mbuti society. Marriage was based on reciprocal exchange. Men of different bands exchanged their sisters, or other female relation. The band was Mbuti's most typical and highest form of social organization. It had no established leadership. Instead, leadership was activated via net-hunting parties. Each band had its own hunting lands, although land boundaries were hard to establish. Fire camps served as forums for discussing community issues, and decisions were reached by consensus. Men and women participated in the discussions equally. Cooperation and food sharing were highly regarded as foundational principles of communal living. Major offenses were punished by banishment or beating; minor ones, by ridicule.[7]

Ambum Lineages. The Ambum who live in the Bandundu-Kwilu region were divided into matrilineal clans.[8] The nuclear family was subordinated to the extended family (*nzo*). Descendants of a common grandmother, living or dead, formed the nucleus of the extended family. Extended families were integrated into lineages. Above the lineage was the clan, a totemic and exogamous community whose members are not allowed to intermarry. Traditionally Ambum clans were not subjected to a common political authority. However, clan members maintained a high level of solidarity, which was expressed through kinship terms, sharing practices and a constant concern for one another's welfare.

Although the Ambum lineage was only a branch of the clan, it formed the largest territorial and organized community in the Ambum political system. It was autonomous and served as the basic administrative structure of the Ambum society. The lineage was headed by its eldest male member. Sometimes the elder overseeing the lineage was designated by the outgoing incumbent or elected by the other elders.

Above the lineage was the village, which included several lineages and served as their coordinating structure. Member lineages of a particular village belonged to different clans and were unequal in size and power. Usually, the prominent lineage had the upper hand in village politics. The village chief was chosen from the prominent lineage and often combined this function with that of lineage head. The function of village chief was passed from the incumbent to his uterine brother (sibling by the same mother) or his sororal nephew (sister's son). A council of lineage heads helped the village chief in carrying out his functions. The latter included cases related to adultery, homicide, property damage and theft. The chief was also in charge of relations with other village chiefs.

Luba Chiefdoms. The Luba of Kasai are one of the many ethnic groups claiming descent from the historical Luba Empire. Oral traditions and historical records suggest that they arrived at their present location after the dislocation of the empire, traveling in small familial groups as escapees of war or famine. Their political organization was an extension of the family system.[9]

The next descent level of the family system was composed of a variable number of extended families descended from a common ancestor. The most significant feature of this level of common descent was communal ownership of ancestral lands by all legitimate members. In turn, many such land-owning groups claiming descent from a son of the chiefdom founder formed the second highest level in the Luba political hierarchy. Collectively, members of this descent group were entitled to a specific function in the operation of the chiefdom. Functionally, this level of the Luba descent hierarchy could be called a political segment. Finally, all the political segments whose members claim descent from a common ancestor credited for being the original founding father formed the highest political level in traditional system of the Luba of Kasai; the chiefdom. This was the level of common citizenship. There was no overarching authority. The Luba society was a mosaic of independent chiefdoms of variable sizes.

Access to the throne of the chiefdom was determined primarily by descent. Customarily, only descendants of the chiefdom founder by his senior wife were eligible to become chiefs, whereas the descendants of the founder by his other wives monopolized the authority to confer power to eligible candidates. Originally the two functions were supposed to rotate among the entitled political segments in decreasing order of their founders' seniority. Rotation was conceived as a device guaranteeing balance in the exercise of power. There also existed political segments other than those descended from the chiefdom founder. Lineages founded by foreigners who had been incor-

Men, traditional and modern: left to right, *abacos* (Mobutu-era suit) with neck foulard; Chief Mbuyamba Konji of Bena Nshimba, Eastern Kasai, in *abacos* with symbols of authority—axe on left shoulder, ceremonial sash and hat; Chief Kabeya Nkashama of Bakwa Kalonji, Eastern Kasai, in full traditional regalia with leopard skin; men in European dress—white suit and tie.

porated into the chiefdom as refugees or prisoners of war fit this category. These groups were excluded from the two functions. However, they were represented in the chief's council, along with all other political segments. Both the rotation and the representation contributed to generalized participation in the political process.

The transfer of power involved the payment of some wealth by the contender to the incumbent and to power-conferring notables. However, with the passing of time, both the number of contenders to the throne and qualified dignitaries anxious to install them in power increased. Thus, power became more plutocratic (held by the wealthy). Consequently, only those lineages whose members were rich enough to satisfy the ever increasing demands for wealth from the incumbent chief and from the power-conferring notables could afford to compete for the position of chief. The situation worsened during colonization. During this period, the Belgian colonizers generally intervened in power disputes among the Congolese by supporting the candidate most likely to agree with their imperialistic gains, often in violation of traditional rules.

The Luba chief ruled with the cooperation of four different bodies: a cabinet of appointed officials, a council of titled notables, subchiefs representing chiefdom segments, and a closed circle of influential family members. His political powers included the obligation to negotiate and conclude pacts of nonaggression with neighboring countries. Administratively, the chief took a leading role in establishing policies, but he did not personally carry them out. He had to delegate the implementation to members of his cabinet. On the judiciary level, the chief, as the supreme authority, was expected to be governed by the principles of transparence (justice had to be rendered publicly) and fairness. The chief exercised mystical powers as well. Inauguration rituals played the double function of legitimizing the chief as the chiefdom ruler and making him the mystical peer of the spirits of past chiefs. In the latter capacity, he could avert calamities threatening the chiefdom and the subjects. The chief's cabinet members were assigned specialized functions, such as defense, order, chief's personal security, and hosting of guest dignitaries.

The Kingdom of Kuba. The Kingdom of Kuba was founded in the sixteenth century by a federation of eighteen groups of immigrants called Bushoongs.[10] They had initially settled in a wide area along the Kwango River, having escaped encroachments by Portuguese slave raiders along the Atlantic coast. Under the leadership of Chief Woot, they later moved to the area along the Kasai and Sankuru Rivers, fleeing Jaga invasions. Besides the eighteen Bushoong groups, the Kuba federation incorporated among its members the original inhabitants of the region, the Twa and the Kete, who had welcomed the newcomers. Several other ethnic groups joined the federation as well, with the original eighteen groups serving as the core organizing body. All became speakers of the Kuba language. At the beginning, the Kuba king was elected for a four-year term. Later, the term was extended, but not to exceed ten years. Both men and women were eligible. The kingdom lasted from about 1568 to 1910, during which, twenty-six rulers presided over its destiny.

Through intermarriage and cultural assimilation, the original indigenous Twa population disappeared as a distinct ethnic group. The land occupied by each surviving ethnic group incorporated in the state became a distinct administrative province of the kingdom. The organization of state power included and expanded the family structure. The lowest level of the political structure was the village council. Initially, villages were the residential communities of particular clans. Clan elders formed the village council. This is to say that traditional village councils of elders became state councils. Each

Male and female authority figures: Chief Mukenge Kalamba of the Luluwa, Western Kasai, in dark *abacos* and ceremonial hat and Queen Mother Nyand Kum of Kuba Bash Byeng in full ceremonial dress, flanked by escorts in ceremonial dresses.

clan had the opportunity to participate in the politics of the kingdom through the village council. With the passing of time, increasing immigration transformed many villages into larger agglomerations. Clans in these urban areas came to coincide with wards (sections of the town or city). Residents of each ward sent their elder to the town or city council to represent them. The village headman, the town subchief and the city chief presided over their respective councils and represented their constituencies in the provincial council. The latter was headed by the chief of the entire ethnic group, who was the paramount chief. Above the provincial councils stood the central state council. Membership in this highest council was reserved for the paramount chiefs of the original eighteen Bushoong founding groups of the kingdom. It was this group that elected the king. Thus, the other ethnic groups, having been labeled latecomers, were excluded from participating in the highest political function of the kingdom.

State councils at all levels were headed by their own elders consistent with their respective ethnic customs. At all levels as well, ethnic representation was equal, despite the numerical importance of the populations represented.

Velour du Kasai: Woven Raffia Cloth (Kuba). Collection of the author.

Besides equal representation, the Bushoongs elevated to national culture status the best cultural contributions of the various ethnic groups composing the kingdom. Thus, cultural practices such as dances, arts, agriculture and house building, in which particular ethnic groups excelled, were promoted as Kuba dances, Kuba arts, and Kuba agriculture, and Kuba architecture. The Bushoongs themselves were expert bootmakers, fishermen and hunters. Thanks to state encouragement, these activities, along with others, such as cloth-making and ironsmith crafts experienced high levels of prosperity. However, generalized cultural promotion along ethnic lines had serious limitations in certain sectors of production. For instance, a few ethnic groups who had traditionally excelled in it practiced all agriculture. Because of these groups' numerical paucity, however, food production remained insufficient and limited in variety, in spite of state encouragement.

The Luba-Lunda Empire. The Luba and the Lunda were two distinct empires. However, because of a significant genetic link that unites them, they are generally presented together or as a single, two-phase phenomenon.[11] The Luba Empire is not to be confused with the collection of Luba chiefdoms discussed previously in this work. The empire was older and much larger.

Raffia basket for personal items. Weaving is practiced all throughout the Congo. This basket uses the same technique as the woven raffia cloth. It is both functional and decorative. Collection of the author.

The chiefdoms are one of the many surviving branches of the empire that draw their names from it. The empire was started during the sixteenth century near Lake Boya in the Katanga region by Songye invaders called the Balopwe. The founder of the empire was Nkongolo Mwamba. The siege was at Mwibele. Nkongolo was later replaced by Ilunga Kalala, son of his sister Bulanda, in a power fight that Kalala won.

Around 1600 a disgruntled Luba candidate to power named Chibinda Ilunga left the empire to conquer a foreign land and founded what became known as the Lunda Empire. This conquest inspired individuals from the Lunda to leave on similar campaigns. For example, some Lunda groups migrated to the valley of Kwango, where they founded the Kingdom of Kasanje. Likewise Kanyama, a Lunda noble man, traveled south and founded the Kingdom of Lwena. Lunda groups who had participated in these movements became rulers in the countries of Cokwe and Songo. Others migrated to the valley of the Luapula River, where they became known as Hemba. Their chief bore the title of *mulopwe wa bantu* (the people's chief). The Bemba of

Malawi and Zambia have been presented as having come from the Lunda Empire by some and directly from the Luba Empire by others. The Lunda group colonized many other peoples.

Chibinda, the Luba immigrant who founded the Lunda Empire, brought to Lunda the basic governing principles of the Luba Empire and adapted them. In each case, the immigrant warrior united numerous preexisting smaller political formations into a large kingdom. In both cases, the occupant sought to legitimize and consolidate his power over the new entity by marrying into the subjugated nobility. The new rulers in both cases practiced indirect rule by keeping the conquered chiefs in place and limiting the intervention of the central government in the provinces to the periodic levying of in-kind tributes payed in local resources. Militarized expeditions of traveling chiefs called *kawata* were sent to the provinces of the empire to collect tributes and communicate the king's messages to local chiefs. *Kawata* expeditions were not used around the capital or in the king's own homeland. Instead, a small police corps enforced the king's orders around the capital. *Kawata* expeditions were more frequent in provinces close to the capital than in distant ones. They traveled to the outer chiefdoms once a year.

Apart from paying the annual tributes, distant provinces could conduct their business as they pleased. In other words, their adherence to the empire was not militarily imposed. What kept their loyalty to the king (*Mwaant Yaav*) intact? It is here that Lunda political inventiveness dwarfed that of the Luba. The Lunda invented two inseparable mechanisms, positional succession and perpetual kinship. According to this double principle, whoever took on the political position of *Mwaant Yaav* automatically inherited the kinship statuses and relations of the preceding *Mwaant Yaav*. He and his relatives become relatives of the previous king's kinsmen, with the same mutual rights and obligations forever. Additionally, conquered local chiefs were kept in their traditional position and given the title of *Mwaant a Ngaand* (owner of the land). Newcomer groups were given the purely political title of *Cilool* (subchief) and were made to understand that the lands on which they lived continued to belong to the original owners.

Made strong by these new principles, the Lunda were more able to expand their power and maintain control over many distant societies in central and southern Africa. The Luba did not achieve comparable success because they did not develop any built-in mechanism enabling them to integrate conquered groups into the Luba society as equal partners. The two government systems, however, shared a common potential seed of civil rebellions: the relations between the central government and the provinces were generally limited to levying tributes. No effort was made by the central government to provide any service to the provinces. Even protection against external attackers was missing. Central control could be seen as pure exploitation.

MODERN HISTORY: THE LONG PLIGHT

The Kongo Kingdom epitomizes in Central Africa an exuberant African civilization that became a victim of European imperialism. At the Berlin Conference of 1884–1885, the participating European powers conceded to King Leopold II of Belgium the sovereignty rights over the Congo and charged him to take the lead in developing policies that would benefit themselves at the expense of the Congolese inhabitants. In 1908 the king passed sovereignty over the Congo to the Belgian nation, and the colony became known as Belgian Congo. On June 30, 1960, the Congo officially became an independent country. However, because of the neocolonial system and military dictatorship that followed, ordinary Congolese people never experienced independence worthy of the name. To the contrary, their life has continued to be a struggle.

The Slave Trade and the Kongo Kingdom

This is the story of two countries, one European, and an adventurous intruder, and the other African, a betrayed host (Portugal and the Kongo Kingdom, respectively).[12]

Kongo Kingdom's Origins and Prosperity. There are two versions as to the kingdom's origins. One version says that the kingdom was founded around 1400, following the unification of prosperous farming, fishing, metal-producing and trading communities that had formed since the early 1300s around the Malebo Pool on both sides of the Congo River, which then was called Nzadi in the Kikongo language. The river and its surroundings offered enormous possibilities for development, which the Kongo people successfully put to use: plentiful rainfall and fertile savannah woodland soils; proximity to sources of copper, iron and salt; fishing grounds along the Nzadi River and its tributaries; and transportation by waterways across the pool and along the rivers.

The other version is that the kingdom started around what became its capital city at the location of the present city of San Salvador, in northern Angola. The founder, Ntinu Wene (also known as Nimi a Lukeni), had come from Bungu, a small chiefdom around Boma, near the mouth of the Nzadi River. Ntinu Wenu allied himself with local authorities by marrying a woman of the Nsaku Vunda clan, a custodian of spiritual rights over the lands. Mani Kabungu, the clan chief and priest to whom the rights over the lands were entrusted recognized him as Mani Kongo (King of Kongo). Mbanza Kongo became the capital of the new kingdom. Following his recognition as king of Kongo, Ntinu Wene conquered the provinces of Mbamba, Mpemba, Nsundi and Soyo. Later, he annexed the provinces of Mbata and Mpangu.

By the early 1500s, the kingdom had reached a high level of prosperity in arts and crafts. The people of the Kongo Kingdom were skilled metalworkers, potters and weavers. They traded fine raffia cloth as far as the Atlantic coast, where it was exchanged for salt and seashells for use as local currency. Trade and the tribute system operated by Kongo kings stimulated interregional trade. By the early 1500s, the *Mani Kongo* (king of Kongo) held authority over the region from the Atlantic in the west to the Kwango River in the east.

The Portuguese and the Kongo Royalty. The Portuguese torpedoed the development process in the Kongo Kingdom by combining various strategies. On their first arrival, in 1484, they initially presented themselves as friends. This allowed them to gain the confidence of Kongo's rulers and to penetrate their inner circles. The penetration was so deep that the king of Kongo and his entourage converted to Christianity and adopted Portuguese names. As a monarch and a Christian, the king of Kongo considered himself the equal of the king of Portugal. Indeed, they addressed each other as brothers. The two brotherly nations exchanged ambassadors, and the brother in Kongo asked for technicians, teachers and more missionaries from the brother in Portugal.

The king of Kongo did not know, however, that his Portuguese counterpart and his emissaries in the Kongo had a hidden agenda and were only awaiting a propitious moment to carry it out. When the moment came, citizens of Kongo began to disappear as they were secretly captured and sent to work as slaves on plantations in the Atlantic islands of São Tomé and Principe. The Portuguese positioned themselves as arbitrators in succession rivalries among the Kongo people in favor of the Christian candidates. Thus, in 1506, a Portuguese-supported candidate won over his opponents who rejected him as too much under foreign control. He became King Afonso I. His reign lasted until 1543. Highly conscious of being a Christian king, Afonso I established relations with the Vatican as well. Internally he used his increased powers to undermine the authority of regional leaders, whose religious powers relied on the respect for ancestral traditions.

The Slave Trade and the Kingdom's Ill Fate. By these acts King Afonso I lost the traditional sources of legitimacy and support and became totally dependent on the Portuguese settlers. He increasingly relied on Portuguese mercenaries and guns to collect tributes from his subjects, control long-distance trade and to expand the kingdom. Having become the only power behind the king, the Portuguese began making express demands for slaves. To meet these demands, they would instigate wars between the king and his subjects in targeted regions. When the situation had become impossible, the king complained to his counterpart in Portugal about the crimes of Portuguese citizens in Kongo. He even tried unsuccessfully to stop the slave trade on his own.

The king of Portugal responded by sending a document called Regimento to the king of Kongo, which laid out Kongo's obligations to Portugal, including payments to be made to meet the cost of Christian civilization, Portuguese expeditions to the Kongo and the education of Congolese children in Portugal. The expected payments included slaves, ivory and copper to be levied on the Congolese populations. The king of Portugal also appointed an ambassador with the mandate of advisor to the king of Kongo in all matters and who, in reality, was meant to be and acted as his supervisor instead, a sort of governor general.[13]

Afonso I's successor, Diogo I (1545–1560), succeeded in limiting the slave trade, and in establishing effective control over Portuguese residents, and he distanced himself from the missionaries. Nonetheless, he lost control over the southern province of Ndongo in Angola. Ndongo seceded from the Kongo Kingdom. In 1568, Alvare I was inaugurated as king of Kongo. In the same year, a group of invaders from the east, the Jaga, interrupted the course of events in Kongo Kingdom. They forced the king into exile until 1574, when the Portuguese reinstated him by means including mercenaries from São Tomé. The Portuguese took advantage of this momentum to solidify their control over the Kongo Kingdom, including arming the province of Ndongo against the kingdom and encouraging other provinces—Nsundi, Mbata, Matamba—to secede. At the same time, in the northern region, near Mbanza Kongo (the capital), the number of contenders to the throne, the *Infantes,* grew beyond measurement and rivalries among them intensified beyond control. The slave trade intensified as well, converging toward the port of Pumbo on the shores of Malebo Pool. A group of Euro-African mixed-race people, named *Pombeiros* after their connection with Pumbo, became specialized slave traders between the interior and the port.

In the south, wars raged endlessly, opposing the Kongo Kingdom against seceding provinces, the kingdom against the Portuguese, the Portuguese against the provinces, province against province and ethnic groups against each other. Some persons involved in the wars resisted the slave trade, but others promoted it. Queen Anna Nzinga of Angola, Dongo and Matamba distinguished herself as an indomitable slave trade fighter over a period of thirty years, from 1625 to 1655. The Imbalanga were among the ethnic groups that became prodigious suppliers of slaves. The Mbundu were among the most victimized populations. Luanda became the bastion of Portuguese and mixed-race slave traders and a major slave export center, with more than ten thousand slaves exported every year. The final destination was now Brazil; SãoTomé only a transit post.[14]

Colonialism in Congo Free State and the Belgian Congo

King Leopold II's vast African empire was called Congo Free State. As the king's heir, the nation of Belgium renamed it Belgian Congo. After occupying the Congo, the king and his successors sought to fulfill their mandate through, among other things, degrading and alienating traditional leadership in the Congo, expropriating resources and subjecting the Congolese to forced labor.[15]

Leadership Degradation and Alienation. The first measures taken by the king included dispossessing the African people of the legitimizing powers of their leaders, as exercised through lineage elders' councils, chief's councils and king's councils. King Leopold II instituted the function of district commissioner, to be assumed by a European member of the colonial administration and charged with the powers to revoke traditional chiefs and kings and to dismantle kingdoms and large chiefdoms and replace them with minuscule entities. The new entities were to be headed by appointed chiefs selected only from among the contenders whose loyalty to the European masters was unquestionable. To further alienate the chiefs from their subjects, the district commissioner made them responsible for enforcing the very policies designed to oppress their subjects. They were required to recruit soldiers for the colonial army and organize corvées, unpaid collective tasks imposed by a dominant group over a subordinate one, which were sometimes rationalized as taxation via labor. Those chiefs who resented having to betray their subjects in the prescribed manner or who failed to perform to the satisfaction of the new master were eliminated from power in favor of more compliant competitors. They were subjected to public humiliation such as flogging in the presence of their subjects, including women and children.[16]

In 1908, King Leopold II passed his sovereignty rights over the Congo to the Belgian nation. In 1910, in pursuit of the king's legacy, the new authorities of the Congo reconfirmed the district commissioner as the controlling authority over the customary chiefs. Similarly, they gave the district commissioner the authority to recognize subchiefs as agents of the colonial administration and to displace villages as he saw fit. Consequently, the district commissioner appointed subchiefs throughout the colony, even where chiefdoms had never existed. As a result, the number of artificially created chiefdoms and subchiefdoms increased so much that the colonial administration ceased further appointments in 1921. All appointments now went to candidates who were most loyal to the colonizing power. In 1933, chiefdoms and subchiefdoms deemed too small to function effectively were regrouped into administrative districts called *secteurs*. Because of this long process of marginalization, the chief became totally incapacitated. In particular, he was unable to resolve the conflict between the interests of his people and those of the colonizers.[17]

Expropriations. The first colonial policy in the Congo Free State affected lands and connected resources. On July 1, 1885, the king issued a decree expropriating all lands that the Europeans in the Congo considered vacant. This was an absurdity because there was no land that did not belong to any community. Moreover, often what the Europeans claimed as unused lands were actually lands left fallow to allow the soil to regenerate. Expropriated lands were kept as state property or conceded to colonial companies or state agencies. Cultivation, gathering, hunting and fishing were prohibited on expropriated lands. Land shortage became a chronic problem among the Congolese people, so much so that in 1906 the colonial administration authorized territorial administrators to leave to each community three times as much land as it actually occupied (built on or cultivated)—which was insignificant in most cases.

In 1908, when the Congo Free State became the Belgian Congo, 66.69 million acres of expropriated lands had been transferred to private interest groups. After that, land contracts were renegotiated and replaced by others allowing only the transfer of good quality lands. As a result, the total of lands transferred to private interest groups decreased to 17.59 million acres in 1919. The Lever Brothers Company, later renamed Unilever, was allowed to select 1.85 million acres of good-quality lands from a total of 13.83 million acres of lands scattered in five different regions. The largest expropriations of this period went to a privately managed government agency, the Comité Spécial du Katanga (111.15 million acres) and another to the Comité National du Kivu (29.64 million acres). Each of the two Comités was a privately managed government agency.

Through these massive expropriations, the Congolese people lost more than arable lands; they lost fishing, hunting and gathering grounds as well. Their losses included a gamut of such resources as rubber, copal (a tropical tree), palm oil, ivory, kola nuts, palm nuts, and raffia. Rubber and ivory were in high demand on European markets in the nineteenth century. Rubber was obtained by making incisions in latex-yielding trees, from which latex was extracted, to be made into rubber. Latex was sold at trading stations along the Atlantic coast. Rubber usually came from the liana, which grows in abundance in the Congolese forests. It can also be extracted from other plants common to the Kwango region. Ivory was used in manufacturing household items, particularly utensils, which were also sold. Ivory was gathered or else obtained by slaughtering elephants. The Congo Free State prohibited the trading of these products and elephant hunting, even on lands that the state had not taken. In Upper Congo, ivory was part of a flourishing commercial network extending from Singitini (presently Kisangani) to the Indian Ocean. Arabs and Swahili-speaking people, who played an important part in the ivory trade, became the target of an open war by King Leopold's emissaries in the Congo. They only allowed general hunting seven months in a year on lands still owned by Congolese communities. In 1910, the colonial administration authorized limited hunting on some state-owned lands. Beginning in 1934, it prohibited all hunting on lands designated to become national parks. Transgressions of these regulations, which included trespassing, were punishable by colonial laws.

Accumulated Property. Like natural resources, accumulated property from Congolese people's labor was subject to expropriation policies. Palm trees were one such type of accumulated property. Long before the coming of the Europeans, the people of the Congo had planted palm trees around their habitations or in distant fields. It is a common practice in Africa for peasants to abandon their fields and even their villages after a certain number of years of occupation to allow the soil to regenerate. The practice is called the fallow system, itinerant cultivation or shifting cultivation. Because of this system, palm trees were generally scattered in small plots coinciding with former places of residence or old fields. These trees continued to belong to the communities that had planted them.

Palm trees were important sources of oil and wine. They also gave the owners a variety of household items, such as baskets and brooms, various

condiments such as salt and bicarbonate, medical products, and edible caterpillars. Dead palm trees provided wood for cooking and heating. Expropriations ended all these benefits, without any serious consideration of legality
or compensation, simply under the pretext that the natives were destroying
the palm trees.

Movable property was subject to expropriation measures, too. The colonial
administration took large quantities of comestibles from the peasants to feed
its personnel, white and black. The request for these products was justified
as in-kind income taxes. The black personnel mainly comprised the Force
Publique (the Colonial Army). The soldiers and the civilian personnel had
been recently recruited from the villages. Recruitment favored able-bodied
young men. Their departure deprived the villages of the most valuable producers. The greater the number of recruits, the larger the quantities of food
needed to feed them, and the smaller the number of food producers remaining in the villages. In other words, the task of producing the required quotas
of food was made more difficult.

The kinds of food that were demanded differed from region to region.
For instance, a village around the location of the present city of Kinshasa,
was required to supply 350 loaves of *kwanga* (cassava bread), each weighing
about 2.2 pounds. It took about one hundred working hours to produce this
quota. The *kwanga* is usually eaten with fish (preferably smoked, for better
preservation). Thus, the populations of certain regions found themselves required to pay their taxes in fish. Such was the case in Upper Congo, particularly around Nouvelle Anvers.

Besides the food for the workers and the soldiers, the Congolese populations had to provide fresh meat (poultry, goats and other domestic animals)
for the European personnel of the colonial administration and companies.
This obligation caused livestock depletion in the villages. Under national and
international pressure, the colonial authorities appointed a commission to
inquire into the massive devastations inflicted on the Congolese by King
Leopold's regime. The commission made its findings public in 1905. The
1905 *Report of the Inquiry Commission* confirmed that sheep, goats, chickens
and ducks had become scarce and more expensive. They were frequently
taken away arbitrarily from the owners as tax payments. Moreover, accumulated frustrations had led the peasants in many villages to stop raising
them.

The obligation to provide food for government officials continued until
the end of colonization. Initially, it was justified as a substitute for money
taxes. After the introduction of money taxes in the 1910s, however, it continued because of conditioning and fear or as a bribe to unfair officials. Until

the 1950s, the last decade of colonization, administrators of territory and agricultural and health officials were all fed during their visits to the villages with eggs, chickens, goats or game provided by local populations, who received no other compensation than the hope of not being brutalized.

Art objects were among the accumulated properties subject to expropriation. From all the corners of the colony, Europeans, lay and clergy alike, took all kinds of Congolese art pieces under various pretexts, including the fight against paganism. The Museum of Tervuren (Belgium), one of the largest and most impressive in the world, is a living testimony, not only to the creative spirit and productive capacity of the Congolese people, but also to the enormity of the losses inflicted on their communities by the agents of colonization.

Forced Labor. Initially begun on a limited scale, forced labor became generalized when Leopold II ordered his representatives in the Congo to take all measures necessary to develop state lands and to have the natives plant in a state domain a number of palm trees proportional to the size of their population and to the amount of available lands. In carrying out the latter measure, the governor-general fixed the number of palm trees to be planted in every village at one-hundred units per hut, for an estimated population of four persons per hut.

The colonial administration forced the Congolese to perform all kinds of corvées for the benefit of the Europeans, such as paddling; supplying wood for powering steamships; clearing fields and planting; building and maintaining roads and bridges, government stations, prisons and court houses; and clearing river banks and the land around telephone lines. The forced labor was frequently abusive. It became common practice for any supervisor of a government station or private factory to demand all kinds of duties in work or in goods to meet his own needs or those of the station or to exploit the land's resources. Many officials were anxious to obtain the most within the shortest time possible. Their demands very often became excessive.

The abuses relative to rubber gathering were among the most notorious. The demands for rubber were often insatiable. Each time the harvesters met a quota, the agents set a higher one for the next delivery. In most cases the harvester had to walk for several days or more every two weeks to reach the places in the forest where rubber trees could be found in abundance. There he led a miserable existence, living in an improvised shelter, deprived of his habitual food and exposed to bad weather and attacks by wild animals. Prior to returning to his village, he first had to take his harvest to the government station or to the company. Hardly could he stay two or three days in the village before the demand for rubber pressured him to go again. Consequently, harvesting rubber absorbed most of his time, due to the many trips imposed on him. The villages whose inhabitants were fed up and refused to go to the station were punished with police raids and killings. Maiming and amputation were common punishments inflicted upon the Congolese people during the Congo Free State period.

Forced labor in the Congo was first justified as a substitute for income taxes. The government introduced monetary taxes in 1910, yet it maintained, and even increased, its demands for forced labor. In 1933, the official duration of forced labor was set at 60 days per year in peacetime and 120 days in wartime. Porterage was among the imposed corvées. This was a very harsh task, involving hauling heavy vehicles across tortuous regions, climbing up steep mountain sides and descending into swamps and across rivers. Porterage was a generalized practice for carrying people, luggage and cargo: travelers and merchants with their goods, state personnel and materials and farm products taken from the peasants all traveled by porterage. This was an endless imposition. Whenever new territories were to be opened or new imports from Europe were to be moved, it was the duty of the Congolese to carry the white man, his luggage and whatever else to their destination, no matter how far.

Neocolonialism and Dictatorship in the Congo

Republic of Congo (1960–1964). On June 30, 1960, Belgian Congo became la Republique du Congo (Republic of Congo), also called Congo-Leopoldville. The new republic was supposed to be a free nation. It was prepared to become a neocolonial state instead.

Neocolonialism is colonization by proxy. Under neocolonialism, the destiny of the nation is officially in the hands of national leaders. In reality, however, these leaders operate as subordinate agents of foreign powers. Dictatorship makes things worse, as dictators rule by coercion and terror under neocolonialism. The Democratic Republic of Congo (DRC) is a misnomer.

Democratic Republic of Congo (1960–1971). The plight of the Congolese people after independence carries many names, including crisis of independence, mass rebellions, dictatorship and *le mal Zairois* (the ills of Zaire).

Crisis of Independence. Upon the independence of the Congo, Joseph Kasa-Vubu and Patrice Emery Lumumba became president and prime minister, respectively. During independence celebrations, Kasa-Vubu spoke to thank the Belgians for granting independence to their former subjects and promised to continue to work closely with them for the mutual benefits of the two nations. Lumumba spoke to the Congolese people, reminding them of the sufferings they had endured during colonization and promising to work with them for a change in their favor. King Beaudoin of Belgium and other Belgians took offense at Lumumba's speech and, with their allies, including the United States, began plotting for his elimination from power.

Within a week of independence, Belgian military officers of the Force Publique (the Colonial Army), incited the Congolese soldiers to revolt against Lumumba, accusing him of denying them the fruits of independence. Lumumba responded with hasty appointments, including Joseph Mobutu as commander in chief of the Congolese army. Not long after, the Belgians invaded Matadi in a move to reconquer the Congo. At the same time, their protégé Moise Tshombe, declared the secession of Katanga, the country's richest province. In addition, in Kasai, the Luba, who had been evicted from Kananga for reasons of ethnic cleansing instigated by the Belgians and had failed to gain high positions in the central government in Kinshasa, declared their autonomy.

Lumumba had thus to fight several simultaneous battles, which proved fatal to the Congolese nation. His enemies, internal and external, succeeded in portraying him as a communist to rationalize their plans to eliminate him because of his goal of attaining true independence for the Congolese people. In the midst of all that, Lumumba and his government appealed to the United Nations for assistance. United Nations troops arrived, but to Lumumba's great disappointment, the forces of the United Nations were apparently there to sink him rather than to help his government put the country back together. His enemies instigated a coup d'état by Mobutu, a man known for having connections with the U.S. Central Intelligence Agency (CIA). They arrested Lumumba, whom they sent to his staunchest enemies in Katanga, the Belgians, Moise Tshombe and Godefroy Munongo, respectively the president and prime minister of the secessionist state. Lumumba was killed between Lubumbashi airport and the city. Confusion still reigns about what happened to his body.[18]

Conflicts surrounding Congo's independence inaugurated an era of insecurity and destruction that has persisted to the present in many parts of the country. Kananga (then Luluabourg) was the provincial capital of Kasai. The Luba had served as the backbone of the colonial administration in Kananga. They made up the largest number of lower-level personnel beneath the Belgians, who had reserved the command positions for themselves. Outside the city, the Luba played a vital role in agricultural production in several regions of the province. (Kananga and the surrounding regions are on the lands of the Lulua people.) In 1959 and 1960, the Belgians frightened the Lulua of Luba domination after Congo's independence. They fomented interethnic conflicts between the two groups, which culminated in the Luba being expelled from Lulua lands and forced to return to their own homeland, around the present city of Mbuji-Mayi. That was the beginning of the destruction of Kananga and its hinterland. The economy and the administration of the area have never been revived.

The victimized populations did not receive any compensation for lost lives, property or jobs. They arrived to the Mbuji-Mayi area as refugees. Local economic, administrative and health infrastructures were not adequate to support an unexpected multitude, and a long period of suffering followed. Soon the situation worsened. In 1961–1962, the Belgians and the local authorities in Katanga conspired to expel the Luba and other Kasai peoples from their homes and jobs. Thousands of people spent months in refugee camps before being expelled to Kasai. Their influx worsened problems deriving from the region's low carrying capacity.

Two camps emerged from among Lumumba's major enemies, who were now in power without him. One, the Kinshasa group headed by Mobutu, had the strong support of the United States and the United Nations. This group was often identified by the clique that dominated it, the so-called Binza Group, consisting of Joseph Mobutu, Victor Nendaka, Justin Bomboko, Damien Kandolo and Albert Ndele. It was through this group, particularly Mobutu, that the United States established and solidified control over Congolese leadership. The other group consisted of Moise Tshombe and his government in Katanga; it was supported by the Belgian government, Belgian settlers living in Katanga and the Union Minière du Haut-Katanga, the mining company that controlled Katanga's minerals and an affiliate of the Belgian mining giant, the Société Générale de Belgique.[19]

Mass Rebellions. Lumumba's elimination threw nationalistic parties that had supported him into opposition. They included the Mouvement National Congolais (MNC)–Lumumba; the Parti Solidaire Africain (PSA)–Mulela and Gizenga wing; the Centre de Regroupment Africain (CEREA), led by Anicet Kashamura; and Balubakat, the party of Jason Sendwe. The regions where these parties dominated became the scenes of bloody wars called rebellions in Congo history.[20] The North Katanga rebellions, both in 1960–1961 and in 1964, were led by Balubakat against the provincial government of Katanga. The Kwilu rebellion was the work of PSA–Mulele wing, with Mulele as its mastermind. After Lumumba's death, Antoine Gizenga became the uncontested leader of MNC–Lumumba. His party led the rebellions in Kisangani, Uvira and Fizi. A different phase of the Uvira-Fizi rebellion was led by the Conseil National de Libération (CNL), which was founded in 1963 and headed by Gaston Soumialot after 1964. Soumialot kept close contacts with the leaders of MNC, notably Gizenga and Christophe Antoine Gbenye. He also intervened in the 1964 North Katanga rebellion, while Anicet Kashamura's CEREA played a part in Uvira-Fizi rebellions.[21]

Many factors drove the masses into the rebellion. Stories of the arbitrary arrests, torture and killings of opposition leaders who seemed to speak for the masses and customary chiefs suspected of supporting them were abundant. Local populations throughout the Congo were frustrated by the indifference and corruption of the administration. Higher-level administrators in the provinces were selected from groups that were strangers to the area. Usually they showed little sensitivity to the needs of the local populations. Instead, they used public funds for personal gains. The masses thus felt left out in sharing the fruits of independence. The gap between the haves and the have-nots was growing wider. In the eyes of the Congolese, political leaders had failed to deliver the better life they had promised them as the fruit of independence. For this reason, they nicknamed the rebellions "struggles for the second independence." The youth was part of the frustrated populations who joined the rebellion searching for a change. Government officials, assimilated customary chiefs and others whomever was suspected to oppose the revolution were targeted for elimination. They also targeted Europeans as symbols of prolonged colonial oppression. In some places missionaries were among the targeted Europeans, but elsewhere they were seen as the only ones still caring for the ordinary people.

In all cases, both the repression and the resulting revolt had an ethnic character. Mulele, the champion of the Kwilu rebellion, was a Mbunda. Gizenga, his closest ally, was a member of the Bampenda ethnic group. The Mbunda and the Bampenda were the backbone of the Kwilu rebellion. Ethnically, the Uvira-Fizi rebellion was primarily the work of the Bafulero and the Babembe. Here, most of the MNC-Lumumba membership and leadership were the Bakusu, who had established control over the region's political institutions during the 1960 occupation of the area by the forces of the Gizenga government from Kisangani. For this reason and because they were perceived as strangers, the Bakusu became the target of political repression by subsequent governments and by the rebels.

A constellation of politicoethnic antagonisms contributed to the climate that produced the rebellion. Rivalry between Bakusu who were considered immigrants from Maniema and the natives of South Kivu was such an antagonism. There was also conflict between the two Bashi chiefdoms, Kabare and Ngweshe. Still a third one involved the opposition of all ethnic groups to Bashi numerical dominance and control over the land. In North Katanga, different factions of the Luba populations participated in the 1960–1961 and the 1964 rebellions. The 1960–1961 rebellion in North Katanga was led by Jason Sendwe and other members of the older generation, who had participated in the independence movement. The 1964 was the work of a younger generation, among whom was the late Laurent Kabila, later self-proclaimed Congo president (May 1997–January 2001).

There were thousands of human casualties and enormous losses of public and private property. Infrastructure destruction and other material losses were considerable as well. Roads and bridges were destroyed in an attempt to isolate the affected regions from counterattacks and from the rest of the country.

Dictatorship and Le Mal Zairois. The list of bloody events that contributed to plunging the Congo into endless chaos exceeds the cases that were already mentioned. For example, there were other rebellions in Mushie, Bolobo and Kisangani. There was also a civil war to end the Katanga secession. Here and in Kisangani, the Congolese government had resorted to mercenaries to win the war and had to fight them out once the domestic war was over.[22]

Les Pendus de Pentecôte. A tragic event took place in Kinshasa after Joseph Desiré Mobutu assumed the leadership of the Congo in a military coup. Four innocent men were hanged in public on the day of Pentecost, 1966. In French, Les Pendus de Pentecôte means "those who were hanged on the day of Pentecost." Mobutu gave the Congolese people a foretaste of his rule of terror by making up charges against these men who were members of the government he had overthrown with his military coup: Jerome Anany, Emmanuel Bamba, Evariste Kimba and Alexandre Mahamba.

From Congo to Zaire. In 1971, President Mobutu decreed a generalized name change, renaming the country Republic of Zaire and himself Mobutu Sese Seko. Presumably, Zaire and other new names were supposed to be consistent with a movement of return to African values called Authenticity. Ironically, *Zaire* is a Portuguese alteration of an authentic African word, *Nzadi*, which the Kongo people used during the Kongo Kingdom to designate the River Congo at the time of Portuguese exploratory voyages along the African coast.

Military dictatorships of the 1960s and 1970s: President Mobutu Sese Seko of Zaire (center left); President Jean Bedel Bokasa of the Central African Republic (center right).

Shaba I and Shaba II. A staunch ally of the United States, Mobutu became a proxy in the war against the Marxist government of Angola, supporting the opposition and transporting American weapons to them. To repay him, Angola armed and sent back members of the former Katanga army, who had taken refuge there when Katanga secession was defeated. They penetrated southern Katanga in 1977 and 1978. The two invasions are known in Congo history as Shaba I and Shaba II. In both cases, the Congo had to appeal to foreign troops to dislodge them.

Le Mal Zairois* or *les Fléaux du Zaire. Mobutu stayed in power until Laurent Kabila and his Rwandan and Ugandan allies drove him out in May 1997. Throughout his reign, he ruled by terror and corruption. These and many other forms of impropriety created among the population a permanent state of generalized disorder, frustration and suffering that became called in French the Mal Zairois (the Zairean Evil) or, in plural form, the Fléaux du Zaire (Zaire's Scourges). The elimination of real and imagined political rivals, both openly and clandestinely, haunted the Mobutu regime. Many people were assassinated on Mobutu's orders. Names such as Pierre Mulele, Kudia

Kubanza, André Lubaya and Honoré Mpinga Kasenda are only a few for whose death the Mobutu regime was responsible.

Brutality practiced by Mobutu's soldiers; his ruling party, the Mouvement Populaire de la Révolution (MPR); and its youth wing, the Jeunesse du Mouvement Populaire de la Révolution (JMPR), along with the resulting general state of insecurity, became a way of life in every corner of the Congo. Arbitrary arrests and beatings, expropriations, pillages and killings, student massacres, rapes and bribes at all levels of public administration were frequently denounced by human rights observers, the international press, and the local press (when not muzzled).

Thirty-two years of systematic pillage by Mobutu, his immediate political and familial entourage and their foreign allies have brought the Congo to a despicable level of poverty. Once a prosperous country, the Congo is now cited among the poorest and most desperate nations in the world. To ensure the longevity of his rule, Mobutu attempted to prevent the formation of any organized force capable of challenging him militarily from within. By so doing, however, he prepared the way for the unthinkable military occupation of the Congo by Rwanda. The absence of any internal force compelled Laurent Kabila, a rebel from the 1960s, to rely on Rwandan soldiers to confront the handful of Mobutu's generals and colonels, whom Mobutu had practically reduced to a force of personal guards.

Back to Democratic Republic of Congo. In May 1997, Laurent Désiré Kabila drove Mobutu out of power and out of the country. He then proclaimed himself president, inaugurated himself and returned to the country its previous name of Democratic Republic of Congo. Notice that the qualifier *Democratic* attached to *Congo* remains misleading. Now, as during the Mobutu regime, the country is far from a democracy. To begin with, Kabila drove Mobutu out with military assistance from Uganda and Rwanda. Rwandans occupied key functions in his cabinet and had the command of the so-called liberation army. The army reinstated public flogging, the most significant symbol of colonial oppression. From the very start, Kabila refused to cooperate with the genuine internal opposition, which had fought against the Mobutu dictatorship by democratic means. Rwanda and Uganda control large Congolese territories with the complicity of former Rwandan members of the Kabila government turned political enemies and of former military supporters of the Mobutu regime. Elsewhere, Kabila reigned by military rule, which he justified as war effort. Even before coming to power, he had begun granting exploitation rights for Congolese minerals to foreign companies or companies that he himself founded, with no interest in improving living conditions for the Congolese people.

NOTES

1. The information on the geography of the Congo is drawn from Siradiou Diallo, *Le Zaire Aujourd'hui*, 3d ed. (Paris: Editions Jaguar-J.A. 1989); National Geographic Atlas of the World, Revised Sixth Edition, 1995; and the *Hamond International Atlas* (Maplewood, NJ: 1971).

2. Jacques Maquet, *Civilizations of Africa* (New York: Oxford University Press, 1972), 33–87, 106–132.

3. See Jan Vansina, *Introduction à l'ethnographie du Congo* (Kinshasa, Zaire Editions Universitaires du Congo, 1965), 53–54. See also Diallo, *Le Zaire Aujourd'hui*, 62.

4. The linguistic foundations of Bantu migrations are discussed in two chapters in Collins, *Problems in African History*: Joseph Greenberg, "The Languages of Africa," 78–85, and Thomas Spear, "Bantu Migrations," 95–98.

5. Jan Vansina, *Introduction à l'ethnographie du Congo*, 202–204.

6. On traditional political institutions in the Congo, see Jan Vansina, *Kingdoms of the Savanna*, (Madison: University of Wisconsin Press, 1968). For particular reference to the Kongo and the Kuba, see Chancellor Williams, *The Destruction of Black Civilization*: Great Issues of a Race from 4500 B.C. to 2000 A.D. (Chicago: Third World Press, 1987); and for the Ambum, see SN. Sangmpam, *Pseudocapitalism and the Overpoliticized State* (Brookfield, VT: Ashgate, 1994), 45–54.

7. For further discussion of the Mbuti, see Vansina, *Introduction à l'Ethnographie du Congo*, 56–60.

8. For the Ambum, see Sangmpam, *Pseudocapitalism and the Overpoliticized State* (Brookfield, VT: Ashgate, 1994), 45–54.

9. The information on the Luba of Kasai comes for most part from Leonard Mukenge, "Croyances Religieuses et Structures Socio-Familiales en Société Luba: Buena Muntu, Bakishi, Milambu," in *Cahiers*, Vol. 1 (Kinshasa: Institut de Recherches Economiques et Sociales [IRES], 1967), 3–95; and M.T.M. Kanyinda-Lusanga, *Les Institutions Socio-Politiques Traditionnelles et les Institutions Politiques Modernes au Zaire: Le cas de la Societé Luba du Kasai* (Louvain: Université Catholique de Louvain, Ph.D. Thesis, 1974).

10. The discussion on the Kingdom of Kuba is based on Williams, *The Destruction of Black Civilization*, 221–242.

11. On the Luba-Lunda Empire, see Vansina, "Kingdoms of the Savanna," 70–97. Two updated and condensed discussions of the Luba-Lunda Empire for classroom use are Vansina's "Kingdoms of the Savanna," 115–120, and Thomas Reefe's "The Luba-Lunda Empire," in *Problems in African History: The Precolonial Centuries*, ed. Robert O. Collins (New York: Markus Wiener, 1994), 121–125.

12. Williams, *The Destruction of Black Civilization*, 243–272. Also Kevin Shillington, *History of Africa*, rev. ed. (New York: St. Martin's Press, 1995), 144–145, 198–201.

13. Williams, *The Destruction of Black Civilization*, 251.

14. Edouard Mendiaux, *Histoire du Congo* (Bruxelles: Charles Dessart, 1961), 61–62. See also Albert Doutreloux's "Les Kongo," in Vansina, *Introduction à l'Ethnographie du Congo*, 115–127.

15. For political life in the Congo in colonial and early post-colonial periods, see Crawford Young, *Politics in the Congo* (Princeton, NJ: Princeton University Press, 1965); Patrice Lumumba, *Congo My Country* (New York: Frederick A. Praeger, 1966); Michel Merlier, *Le Comngo de la colonisation a l'independance* (Paris: Maspero, 1962); Kanyinda Lusanga and Guy Malengreau, *Continuité et Discontinuité de l'Action Administrative dans l'Organisastion Territoriale du Zaire* (Kinshasa: Centre interdisciplinaire d'Etudes et de Documentation Politique [CIEDOP], 1985); Georges Van Der Kerken, *Les Sociétés Bantoues du Congo Belges et les Problèmes de la Politique Indigène* (Bruxelles: Etablissement Emile Bruant, 1919).

16. Kanyinda Lusanga and Guy Malengreau, *Continuité et Discontinuité de l'Action Administrative dans l'Organisastion Territoriale du Zaire*, 115; Rene Lemarchand, *Political Awakening in the Belgian Congo* (Berkeley and Los Angeles: University of California Press, 1964), 39.

17. Kamitatu Cleophas, *La grande mystification du Congo-Kinshasa: les crimes de Mobutu* (Paris: François Maspero, 1971), 55–88; Benoît Verhaegen, *Rebellions au Congo* (Bruxelles: Les Etudes de CRISP, 1966), 32–33.

18. Kamitatu, *La Grande mystification du Congo-Kinshasa*, 98.

19. On rebellions in the Congo, read Verhaegen, *Rébellions au Congo*, 1.

20. These regions included Kwilu, Bolobo-Mushie, Uvira-Fizi and North-Katanga. See Veraegen, *Rebellions au Congo*. In addition to rebellions, there were mutinies. On this subject, see J. Gerard-Lebois et al., *Congo 1967* (Bruxelles: Centre de Recherche et d'Information Socio-Politique [CRSP], 1969), 365–415.

21. On the Mobutu dictatorship, see Michael G Schatzberg, *The Dialectics of Opression in Zaire* (Bloomington: Indiana University Press, 1991); and Kamitatu, *La grande mystifications du Congo-Kinshasa*.

22. An example of such contacts is the one with the American Mineral Fields of Hope, Arkansas, reported by James C. McKenley Jr. in "Rebels' New Allies: Men Armed with Briefcases," *New York Times*, Thursday, April 17, 1997.

2

Religion and Worldview

THE BELIEF in the existence of supernatural forces and in their intervention in human life is the key to understanding Congolese people's religious behaviors. To begin with, they believe that there is a supernatural power inside each human being as a product of divine creation. This innate power, called vital force, animates the body and sustains life.[1] Hence its other name, principle of life. At death, the principle of life leaves the body, becomes a pure spirit and joins the spirits of departed relatives to become an ancestor. The ancestors continue to be active in the lives of their living relatives, regulating their behaviors by rewarding them for conformity and punishing them for disobedience. Other than the ancestors, daily life is influenced by individuals who, through initiation or divine revelation, have acquired the power to incorporate spiritual forces and powers from nature. Rain, lightning and certain strong animals provide these powers. Diviners, witches and healers can alter a person's condition by energizing such supernatural forces.

The ancestors and the persons who are endowed with supernatural powers operate at the individual and family levels. Their actions, whether beneficial or harmful, affect the target adult person or his or her progeny or undertakings. Collective endeavors, organized at the village or intervillage levels, are often accompanied by religious ceremonies involving members of different clans. They address nature spirits or spirits of historic heroes, such as famous leaders who have died. Collective hunting or the conjuration of a calamity, for example, often bring together individuals who are not related by blood. They invoke the spirits of famous hunters or forest spirits for protection and success. Standing above all other supernatural powers are the unlimited and sovereign powers of the Creator. The Creator's interventions are often acknowledged in principle, but they are not often related to specific circumstances. For example, except for death in old age, misfortunes are generally attributed to ancestral punishment or to malevolent actions of evildoers. People admit that God is the ultimate cause of death, but when death occurs, generally ancestors or witches, rather than God, are held responsible.

With Belgian occupation, following the 1885 partition of Africa at the Berlin Conference, traditional religions in the Congo became the target of oppression by the colonial government and Christian missionaries. Catholic missions were an integral part of the colonial power structure. They used methods of coercion at will. Protestant churches, which were staffed by non-Belgian personnel for the most part, were less coercive but nonetheless determined to convert the Congolese from ancestral beliefs to the Christian faith. Congolese prophetic movements that followed the paths of Christian mission stations and protested against human exploitation were met with severe repression. Their leaders were sentenced to death or exile. Congo's political independence from Belgium, which it acquired in 1960, reinstated the freedom of religion denied to the Congolese in colonial times. As a result, the Kimbanguist Church, which was born from a prophetic movement that had operated clandestinely during colonization, joined the mainstream. It is today a national church, along with the Catholic Church and Protestant denominations. Independence has also opened the door to prophetic churches of all sizes. As products of a double inheritance, the new prophetic churches are hybrid in their decor and their teachings. Not only do they readjust the rituals and dress, in some way they also redefine theologies in relation both to ancestral beliefs and to the Euro-centered Christian faith.

The next section examines six elements of traditional religions in the Congo: the human as a spiritual being, the ancestors, nature spirits, the spirits of historic figures, practitioners of supernatural powers and the Creator.[2] The following section illustrates the phenomenon of religious hybridization, first within the Catholic Church and then in the Kimbanguist Church and other prophetic churches.

ELEMENTS OF ANCESTRAL RELIGIONS

The Human as a Spiritual Being

The vital force that is the principle of life (*moyo*) is the essential element in the human as a spiritual being. It represents the divine presence in every creature. The divine presence permeates the human body and makes it sacred, that is, set apart as a high value. Therefore, the Kongo people differentiate the human body as a sacred reality (*nitu*) from the flesh (*nsuni*), which humans and animals share and also from the body as a physical structure (*vuvulu*). The life-sustaining principle also permeates the human blood (*menga*), another essential element of life. Therefore, tampering with the blood affects the principle of life. For instance, magical manipulation or shedding of the blood can debilitate the essence of a person. As *nitu* (that is, for being permeated by the principle of life), the human being has the capacity to leave the flesh and the bodily envelope and operate independently. Thus, for instance, at an individual's death, his or her principle of life survives and moves to *ku masa*, a location by the water where life is eternal.

Also inherent in the human's essence is the shadow. Wherever the individual is, his or her shadow is also. The shadow projects the individual so closely that a damage to the shadow affects the individual in real life. Consequently, an adult person would not tolerate someone walking on his or her shadow. Worth mentioning also is the concept of a name. One's name is part of one's personality. Therefore, it changes with one's social status. When one's personality is transformed, for example, through initiation ceremonies, the neophyte takes on a new name reflecting a new identity. Just as with the principle of life, a person's name survives his or her death.

The Spirits of the Land

Through death, a person becomes a pure spirit and joins the spirits of departed relatives, thus becoming an ancestor. Unlike the ancestral spirits, nature spirits have never existed in human form. They have been spirits from creation and continue to be such. Great spirits are spirits of past heroes. Like the ancestors, they have existed in human flesh. The three types of spirits are sometimes referred to collectively as spirits of the land.

Ancestral Spirits. The Kongo people distinguish several categories of ancestors, depending on how a person lived on earth and how he or she died. The most venerated ancestors (*bakulu*) are those departed elders and noble members of the clan who lived exemplary lives on earth; they now live a peaceful and happy life in the ancestral village. Ancestral villages, located underneath the earth near forests and rivers, are organized on a model similar to human villages, with men and women, chiefs and subjects, fulfilling the same functions as they did on earth. Relatives who lived undeserving lives on earth (*matebo*) and sorcerers are denied access to the ancestral village. They are generally represented as small in stature, ugly and foul smelling.

Stylized Ceremonial Head Mask. Collection of
the author.

They feed on human flesh and build their shelters near springs of water,
which they leave only to steal chickens, goats and clothing. Persons who died
violently, such as the founding fathers who perished in conquest wars and
victims of assassination or suicide, form a separate category of ancestors
(*bankita*). Finally, there are the water spirits (*bisimbi*), who live by creeks,
springs and ponds. It is prohibited to fetch water from these locations or go
near them. *Bisimbi* have the habit of crouching underneath stones and roots.
Individuals who step on them become sick.

Ancestral Rituals.   Each Kongo clan had a day of the week designated as
a holiday. On that day, the priest of the ancestors would bring a small calabash filled with palm wine into the ancestors' house. He would plunge some
leaves from a certain tree into the calabash and sprinkle the wine on the
ancestral basket. Then he would kneel down, pour some wine on the ground,
pick up some wet soil and rub it on his chest three times. Before vacating
the house, he would greet the ancestors three times by clapping his hands.
The ancestors are the providers of everything, including success in reproduction, farming, business and hunting. Four-legged animals with claws are
ancestral property. The hunter who has killed such an animal must show his
respect for, and gratitude toward, the ancestors by honoring all hunting
traditions concerning that particular animal species. The chief selected the

day for such hunts and the day and time for supplication prayers in the ancestral cemetery before the hunt. Hunters would bring their dogs and guns to the cemetery, the chief would pour palm wine on each tomb and all the hunters would then kneel behind him. He would address the ancestors as fathers, mothers and elders, inviting them to drink wine and imploring them to bless their descendants with fecundity and success in the enterprise of the day by making the game available to the hunters and reachable by their weapons. Everyone would greet the ancestors with a triple hand clap and then leave for the hunt.

Nature Spirits. The veneration of nature spirits was widespread among the Mongo people, who live in the Equatorial province. Mongo nature spirits (*bilima*) were believed to live sometimes in village communities as husbands, wives and children. The most generous *bilima* favored human beings with abundant progeny; they were addressed as grandmothers. It is a quite widespread African custom for a person who is a source of generosities to be affectionately referred to as mother even if that person is a male. Grandmothers here is used in the sense of those who have provided for their offspring unceasingly and for a long time.

Nature spirits resided in mysterious locations, such as whirlpools, springs or steep slopes. They exercised supernatural powers to the benefit of humans, such as helping them to discover thieves, take revenge on an enemy or achieve success in hunting and fishing. The greatest gifts expected from these spirits were fertility and progeny. In general terms, their role was to intercede before God for the humans and secure for them success in their undertakings and all kinds of blessings. By their social position, certain individuals could establish alliances with particular spirits, to whom they would regularly make presents of food. Sometimes an individual would give food to a spirit simply for survival. Such a gift was different from offerings of food (not sacrifices) made at his home for the specific purpose of obtaining blessings for children.

Great Spirits. The Bashi of Kivu, in eastern Congo, venerate a great spirit called Lyangombe. They share this practice with related ethnic groups who live in neighboring Great Lakes countries (Uganda, Rwanda, Burundi and Tanzania). The Bashi believe that Lyangombe lived in Rwanda, where he died as a hero. They believe his father was a leader of a religious sect (*manduwa*). Lyangombe, a formidable magician frequently consulted by monarchs, succeeded his father at the head of the movement. He once had a dispute with King Ruganzu Ndori (Ruganzu II) of Rwanda. After that, he died while in a hunting party, killed by an antelope. To elevate Lyangombe's death to the hero's greatness, oral tradition later transformed the antelope into a buffalo and turned his followers into heroes who committed mass suicide at his death out of loyalty to him. Their sacred death was later avenged by a severe epidemic that befell Rwanda during the reign of King Mutara I, the son of Ruganzu II. To cool the anger of these formidable spirits, the king and the noble men ordered the initiation of the entire Rwanda country to the cult. This is the account of a national religion originating from ancestral veneration.

Secret Society. Practitioners of the Lyangombe cult have been initiated into a secret society (*kubandwa*). To the initiate, the society stands as an adoptive family. Initiation is carried out in two phases, respectively designed to set the adepts apart as novices and to confirm them as new spiritual ministers. The initiation process begins at a sacred tree with a libation by the officiant (a type of priest) standing for the spirit Lyangombe. He sprinkles the tree with water and then gives the candidates instructions. Each initiate must repeat every word of commitment after the officiant. He must pass a test of the names of the grand spirit members of the Lyangombe pantheon. The initiate swears never to reveal the secrets of the society to nonmembers and calls upon Lyangombe to curse him with miseries of all kinds if he ever does.

Supernatural Power Practitioners

Many Congolese stories tell of fetish owners and witches who harm persons they dislike, dream interpreters and diviners who uncover hidden causes of misfortune and healers who counteract wicked actions of malevolent persons and restore health to their victims. Most of the following examples come from the Yansi culture.[3]

Fetishes. Fetishes are empowered objects (*nkisi*). The powers in such objects are not natural to them. They are infused and controlled from without by persons of a certain social status who are endowed with special supernatural might acquired through certain mystical operations, purchase or inheritance. Authority figures, such as elders, are often the focus of suspicion in cases of bad luck, sickness, sterility, accident or death affecting their subordinates. The victim may be the price that the authority figure has paid to obtain his supernatural powers and the expected outcome, such as wealth or promotion on the job. Likewise, violations by younger relatives of family rules (such as respect for the hierarchy, the obligation to share wealth or sexual taboos) are often suspected as the motive for their victimization. The victim may not be the very person who has committed the implicated infraction against the custom. Often one of his children may be harmed instead.

Witches. The supernatural power in fetishes resides in a material object, such as a statue, a bag, a basket or a walking cane. Some supernatural powers reside in the individual who exercises them intentionally or unintentionally. Individuals endowed with such powers (*ndoki*) operate immaterially. They do not use physical objects to reach their goals. Witches, like fetish practitioners, are often older persons of a certain social status who exercise a certain authority over their victim: an uncle in relation to a nephew, a father vis-à-vis a son, a village chief versus a subject. Here, too, the victims are individuals who have disrupted some balance prescribed by custom. Witches operate in the darkness of the night. They may kill their victims or keep them alive only physically while in essence they have already eaten them.

Dream Interpreters. Dreams are carriers of hidden messages about a person's future or indicative of the will of the ancestors. They are also a medium of communication between an individual and his or her fetishes. Fetish owners keep them next to their bedside at night in hope that the fetish will bring them some meaningful messages through their dreams. Overall, dreams may express the ancestors' discontent or a threat of menace by a living person. A person who has carried out the recommendations of a diviner on a particular case will be informed in a dream about whether his or her efforts will succeed. Dream messages are often inversions of reality. For example, among the Yansi, dreaming of a child dying by a tree may mean to a hunter that he will kill a big game in his next hunting adventure. A dream featuring two foxes catching roosters from the village may announce imminent death of children from that village.

Diviners. The most important role in discovering the hidden sources of misfortunes is played by diviners. When they are consulted, their judgement is binding. Some have the ability both to identify and to kill the person responsible for an unfortunate situation, if it is the client's wish. Some are consulted exclusively for children's diseases; others are consulted only for cases of sterility. Divination methods may include shaking a bag filled with cowries or coins to study their reactions and movements. Sometimes a diviner places a coin on his or her forehead while holding a fetish pot on his or her lap and shaking his or her head after asking the pot a question. If the coin falls into the pot, the response is positive; if it falls outside, the response is negative. Sometimes the diviner's task is to identify the image of the person responsible for a particular condition by looking into a special cooking pot. He or she may scratch the soil with a stick while enumerating different possible causes that the stick suggests and ask the client to choose.

The Creator

Congolese peoples acknowledge the existence of the Supreme Being who is the ultimate maker of all that exists, both material and immaterial. All have elaborate notions of how the creation process unfolded. All ethnic groups have notions of God's demands on the humans and have developed formulas for expressing God's greatness and other attributes as well as relations with the humans and other creatures. All also confront God with philosophical questions about human disparities, hardship and death. Mufuta Kabemba and his students at the National University of Zaire, Lubumbashi Campus, studied these issues among twenty ethnic groups. The following information is drawn from their work.[4]

Belief in the existence of a Supreme Being who is the author of all creations is universal.[5] People know God and address God by one or several names. Etymologically, some of God's names among the Chokwe and the Sanga, for example, derive from a root meaning *father* or *maker*, thus acknowledging the Supreme Being as the author of all creation. Some names are specific in their knowledge of the Creator's spiritual nature and on identity as the original spirit, who is older than any other. Such is the case among the Hemba, Kete and the Songye. The Binja and many other groups say that God's residence is everywhere; other groups, the Chokwe and the Luba among them, situate it in the sky.

The Supreme Being's relation to the humans is one of a father to a son, a protector to a protégé; in brief, it is one of dependence. For most groups, God relates to members of a particular group collectively through their ancestors. A few, including the Luba of Shaba, assert a direct individual relationship. All groups see respect of the law, love for their fellows and solidarity among family members as divine prescriptions. As a rule, God's demands and the ancestors' demands coincide. Both aim at maintaining unity and solidarity among humans.

Human interaction with God involves prayer. Persons who have received blessings or who experience some form of hardship may address individual prayers to God. Groups going through special circumstances, whether a prolonged drought or an abundant harvest after a long period of scarcity and epidemics, often address collective prayers to God. Prayers to God often begin with an invocation of one or another of the "praise names" and end with an invocation of the ancestral spirits. Sometimes, the ancestral spirits are invoked before God.

Praise names appeal to God's goodness and magnanimity: For example, they may identify God as the One who created mountains and valleys or the Most High One, who gives to the elders and the youth alike. The prerogative of presenting collective prayers belongs to the authority figure who represents the ancestors: the oldest member of the group (a male among the Bemba; a person of either sex among the Chokwe or the Binja; a male head of the clan among the Hemba, the Kete and the Luba of Kasai; the oldest male descendent of the lineage founder among the Luntu).

Collective prayers generally accompany some ceremony or ritual performed in special locations: in the forest under a sacred tree or on a rock among the Bemba; in a grotto near a waterfall among the Binja; at a crossroad or under a palm tree among the Kete. Collective ceremonial prayers to God were said at specific times of the day: in the evening among the Songye; at dawn among the Soo; either at dawn or at sunset among the Vira. During collective prayers to God, people cover their bodies with white kaolin or wear white clothes. The white color is a symbol of purity of heart. The extremities of the white cloth sometimes form a knot, a symbol of unity with the Supreme Being.

TOWARD AFRICANIZING CHRISTIANITY

The Jamaa movement, the Dieudonnés diviners, the Kimbanguist Church and the new prophetic churches illustrate four types of connection between Christianity and African values. The Jamaa movement was an attempt to revamp Christianity by organizing its teaching around selected compatible principles of the African worldview. Kimbanguism was born as a revolt against European hostility to Congolese peoples' values and interests. The Dieudonnés diviners used the Holy Spirit, a Christian weapon popularized by Kimbanguism, to fight sorcery; this was a deep-seated need in the traditional African belief system. Prophetic churches represent an amalgamation of elements from the two religious traditions designed to meet the spiritual and material needs of urban migrants, underpaid workers and middle-class individuals experiencing downward mobility.

The Changing Catholic Experience

The Catholic Church dominated the religious scene in the Congo. Throughout the colony, Catholic missionaries tried to convert the Congolese from ancestral religions, which they pejoratively referred to as paganism, to Catholicism, which was presented as the only true religion. All the methods they employed to this end were exclusively based on European customs. Slight elements of change began to appear toward the end of the colonial period. Independence brought the Congo more changes.

From Organ to Drum. Conversion to Christianity begins with baptism. Candidates for baptism followed several months of instruction. They generally administered baptism on a Saturday. On the previous Friday, the candidates were taken to church to confess their sins, repent, obtain pardon and blessing from the priest and carry out the penance prescribed by him. The most common penitential punishment consisted of performing the stations of the cross or the Virgin Mary rosary recitation. Baptism was administered by pouring water on the candidate's completely shaved head. On Sunday, the novices attended the mass in their nicest clothes and received the first communion. Children of Christian parents were baptized at a young age. Around age twelve, they were confirmed and received their first communion.

Catechism and instructions for the baptism, confirmation, first communion or wedding ceremonies were given in church. All the sacraments were administered in the church except the last anointment, which took place wherever the dying person was. The order of the mass followed a very rigid canon. The officiant recited the same prayers and the same songs in Latin in a prescribed sequence. The "Lord's Prayer," the recitation of the rosaries of the Virgin Mary and the sermon were given in the local vernacular in services for the masses and in French in those for the educated ones. The reading of the Bible was in most part restricted to clergy, both actual or in training. The sitting section for the parishioners was filled with benches facing an elevated pulpit. In cities where the Congolese and Europeans coexisted, three scenarios were possible. In some places, Europeans and Congolese attended different churches in their respective neighborhoods. In others, they attended the same church but for different services. Sometimes they attended the same service, but the Europeans sat in chairs up front and the Congolese sat on benches in the back. The reed organ and the bell were the dominant musical instruments used during the mass. Not unexpectedly, the grander churches, such as cathedrals, had more impressive instruments.

In the late 1950s, African elements began to appear in the church service. The first was *Misa Luba*, composed by Gregoire Luntumwa, a native of Western Kasai and former student of the Kabwe Great Seminary. The *Misa Luba* was sung in Latin but with melodies borrowed from "Kasala," the heroic song common to various Kasai ethnic groups tracing descent from the ancient Luba Empire. Congo independence opened the door to additional influences.

Gradually, in many places, the church service for the masses took the form of what is sometimes referred to as folkloric mass. These masses incorporated African songs, rhythms and musical instruments. The most common African musical instruments in the Christian service are the maraca and the drum. Sometimes dances that were once precluded as pagan are executed in the church for the Lord.

From Catechism to Storytelling. The catechism is the most typical training instrument in Catholic tradition. In catechism, Christian doctrine and practices are simplified and presented as questions and responses. When the catechism was not the core of training for a particular session, selected questions or passages from the Bible were used to introduce the subject of the day. In the 1950s, in the city of Kolwezi, in Katanga province, there developed a practice of introducing the teaching of Christian messages with African stories. From its origin in Kolwezi, the practice expanded to the rest of Katanga and into the two Kasai provinces, especially in the aftermath of the bloody events that followed Congo independence. Known as the Jamaa movement, the practice remained within the original Roman Catholic Church as a necessity for preserving the principle of unity on which it is founded. Father Placide Tempels, from whose teaching the movement derived, defines it as a search for *bumuntu*, a trio of values central to the human in every individual as conceived by the African people.[6] The three values are the vital force, fecundity and bonding love. Both Father Tempels and his disciples characterized Jamaa as a state of mind or a consciousness that should animate every true Christian person.

In practical terms, Jamaa is, above all, an approach to teaching that employs African tactics. Tactically, Jamaa teachings (*mafundisho*) are conveyed through fables, animal stories and myths from various ethnic groups; this is done in hopes of fostering interethnic unity among Jamaa members. Particular didactic (teaching) stories emphasize particular values. A good example is the story of a blacksmith's son who thought he was more skilled than, and thus superior to, his father. Later, however, he was forced to come to his father for advice upon encountering an unsolvable and life-threatening problem. The moral of the story is that there is no survival away from the source of life and that victory resides in the application of the collective ancestral wisdom, as passed down from father to son.

The Antisorcery Movement

The belief in sorcery is deep-seated in the souls and minds of the Congolese people. Sorcerers are evildoers who use supernatural powers to harm other individuals. They can kill their victims by eating them mystically. The fight against such individuals is continual. Where a strong sense of community existed, the fight against sorcery often took a collective form designed to protect and promote the welfare of an entire village rather than a single family.

A Community-Based Approach to Sorcery. In the 1920s, there developed a strong village-based antisorcery movement in different parts of Equator, Kasai and Kwango.[7] A particular village joined the movement by taking a public oath against sorcery and using harmful charms in a collective initiation ceremony. Violators of the oath would get sick and die if they did not confess their crime. Periodically, or at the occasion of a misfortune affecting the community, the village held collective rituals through which all the participants rededicated themselves to combating sorcery.

Although this movement started before the Belgian colonization of the Congo, its influence in the twentieth century should not be overlooked. In the early 1930s, in Lower-Kasai and in Kwango, antisorcery ceremonies began to incorporate charms and rituals designed to chase the Europeans from the country. The 1931 revolt of Pende, in particular, included a cult, called *tupelepele*, that was targeted at forcing the Europeans out and bringing the ancestors back into control. Later, under the Christian missionaries' influence, a practice was introduced that consisted of using blessed water in rituals designed to remove evil powers from sorcery victims. In 1937, Vanda, a Methodist catechist in the Upper Sankuru region, founded a cult combining rituals from African, Catholic and Methodist traditions. The steps in carrying out the cult included confession, paying dues, baptism by water, swallowing a potion made out of the barks of a certain tree, or rubbing the potion on an incision on the body of the target person. Reportedly, the Christian elements most adapted to African traditions were more amenable to incorporation. Such was the case with hymns, public confession and dignitary titles. For instance, leaders bore such titles as apostle, monsignor or pope.

The ever present threat of sorcery fosters the need for consulting diviners who have the supernatural power to discover the hidden causes of human suffering and propose the appropriate course of action for rescuing the victims of sorcery. Spiritual incorporation is one of the most powerful forms of divination. It takes place during special ceremonies involving drumming, singing and dancing and culminating in a trance state. The drumming and singing invite spirits expected to reveal the cause of the designated misfortune. During the trance, the spirits utter some inarticulate words that only some specially endowed initiates can interpret. These words reveal the secret for which the spirits were invoked. If the revelation made by the spirits or by any other diviner pointed to a sorcerer, the accused was normally subjected to special rituals designed to make him or her vomit the victim.

Dieudonnés Diviners. In sorcery, the evil powers that cause harm to people or their property are housed in a human being. In a fetish, such powers, although controlled by a person, are housed in an object. In some regions, the antisorcery movement was directed toward the destruction of fetishes. A branch of the antisorcery movement called the Dieudonnés and specifically targeted at fetish destruction developed in the Kwango region out of the missionary and Kimbanguist churches. The Dieudonnés acted in God's name but derived their divination powers from a famous fetish named Lumon.[8] Their mission was to burn down statues and other objects representing fetishes. They carried out the destruction at the request of individuals who, having experienced some misfortune in their lives, suspected the presence of some hidden fetish on their premises.

The state licensed some Dieudonnés to carry out fetish destruction and take individuals to court for practicing fetishes. The divination process, which culminated in a trance state, generally started with self-purification with Christian holy water, followed by invocations in songs to God or to saints. During the trance, the Dieudonnés communicated with the spirits of the dead, who revealed to them the locations where the fetishes for destruction were hidden. Following the discovery, the Dieudonnés would sacrifice a chicken in expiation of the anticipated fault of fetish destruction and, finally, procede with the actual destruction.

The Holy Spirit. With the adoption of certain forms of Christianity, particularly those of the Pentecostal type, the Holy Spirit replaced divination spirits. Like divination spirits, the Holy Spirit reveals secrets during a trance. These secrets, as with those involving fetishes, are in a language that only a few initiates, called prophets, can interpret. The victim-vomiting ritual takes on a new form as well; it is now exorcism. In this Christian version of sorcery, the prophet, who is in a state of trance and empowered by the Holy Spirit, practices exorcism by ordering the evil powers out of the victim.

Prophetic Movements

As early as 1906, Christian churches in the Congo became incubators of religion-inspired revolt movements portraying missionaries as agents of colonial oppression and enemies of the Congolese people. Of these movements, the most massive and most feared by the colonial administration was Kintuadi, which was founded in 1921 by Prophet Simon Kimbangu.[9]

Prophet Simon Kimbangu. Born on September 24, 1881, at Nkamba, in the District of Cataract, Lower Congo, Simon Kimbangu became a catechist in a Protestant mission station after completing training as a Baptist catechumen (which precedes becoming a communicant, or church fellow). On the night of April 4, 1921, Kimbangu recounted, he had a personal encounter with Jesus Christ, who entrusted him with the mission to reconvert and reconcile his unfaithful followers. At the time, Catholic missionaries were an integral part of the colonizing force in the Congo, with all the zeal and extortionary behavior of the conqueror. In addition, Catholics and Protestants in the area—and, in fact, throughout the Congo—were living in discord. Feeling unable to reconcile them, Kimbangu left the village to take on a job in Kinshasa. Still, he explained, a divine voice called him repeatedly to work for Christ. Finally, he returned to the village to devote himself to evangelism and farming.

One day, Kimbangu is said to have healed a sick woman by laying his hands on her. Following this, he is said to have performed many other miracles in Christ's name. As the news of his miracles spread, a crowd of followers from the surrounding villages began to form around him, seeking healing and listening to his words. As a result, the Catholic missionaries became very unhappy with him. Following in their path, the colonial administration asked an account from the Protestant mission stations, because Kimbangu worked for them. Afraid of government sanctions, the Protestant missionaries disavowed Kimbangu. On June 6, 1921, the Belgians arrested Kimbangu, accusing him of inciting the populations to revolt and of engaging in civil disobedience by refusing to pay taxes. On October 3, 1921, they sentenced him to death and set the execution date for the next day. However, King Albert I of Belgium commuted the sentence to life in prison. Kimbangu was jailed in Lubumbashi (Elizabethville), where he died thirty years later, on October 12, 1951.

The Kintuadi Movement. The colonial authorities in the Congo had hoped that Kmbangu's ideas would die with his arrest, but to the contrary. Many followers continued his legacy through collective prayers and sermons. Like Kimbangu, the Kintuadi leaders were arrested and deported to prisons in distant regions of the colony, where they perished. However, the movement continued to operate in secret. From the rural areas, it spread to the city of Kinshasa in the 1950s. The principal proponent was Lucien Luntandila, an employee of the colonial administration, who had access to official files detailing cases of individuals exiled for their affiliation with Kintuadi.

The Kimbanguist Church. In the aftermath of the popular uprising of January 4, 1959, the Kimbanguists opened their own schools and health centers. Finally, on December 24, 1959, Kimbanguism was officially recognized, with its headquarters at Nkamba, Kimbangu's birth place. Joseph Diangenda, the prophet's son, became the church's spiritual leader and legal representative, and Lucien Luntandila assumed the functions of secretary-general. To appeal to a more universal membership, the church changed its official name from Kintuadi to L'Eglise du Christ sur la Terre par le Prophet Simon Kimbangu (The Church of Christ on Earth by the Prophet Simon Kimbangu). Today the church claims to have branches in practically all Congolese provinces and nine African countries. Outside the continent, Kimbanguist leadership claims members in Belgium, France, Germany, Holland, Portugal, Switzerland, Canada and the United States.

Kimbanguist Doctrine. Kimbanguist doctrine is summarized in the official name, The Church of Christ on Earth by Prophet Simon Kimbangu. At the center of the Kimbanguist doctrine stands the belief in Jesus Christ as the Son of God and the Savior of humankind. Prophet Simon Kimbangu is his witness on earth, that is, his special messenger. Kimbanguists believe in the Holy Trinity and in the power of the Holy Spirit, including the power to heal the sick by the laying on of hands. They consider it their religious obligation to love God and their fellow humans through Christ; in other words, all who believe in God as the Supreme Being and Creator of the universe. They do not drink alcohol or smoke. They practice monogamy and condemn polygamy and all forms of violence, whatever the goal, whether in politics or any other domain.

Kimbanguist Spiritual Discipline. Kimbanguist believers are expected to pray before every activity of the day and at specific hours: 6:00 A.M., 10:00 A.M., noon, 3:00 P.M., 6:00 P.M., 10:00 P.M., midnight and, for those who can, 3:00 A.M. Kimbanguist believers also hold spiritual evenings in different wards at the residence of a member. They hold special prayer meetings in anticipation of major events. Sunday service is practically an all-day activity. There also exist days devoted to God, two per month, which are celebrated with a special liturgy and songs and music of glory. At such occasions, they hold meetings in large shelters. Nowadays, in the overpopulated parishes they even hold the regular Sunday service in shelters.

Kimbanguist Social Concerns. The Kimbanguist Church has, in a sense, replaced the community house (*mbongi*) of the precolonial era, where all matters affecting the community were discussed. On Sundays, after the religious service, church members spend the rest of the day at the church debating concerns of community interest. They hold competitions between men and women or youth and elders to raise money for community construction projects, farms, education or health.

New Prophetic Churches. The postindependence era has experienced a resurgence of Pentecostal-type charismatic churches.[10] Congo's independence in 1960 introduced freedom of religion. Mobutu's ideology of a return to authenticity of the 1970s reinforced the motivation for integrating elements from Africa ancestral and Judeo-Christian biblical traditions. For instance, it is the responsibility of the prophet to seek guidance from the Holy Spirit in order to help the followers solve their health problems. The Holy Spirit reveals the illnesses, including their cause and the solutions, to the prophet during a trance. Revelations by the Holy Spirit point to violations of ancestral or divine law, evil spirits, fetishes, adultery, greed or sorcery. Sometimes, the prophet performs exorcism to set the client free from the powers of the sorcerer or of evil spirits. Exorcism rituals have two aspects, one formal and one informal. The formal aspect consists of hymns, prayers, Bible readings and spiritual instructions. The informal aspect includes hand-clapping and dancing, among other rituals.

An economic crisis that reached high proportions beginning in the 1980s favored an explosion in the number of prophetic churches. The crisis left many social categories disconnected from established networks: migrants, single mothers, fallen middle-class employees, the homeless, and others. The prophetic leaders' appeal and their ability to integrate individuals of diverse backgrounds motivated these disenfranchised individuals to look for religious experiences other than those found in the conventional ancestral veneration, Catholic mass or Protestant service. In addition, prophetic churches cultivate a sense of equality among the members. Everyone has an equal opportunity for direct access to the Holy Spirit through prayers, visions and spiritual incorporation. To symbolize their equality, everyone enters the prayer house without shoes, watches or jewelry.

NOTES

1. R.P. Placide Tempels, *La philosophie bantue*, trans. A. Rubbens (Paris: Presence Africaine, 1948).

2. Mulago gwa Cicala Musharimana, *La religion traditionnelle des bantu et leur vision du monde* (Kinshasa Zaire: Presses Universitaires du Zaire, 1973). Mulago summarizes the writings of various anthropologists who have studied the culture of the Mongo, Kongo, Bashi and other Congolese ethnic groups. He also gives special attention to the cult of Lyangombe, a semimythical, semihistoric hero. The cult started in Rwanda but is also practiced in the eastern Congo. See also two works by K. Kia Bunseki Fu-Kiau, *Mbongi: An African Traditional Political Institution* (Roxbury, MA: Omenana, 1985) and *Self-Healing Power and Therapy: Old Teachings from Africa* (New York: Vantage Press, 1991), for an expert analysis of the culture of the Kongo people.

3. Guy De Plaen, "Rôle social de la magie et de la sorcelerie chez les Bayansi," *Cahiers Economiques et Sociaux* 6, no. 2 (1968): 203–235.

4. Mufuta Kabemba, "Croyances traditionnelles et pratiques spirituelles au Zaire," in *L'Afrique et ses formes de vie spirituelle* (Kinshasa, Zaire: Centre des Religions Africaines, 1990), 175.

5. Mufuta Kabemba and his research team have identified one exception: the Ndembo, a branch of the Lunda ethnic group, which appears to lack any notion of the divine or divine attributes.

6. Johannes Fabian, *Jamaa: A Charismatic Movement in Katanga* (Evanston, IL: Northwestern University Press, 1971).

7. Jan Vansina, "Lukoshi/Lupambula: Histoire d'un culte religieux dans les régions du Kasai et du Kwango (1920–1970)," *Etudes d'Histoire Africaine* 5 (1973): 51–97. Vansina investigates the spread of the antisorcery movement to many regions of the Congo between 1920 and 1970.

8. On the Dieudonnés diviners, see De Plaen, "Rôle social de la magie et de la sorcelerie chez les Bayansi," 217–219.

9. Information on Kimbanguism is based on extensive interviews conducted by the author with Reverend Lucien Luntandila and his wife, Mama Jeanne Lukibawo Luntandila. Reverend Luntandila served for forty years as secretary-general of the Kimbanguist Church. He also shared with the author written documentation from his personal library.

10. This section draws heavily on René Devisch, "Pillage of Jesus: Healing Churches and the Villagization of Kinshasa," *Africa: Journal of the International African Institute* 66, no. 4 (1996), 555–585.

3

Literature and Media

BOTH LITERATURE AND MEDIA are methods of communication that use sound and writing to convey messages. Two trends stand out in Congolese literature. One trend seeks to revive ancestral traditions. Writers in this category have undertaken to record Congolese traditions preserved through oral history and mnemonic (memory) aids. Some literary genres pertaining to this trend are verbal competition and play songs, animal stories and legends, proverbs, praise poetry and drama. The other trend confronts the ills of contemporary Congolese society. Through novels, poetry, or other forms of narrative the writers following this trend address such themes as colonial oppression, ethnic conflicts, political treason, power abuse, rebel invasions and ethnic cleansing. The two trends are not mutually exclusive; in fact, many writers belong to both. The themes presented in this chapter are only illustrative. They are far from representative of all those found in modern Congolese literature today.

Mass media are communication methods designed to reach a large audience. Messengers and public speech were, and still are, widely used throughout the Congo. Additionally, authority figures in ancient times employed instruments such as the flute, the slit drum, and the tom-toms for special messages. Modern communication media in the Congo were introduced during colonial rule. For a long time the radiotelegraphy was the only modern medium available. Then came more complex media such as the radio and then the television. Missionaries introduced the written press, and the government soon adopted its use. Some time later, businesses also adopted the use of publications.

RECONSTRUCTING THE ANCESTRAL LITERARY HERITAGE

In Congolese families childhood education for intellectual development takes many forms, such as counting rhymes, the inversion of word syllables, riddles and enigmas. The learning of these forms and others generally takes place in some sort of competition among the learners. The teaching-learning process for counting rhymes and inversion requires automatically supplying the response. Learning riddles, enigmas and other types of learning materials, such as animal stories, legends, proverbs and epic songs, requires a higher level of intellectual effort than counting rhymes and inversion games. Therefore, they stress understanding and application rather than speed.

Verbal Competition and Game Songs

Verbal competition is a literary genre in which children must correctly and rapidly recite counting rhymes, inverted words, riddles or enigmas. The learner is expected to conform strictly to specified rules. Violations are sanctioned with booing and elimination from competition. The purpose is to teach young people the mastery of the spoken word, an important skill in judiciary art and reporting. The most immediate objective is to practice suppleness of the tongue, correct pronunciation, perception and the discernment of sounds, melody and rhythm. Phrases, poems, counting rhymes, enigmas and songs that are the object of competitive recitation are value-laden cultural devices. Therefore, the exercise seeks to achieve more than correct practice of the language. It is also intended to inculcate social values deemed indispensable for cultural continuity.

Counting Rhymes. Counting fingers rhythmically is perhaps the most universal initial strategy for teaching numbers to African children.[1] The counting is to be done in a fixed order by enunciating each finger's name. In many Congolese cultures these names are descriptive, evoking the fingers' respective sizes, positions or functions. A literal English translation of fingers' names from the language of the Banya Bwisha people would read like this: little finger, little finger's big brother (ring finger), long finger (middle finger), finger before last (index), and the shortest finger (thumb). Nguey children normally sang the fingers' names in two rounds, first from thumb to little finger and then from little finger to thumb. An English translation of Ngwey fingers' names would be like this: village chief (thumb), quarrel pointer (index), they track him but never catch him (middle finger), brown skin and beauty (ring finger) and house where there is no junior or senior (little finger).

Other than singing rhythmically, many features help Luba children learn and retain the fingers' names. Each finger's name is composed of two words of approximately the same length. Counting is always done on the left fingers from the little finger to the thumb, by holding the fingers one after the other with the right thumb and middle finger and shaking each finger twice while introducing it with the demonstrative "this is." The counting goes like this:

Eu ntengana ntengana	This is the little finger.
Eu mmulonda ntengana	This is the one following the little finger.
Eu mmunu wa munkulu	This is the middle finger.
Eu mmuinshi kalekele	This is the index finger.
Eu ke tshiala mwabila	This is the thumb.

From the fingers, the counting exercise is extended to the rest of the left arm by including the following:

Eu mbutshila kanyinyi	This is meat holder (closed palm).
Eu nyunguluja diboku	This is put-it-around the arm (wrist).
Eu nkongoloja muana	This is cradle-the-baby (curve of the left arm).

Counting rhymes are used to teach children important features of the immediate physical and social environment. Luba children in their formative years were asked to rhythmically recite the names of ten animals, ten rivers, ten chiefs or ten important marketplaces. Ngbandi children competed for a perfect score of ten, alternating an animal name and a fish name. The Alur people had children recite their own genealogies.[2]

Inversion of Word Syllables. A widespread literary practice used in teaching children the language consists of inverting the order of syllables in words. The inversion game is played in pairs. The first speaker says the word rapidly in inverted form and the second repeats the word instantaneously in its correct form, or vice versa. For example, if Kete children were socialized in Kete culture (in the Congo) using the English language, one partner in the game would say rapidly something like this: "*gerriama sessposupre velo*," expecting the playmate to respond immediately by saying: "marriage presupposes love." In turn the second partner would say, for example: "poverty is vice," and the first would rapidly respond: "*tyverpo is cevi*."

Riddles and Enigmas. Counting rhymes are used with little children. More mature children are taught through other media, such as riddles, enigmas and proverbs, which seek to inculcate more profound meanings and develop higher-level intellectual reflexes. Riddles and enigmas occupy an important place in children's intellectual education. Some ethnic groups designate the two concepts by different terms. For example, the Bemba word for riddle (*ifityoleko*) means "wisdom test," whereas the word for enigma (*ubwilye*) signifies something resembling the spider web, in which discovering the beginning and the end is difficult. The Yaka use two different words as well: *bitsimbwa* or *bitangi* ("what is enunciated to be completed") for riddle and *biswekama* ("what is hidden") for enigma. Other groups use a common term for both concepts. For example, the Bira term *tandakima* and the Hunde term *ngabulira* apply interchangeably to riddles and enigmas.

The riddle competition is executed in the form of a game, which is very fast paced. Before the game, the contenders agree on the nature of the punishment for an inability to respond correctly: either fine or a symbolic curse. Enigmas require a longer time for reflection, so discovering the hidden meaning is given more importance than making a prompt response.

Game Songs. After being introduced to counting rhymes and inversion, small children practice them freely without adult supervision. They do so for other games as well. Luba small girls, for example, play a game called A Wa Nsabweee, which is played in pairs. The players stand facing each other. Then, they hit each other's palms in parallel and crisscross, alternatively. Then each hits her own knees with her palms, again alternatively in parallel and crisscross. As they do so, they jump up and down rapidly and rhythmically while singing "*A Wa Nsabweee.*" The game is played very fast. The person who breaks the rhythm or misses an appropriate hit or jump loses.

Teenagers and adolescents have their own games, in which they talk more freely about certain things that they would not feel comfortable mentioning in the presence of adults. A number of such games take place in the evening, outside, in the moonlight. Many evening games include dances and songs. Young people of both sexes participate in them.

Nsunza Games. Some songs accompanying the young people's evening games convey moralizing messages. The Congolese writer Batukezanga Zamenga relates two stories from game songs of his youth which criticized community members who had secretly engaged in forbidden activities, thinking no one would know about it.[3] One song talks about Ngabidiela and Zelemani, who tasted jackal meat in secret. This meat is forbidden, as the jackal is identified as a wild dog. Their excuse was that the jackal is not really a dog, as the dog is domesticated while the jackal lives in the wilderness. The song reminded them that a dog is a dog whether it is domestic or wild. The other song denounced two boys, Noel and Wanga, who had stolen a big rooster and were caught busy cooking it in the forest. They pretended it was an eagle. The song confronted them with two undeniable facts: one, the feathers of the two birds are different; two, even if their bird were an eagle, the forest is not the place where humans cook and eat their game meat. Humans cook and eat their food in the village, not in the wilderness.

Animal Stories and Legends

Animal stories carry moralizing messages. Legends are unverifiable stories passed over from generation to generation. The story of Chameleon and Leopard, and the Songye legend of Kapongo and Kakutshi come from Kasai. The Chameleon and Leopard story draws attention to the importance of reading the signs and of trusting in one's first intuition. By the same token, it warns one against the high price of credulity and inconsistency. Ultimately, it says, trusting in the friendly words of a person who has threatened your life is stupid.[4] The Kapongo and Kakutshi legend was told to the youth in Songye villages to discourage laziness and thievery. It warned people of after-death torments awaiting perpetrators of social and moral offences, as explained in the title, "In the Land of the Dead."[5]

"Chameleon and Leopard." Leopard had befriended Chameleon by sealing a friendship pact with him and throwing a banquet in his honor. However, Chameleon was skeptical of Leopard's good intent. When Leopard visited Chameleon in return, instead of welcoming him, Chameleon climbed into a tree. When Leopard yelled asking him to go down and greet his trustworthy friend, Chameleon threw down a stick, saying: "Here I am." Leopard jumped over the stick, caught it with his teeth and broke it into pieces. Realizing that Chameleon had not really come down, Leopard asked him to do so in honor of their mutual pact. Chameleon told Leopard he was afraid that Leopard would do to him what he did to the stick. Leopard went back home. Chameleon then paid Leopard a second visit, Leopard slaughtered a big goat and they feasted together. Leopard visited for a second time as well, and again Chameleon climbed into a tree. Once again when Leopard asked him to come down he threw down a stick, which Leopard immediately broke into pieces with his teeth. Chameleon says: "You see, what tells me you will not do to me what you did to the stick?" Leopard retorts: "Did we not seal our friendship over a meal?" On that note, Chameleon descends

from the tree, whereupon Leopard jumps over him and breaks him into pieces. Chameleons have stopped jumping down from the trees ever since.

"In the Land of the Dead." This is the story of an individual called Kakutshi, who had been stealing people's crops and other property. Each time he would escape earthly justice by practicing magic. Finally, he was expelled from the village after a boy testified he had seen him stealing a chicken. He went into the forest. There, a voice called him, asking him to come closer. He did so, but all he saw was a huge tree standing in the pathway with a big hole on the trunk, near the base. The voice invited him into the hole, which proved to be the tunnel that led to the village of the dead. The village was vast. Kakutshi found all the people from the village who had died over the years, including his mother, father and brother. All were very short. Their hair fell down to their shoulders. Their feet were reversed, that is, with the heels in front and the toes in the back.

The mother served him beetles and worms, but he did not touch them even. The mother told him: "That is all folks eat over here." The mother told him she had to hide him since people in the land of the dead did not like the living. At night, the mother hid Kakutshi in a pit, under a mat. Later, the father returned home. He was very small, his feet were reversed, and his hair was very long. The father sat on the mat, right on Kakutshi's neck. Kakutshi thought he was going to die of discomfort, but the father did not get up. The mother murmured to Kakutshi warning him that he would be killed if he cried. After a while, the father went out. The mother quickly put Kakutshi in a basket and hid him in the attic and again warned him against crying, saying that he would be finished if he did.

The father came back and lit the fire. The smoke drifted up into Kakutshi's eyes. Kakutshi began groaning: "I cannot stand it anymore. I am dying, I really cannot stand it, I am dying." The father brought the neighbors over. They searched and found Kakutshi hiding in a basket in the attic. When Kakutshi came down, his father asked him: "Who hid you?" Kakutshi said: "My mother did." The father convened everybody. The full number gathered. They were all very small, and they all wore long hair, falling down to their shoulders. All had feet with the toes in the back and heels in the front. They grabbed Kakutshi and killed him. Then they told the mother to go away. For hiding someone who had committed crimes against the community, her place was no longer among them, so they expelled her.

The mother left, heading toward her former village among the living. However, everyone who saw her ran away, including her surviving son, Kitenga. People were scared by her appearance. She was very old and excessively short. She had her heel where her toes should be and long hair. They panicked, ran away and deserted the village. To make things worse, a torrential rain began to fall. It took away everything: the houses, banana trees and fields. Kakutshi's mother arrived at the site of the village, but it had disappeared completely. She became an errant spirit.

Proverbs

Proverbs are popular adages about observed facts of life. They are the backbone of African philosophy and approach to education. The writer, Clementine Faik-Nzuji, has recorded numerous proverbs from different regions of the Congo in French and interpreted them. Her informants included urban residents who had recorded proverbs from their home provinces in vernacular languages.

Proverbs from Upper Congo and Kasai. Some of these proverbs were originally recorded in Swahili by people living in Kinshasa who traced their descent to Upper Congo province. Six Upper Congo proverbs are paired here with equivalent proverbs from Kasai.[6]

Upper Congo: When you have a brother at the distribution center of a valuable, you will not be overlooked.

Kasai: Lucky is she whom a relative has preceded to the mortar.

Interpretation: It is a blessing to have one of your own in a service where intervention may be needed.

During harvest periods, women in Kasai villages used to husk beans in common mortars. Normally latecomers waited for their turn. Nevertheless, a person who found a relative already there could claim that they were together and thus skip ahead. The previous two proverbs are used to express appreciation to a relative or acquaintance whose intervention has helped one to get a job or obtain some other favor.

Upper Congo: The elephant never gets rid of his tusk.

Kasai: The excrement of the neighbor's child smells.

Interpretation: Parents love their children even if other people find them undesirable.

Parents of disabled or socially ill-adjusted children use the preceding proverbs to silence other parents who might mock, ridicule or criticize them for their children's condition or behaviors.

Upper Congo: Put out the fire before it gets out of control.

Kasai: Silence the croaking bird before it becomes a nuisance for the entire village.

Interpretation: These proverbs are advice to people to stop bad habits before they become too difficult to correct and harmful to the community.

Individual behaviors are reflections of community values. Good behaviors enhance the image of the community. Bad ones tarnish it. The traditional value system holds the community responsible for the faults committed by its members against outsiders.

Upper Congo: Ears do not grow taller than the head.

Kasai: Shoulders do not rise higher than the head.

Kasai: Never will a child outgrow his parents.

Interpretation: Children cannot supersede their parents' knowledge in life experiences.

These proverbs are recited to young people who think they have all the answers and nothing more to learn from adults. It is a reminder to the arrogant one who seems to lack respect for his elders that success, no matter how great, does not exonerate one from the respect and honor due to the elders.

Upper Congo: A poor person is identified by his debts.

Kasai: Pay your debts first, then raise goats and chickens as you wish.

Interpretation: The first proverb means that a person who cannot pay his or her debts is poor.

The second interpretation says that unless you can pay your debts, raising goats and chickens will bring you no wealth.

Upper-Congo: A child always returns to his parents' home to sleep.

Kasai: Child, the time will call you home.

Kasai: The rain showed Kalume the way back home.

Interpretation: In the village, even when young people play out until late in the evening, they end up returning to their parents' home to sleep. When they are in danger, they run back home.

These proverbs address themselves to children who have misbehaved and think they can escape punishment by staying away from home. The proverbs remind them that the darkness of the night or another threat to life will bring them back home.

Praise Poetry and Drama

Birth Homeland. An illustration of praise poetry can be found in the writer Clementine Faik-Nzuji's poetic song titled "Muetu Mundela" (My homeland). In the poem, the writer exalts her birth place as the land of the powerful ones: the crocodiles, the hippopotamuses, the buffalos, the sparrow hawks, the lions, the leopards. It is also the land where harmony reigns between the living and the dead, the old and the young, and pairs of lovers.[7]

Nkenge. In theater, as in other literary genres, tradition and modernity coexist. *The Four Moments of Nkenge* portrays a traditional theme, whereas *I Love Him Foolishly* represents a modern one. Nkenge is the name of a dance theater mirroring the sacred order of the Kongo people's cosmos.[8] In theater the theme of Nkenge is a tradition that speaks of vanity, pride and greed. Vain of her beauty, not only did Nkenge turn down the advances, expressed through the most difficult acrobatic dances, of all the young village suitors as inferior, but also convinced her peers to do likewise. Nkenge's admiration for a charming stranger suitor led her to unknowingly marry a ghost. After the wedding ceremony she leaves to go live with her handsome and rich husband in his foreign land. Nkenge's little brother, worried about her fate, decides to follow the couple, but he has to return home after facing her objections and condescending behavior. He also steals the groom's magical ring, which made him charming and procured him wealth. Deprived, the groom is unable to pay his debts and is striped of his attractive clothes by his creditors. Moreover, his real identity is finally revealed: he is a ghost. The ghost leads Nkenge to the cemetery, the symbol of the dark world of death. Luckily, her little brother, guided by the stolen magical ring, comes to her rescue. Nkenge returns home unrecognizable, in ragged clothes. Having been to the land of the dead, she must be purified through exorcism rituals before rejoining the community of the living, where she becomes everybody's mockery.

In Kongo cosmology, the life cycle follows the four stages of the sun's movements: dawn, noon, sunset and midnight. The conception of a child marks the midnight, which is the moment when the ascending movement of the sun begins; birth represents the dawn, the sunrise; initiation and adult life are midday; death is the sunset. The play has four parts: puberty ceremonies (dawn), celebrations of Nkenge's marriage to the devil (noon); Nkenge entering the terrifying world of the ancestors (sunset); and rescue and exorcism in the village (midnight).

Sister Hélène's Temptation. *Je l'aime à la folie* (I love her madly) is a 1999 reprint from the playwright Charles Lonta Nghenzi's 1977 drama entitled *La Tentation de Soeur Hélène* (Sister Helene's Temptation).[9] Whereas the original title emphasizes the religious status of the main character and the religious nature of the challenge she faces, the reprint stresses the nature and intensity of the character's predicament as one of deep romantic love. *Sister Hélène's Temptation* is the dramatic story of a young woman morally torn between love for the man she wants to marry and monastic vows from which she wants to run away. In the play, Hélène speaks with her conscience, which is identified as "Witness."

Hélène argues with God about her inability to take her mind off the man she wants to marry and think about the monastic life she has embraced. She asks God to speak to her with clarity and a reassuring solution. Her conscience, Witness, reminds her that the Lord has never been her preoccupation. She denies this categorically, enumerating the many things she has given up in her life for the Lord. To this, Witness retorts by saying that hers was only lip service. In reality, she was still holding on to her worldly goods. Hélène follows up with a long list of handsome young men she has turned down as potential marriage suitors and the good times she has had with each, particularly the one she loves most.

The exchange continues, with Witness telling Hélène that what she is experiencing is nothing other than remorse and despair. Although rejecting this statement, Hélène goes on enumerating the troubles that the love of a husband would have helped dissipate: a life filled with bitterness, darkness, uncertainties, the inconsistence inherent in her nature as a woman and the huge prison that earth has become for her. She concludes that all she is left with is the shadow of a man and not a real man. To this Witness responds, "Why then are you bothering the Lord? You never loved Him."[10]

CONFRONTING CONTEMPORARY SOCIAL ILLS

Besides revitalizing and recording traditional literary forms, Congolese writers have taken on the responsibility to write on contemporary topics in modern literary forms such as the novel, poetry and drama. Their works cover a wide range of topics and are written in French, the language of education in the Congo. One such topic is love. A major trend that dominates in their writings, however, is portraying the ills of the Congolese society. They address such themes as oppression and power abuse, rebellions and invasions, ethnic conflicts and ethnic cleansing.

Oppression and Abuse of Power

Colonial Oppression. Resentment for colonial oppression was vivid in the hearts of the Congolese people. T.K. Biaya has recorded in French a poetic rendition of the history of the Luluwa people. It was first written in the Tshiluba language by a Luluwa traditional poet and historian, Nyunyi wa Lwimba. The first part of the poem interprets colonial history in the Lulua districts of the Kasai province. Colonial action is portrayed as destructive of the preexisting order of things: people walked with a rope placed around their necks by their brothers; they were subjected to forced labor, which included growing cotton and building cotton depots, and enclosures around European neighborhoods (*la ville*); they were forced to produce copper and grow peanuts.[11]

Human Abuse. Human abuse did not end with the colonial system. Under the Mobutu dictatorship (1965–1997) it again became severe and widespread. Arbitrary arrests, beating, imprisonment for no cause and without trial, extortion of bribes and sexual harassment were daily events. Poet Maliza Mwana Kintente describes sexual harassment and forced sex by a ticket agent on an unnamed young woman desperate to travel. The poem is entitled "Que cachez-vous dans ce sac?" (What are you hiding in that bag?)[12]

Rebel Invasions. *Congo* and *rebellion* are almost synonymous terms. In the 1960s they coexisted in Kwilu, North Katanga, Kivu, Kisangani and the rest of Upper Congo. In 1977 and 1978 they broke out in Kolwezi and surrounding areas under the nicknames of Shaba I and Shaba II, respectively. Today, the Congo is split among several rebellious factions, including those in control of the capital, Kinshasa. Along with them are foreign occupation forces to whom they pay allegiance: Rwandan, Ugandan, Burudian, Angolan, Zimbabwean and Namibian.

Shaba II Invasion. Valentin Mudimbe, the most prolific and complex Congolese writer, described the nightmare caused by returning former Katanga gendarmes (soldiers) in 1978 to a Congolese Franciscan Sister who worked in a dispensary belonging to a convent, in which she was responsible for novices. Unable to cope, she died. An excerpt from the novel is entitled "Un pur cauchemar" (A pure nightmare).[13] The sister describes the men as dressed in extremely dirty civilian clothes. It was difficult for her to tell whether they were soldiers or civilians. They had maimed limbs and open bullet wounds. They ignored her request that they go to a bigger and better equipped Gécamines (mining company) hospital and instead kept coming. She was angered when, after hearing a big noise and moving to the entrance, she saw a missing hospital coworker standing outside along with another person, both surrounded by police officers. However, in the name of peace, she walked away without saying a word and later died.

Ethnic Conflicts and Ethnic Cleansing

Ethnic Conflicts. Inherent in the colonial action in the Congo was the deliberate cultivation of ethnic divisions among the Congolese as a strategy for preventing the unity of the oppressed against the oppressor. These divisions planted the seeds for the ethnic tensions that surfaced in different parts of the Congo in the late 1950s and early 1960s, such as those between Ngombe and Budja and between Ngombe and Mongo in Equator, as well as those between the Kongo and the Teke in Kinshasa. Sometimes tensions culminated in actual conflicts, such as the Luba-Luluwa conflict in Kasai.

Luba-Luluwa Conflict. In a poetic narrative, poet and historian Nyunyi wa Lwimba praises the Luluwa people for their vigilance, which enabled them to discover the domination plan the Luba had launched against them under their leader, Albert Kalonji. This plan, according to the poet, would have turned the independence won from the Belgians into a bonanza for the Luba alone. The Luluwa would be paying them tributes and property taxes on their own land. They would also be subjected to beatings. Having discovered the malicious plan, the Luluwa assembled in Kananga, in a meeting convened by the great chief Kalamba Mukenge. He instructed them to expel the Luba, and soon a devastating war raged all over the Luluwa country. Soon the war became so damaging, says the writer, that Luluwa chiefs, Luba chiefs, other Kasai chiefs, and Congo president Kasa-Vubu decided to call it off. The Luluwa chiefs consulted among themselves first and agreed to end the war. To signify the end of the war, they ground samples of all edible crops in a mortar, placed a leopard skin on the ground and burned a live dog. Luluwa and Luba representatives swore never to kill each other again. They sealed a pact between the two groups allowing them to live in peace from then on.[14]

Expulsion of the Kasaiens from Katanga. Nyunyi wa Lwimba's poetic narrative describes how the Luba were the object of ethnic cleansing in Western Kasai in 1959–1960. They experienced a similar fate in Katanga in 1961–1962, this time along with the Luluwa and other groups from Kasai, who were identified by the Katanga natives as Kasaiens. Thirty years later, in 1992 and 1993, Governor Gabriel Kyungu wa Kumwanza of Katanga and other Katanga leaders, working in league with President Mobutu, expelled the Kasaiens from Katanga (Shaba) again. In a public speech Kyungu advised Katangese and other Congolese people that he had no remorse for having cleansed Shaba (Katanga) of insects (*bilulu*), by which he meant the Kasaiens.

The Train of Death. Sangalayi, a cultural and intellectual organization of Kasai people living in Europe, produced a tape telling the Kasaiens' story and lamenting the sufferings and deaths incurred by thousands of their people, particularly in the train stations of Kolwezi and Likasi and on the train during the long journey. As this was the second time that they expelled the people from Kasai from Katanga, the Sangalayi called the event "Second Round Katanga" (Katanga wa Tshiakabidi). The tape is in Tshiluba, the most widely spoken vernacular in Kasai. However, the transcript was translated into French by the producers and by others. In the narrative, the authors invite men and women from far and near to come hear for themselves the cries of the slaughtered, dispossessed and evicted Kasaiens, who spent weeks and months in the rain, waiting uncertainly for the train and without food, medicine or shelter. It tells the story of the Kasaiens recruited in the 1930s, who lost their lives building Katanga copper mines, extracting minerals in Kipushi or building the Kamina military base. The song deplores the mistreatment inflicted on the Congolese by the colonizers, the destructive behaviors of the jackals who replaced them in power, and the complicitous silence of the eyewitnesses to the genocides, who say nothing, thus pretending they did not happen. It invites everyone to reject hatred and work toward restoring human dignity and national pride.[15]

COMMUNICATION METHODS

Messengers were the most common vehicles for transmitting urgent messages from village to village. Authority figures in ancient times sent messengers to communicate ordinary messages. Today, some of the media employed in and across networks are simple while others are more complex. Sending messengers and using the drum, flute, or bell are simple methods. Transmitting from radio or television stations is a more complex method.

Simple Methods of Communication

Communication in the Congo circulates within and across social networks. These include ethnic networks, government networks, missionary networks, the networks created by other nongovernmental organizations. All networks are represented both in the rural areas and in the cities. To date, all these networks use simple methods of communication.[16]

Messengers. Today, as in the past, the messenger remains the number one means of communication in both rural and urban settings. Family members send messengers to announce serious sicknesses or deaths to relatives living in distant locations. Traditional marketplaces were the most convenient forums for transmitting messages through messengers. In many parts of the country, markets were located in the villages of the chiefs and held on different days. Relatives living in different villages had as many opportunities to communicate through messengers as there were marketplaces commonly frequented by people from their respective villages. Today, in some places, for intercity or international communications, modern technical services rather than the marketplaces play the role of relay stations in transmitting messages through messengers. For example, the originating family sends a messenger to a radiotelegraphy station, a money order service or a cellular phone owner. There the messenger will charge the operator to contact the operator of a similar service in the destination location with a message for an individual in the city or nearby village. The latter operator will, in turn, send a messenger to the individual in question to deliver the message. Sometimes the message is a specified time for the receiver to come to the phone and have a direct conversation with the sender.

Traditional hierarchies—kings and provincial chiefs, chiefs and subchiefs—communicated with one another through the service of messengers as well. Missionary networks, both Catholic and Protestant, rural and urban, resort to messengers to communicate from station to station. In recent years, the

Reseau d'Education Civic au Congo (RECIC), an association of nineteen nongovernmental organizations, has resorted to door-to-door messengers to discuss mass education issues with individuals at their homes. RECIC also combines messenger use with posters. Messengers move around with mobile posters carrying messages in images and also in both vernacular languages and French. They plant them at locations of mass gathering such as bus stops and stay there for some time to record people's reactions and answer their questions. Because of the collapse of the entire land transportation and post office systems, even the government and the industry, particularly in the provinces, rely on messengers to a large extent. Sometimes it is the only way they can reach certain areas. Even when the post office was operational, the highly centralized Congolese government paid state personnel in the provinces by sending central government officials with stacks of banknotes. Rectors and budget directors of university campuses regularly traveled to the capital Kinshasa to collect cash with which to pay the personnel under their supervision.

Communication Instruments. On special occasions, chiefs and subchiefs, rather than sending messengers, used communication instruments instead. Usually these included the drum, the horn and the flute. Drumming helped communicate a variety of messages. It was often used to communicate death. In some traditions, slow, rhythmic drumming meant death. A slow rhythm played five times meant the death of a chief; four times, the death of the chief's wife; and three times that of the chief's son. A fast rhythm meant urgency and the need to return home right away. Two types of specialists participated in transmitting messages through drumming: those who sent them from the origin and those who decoded and interpreted them at the destination. Sometimes, relay stations passed the drumming on to next villages.

Catholic churches used the bell to remind the parishioners of the schedules of church-related activities. They suspended the bell in the tallest tower of the church. Sometimes it hung on a metal rod resting on two brick pillars or two forked metal pillars in the manner of a beam. Replicating the churches, Catholic schools to date enforce the daily agenda by ringing the bell at fixed hours. Rather than a real bell, some schools use a big copper ingot. In recent years, RECIC has added the tape to the lists of devices used to convey messages to the public. RECIC first organizes a competition among music composers to produce a tape containing particular educational messages. Then it arranges with drivers of mass transportation vans to have them play the tape for their passengers.

Audiovisual Media

When they functioned fully, modern communication methods in the Congo included the radio, the television, telephone cabins, antennas with underground fixtures, and satellite stations.

The radio broadcasting service has been in the Congo since its introduction by Roman Catholic missionaries in 1937. The colonial government followed the path in 1940 with the creation of the official Radio Congo Belge (RCB), precursor of the present day Radio-Television Nationale Congolaise (RTNC).

The Belgians established most radio stations in the Congo before 1960. In 1966, the Congolese Government nationalized the Catholic missionary radio-television station, Tele Star, which later became Tele-Zaire. Its network consisted of four production centers, six production studios and three diffusion stations based in Kinshasa, plus two substations in Kinshasa and Lubumbashi. Government-supported journalism received a boost in 1973 with the creation of the Institut des Sciences et Techniques d'Information (ISTI) (Institute for Information Sciences and Technology) and a studio school for training intermediate-level audiovisual producers and technicians. They built additional facilities in subsequent years: La Cité de la Voix Du Zaire in 1978 and L'Office Zairois de Radiodiffusion et de Télévision (OZRT) in 1981. In 1989, the buildings and grounds of the Former Radio Star were converted into La Radio et Télévision Scolaire (RATELESCO), which was founded to produce educational and cultural magazines. They established local televisions in most provincial capitals, broadcasting for the hosting city and its immediate surroundings. At each of these stages, modernization efforts included the acquisition of new equipment. Apparently, however, due to the absence of a serious feasibility study or adequate technical monitoring, these innovations did not bring about the expected quality services.[17]

Privately owned audiovisual units came to the Congo following the liberalization of the press in 1990. Licensing is done through an official application in the form of a file and the payment of the appropriate fees. One could conduct radio communication on six frequencies from a stationary location or a mobile one, as with a ship. In 1999, the number of operating radiocommunication devices was estimated at 600. The demand for privately operated televisions was very high. The country counted fifty underground stations. Operators paid for reception antennas. The Radio Télévision Nationale Congolaise owned some satellites. The Office Congolese des Postes et Téléphones (Congolese Post and Telephone Office) owned others. Either had the power to sign concession contracts with private operators with authorization from the Ministry of Post Office and Téléphones.

The licence for commercial exploitation of an audiovisual communication station was delivered to anyone who paid the appropriate fees. The fees were proportionate to the importance of the radio or television station under consideration. In Kinshasa, three radio stations—Radio Raga, Radio Kin-Malebo, and Malebo Broadcasting Chanel—and five television stations came into existence after 1990. The five television stations are Raga TV, Télé Kin-Malebo, Canal Kin 1, Canal Kin 2 and Antenne A. All are commercial, broadcasting to the cities of Kinshasa and Brazzaville and their surroundings. Most television programs are local, whereas the radio programs are relays of Radio France International (RFI).

In principle, the Radio Télévision Nationale Congolaise broadcasts in French, the official language, and four Congolese national languages: Kikongo, Lingala, Swahili and Tshiluba. The Office Congolais des Posts and Télécommunications issues broadcast licenses for various communication technologies, such as private messenger services, radiocommunication, radio-television and others. The infrastructure of the Radio-Télévision Nationale Congolaise includes six telephone exchanges in Kinshasa: Gombe, Limete, Binza, Kabinda, Kinshasa I and Kinshasa II. Two transmission and reception exchanges, one in Binza and one in Njili, connect Kinshasa to the provincial capitals by way of a satellite and a radio beam. Each provincial capital has at least one exchange enabling it to connect with the district headquarters under its jurisdiction through telegraph or, in rare cases, telephone. In a very few areas, the provincial capital or the district is connected to some rural territories.

Because of insufficient or badly deteriorated equipment, only a very small portion of the Congolese population can be reached by telephone. For instance, in 1999, there existed only sixty telephone lines in Mbuji-Mayi, a city of 2 million people. In the same year, Kinshasa, with an estimated 6 million inhabitants, had 34,000 telephone lines, or 176 persons per line, without counting the fact that many were often inoperative for considerable periods.

The Written Press

The written press in the Congo reflects the country's political fluctuations. Following seventy-five years of colonial rule (1885–1960), the Congo passed to a stage of political instability (1960–1965), an absolute dictatorship

(1965–1991), a futile struggle for the return of democracy (1991–1997) and the present state of instability, civil war and rebellion.

Evolution of the Written Press. Roman Catholic missionaries introduced the written press to the Congo with the creation of *Minsamu Mia Yenge*, in Matadi in 1892.[18] The press in the Congo remained foreign controlled throughout the colonial period. However, toward the end, a handful of Congolese had established a reputation as professional journalists.[19] From 1959 to 1965, newspapers in the Congo operated under a 1959 legislation guaranteeing the freedom of press. Between 1965 and 1972, the government embarked on buying off newspapers financially and staffing them with figureheads. The government also reorganized and aligned various newspapers with the official ideology. In 1970, President Mobutu signed an ordinance law imposing a deposit for running a newspaper. The deposit was to be placed in a bank account, whose interest would be used to pay fines for any violations of the law regulating the press. Those journalists who rose against government's dictatorial measures lost their jobs, were incarcerated indefinitely in secret prisons or murdered. On the other hand, the amount of the bail was so high that many newspapers simply ceased to exist due to an inability to pay. Thus, the number of operating newspapers went from twenty in 1965 to six in 1987, twenty-two years into the Mobutu dictatorship. These newspapers had operated under complete government control since 1972. The government appointed their directors, supported their printing expenses and payed journalists' salaries. Thus, professional journalism was largely tainted with political patronage. By 1987, those newspapers that resisted subservience to the government had fallen.[20]

The years prior to 1970 were economically prosperous, so the government could grant the newspapers freedoms. The situation changed with the crisis triggered by the 1973 "Zairianization" measures by which the government took over private businesses. Government subsidies to newspapers became selective, with some newspapers, such as *Elima* and *Salongo*, receiving the lion's share. As the subsidies became less regular, the government abandoned its support of the written press. Instead, it concentrated its resources on the official radio-television agency, L'Office Zairois de Radio-Télévision (OZRT) and the official press agency, the Agence Zaire-Presse (AZAP).

Then came the 1981 legislation defining the freedom of press. A journalist satirized it as a press-policing legislation, since thirty-six of the thirty-eight articles in the legislation pointed to restrictions rather than freedoms. Furthermore, none provided for the journalist's freedom of expression or legal protection. Nonetheless, in the same year, various laws were promulgated that regulated the Agence Zaire-Press and the Office Zairois de Radio-Television. Similarly, a legal disposition replaced the financial deposit by a simple authorization to publish. The latter clause generated a multiplicity of newspapers with different statuses and fates. A few began to operate, at least temporarily, as truly independent institutions. The majority remained aligned with government ideology and were given the mission to mobilize and motivate the population in favor of the regime. They continued to rely on financial support from the government, which provoked a fierce competition among them for government favors.[21]

Because of this evolution of government-press relations during the Mobutu regime, the press became a simple propaganda organ of President Mobutu's single party, the Mouvement Populaire de la Révolution (MPR). The situation changed, however, in the early 1990s. Newspapers stopped being simple copies of the Agence Zaire Presse, and the incessant government investigations and denunciations of the press were left behind. Many formerly taboo topics appeared in the press: the 1990 massacre of students in Lubumbashi, the embezzlement of diamonds in Mbuji-Mayi, President Mobutu's fortune and kidnapping and assassination cases, to name a few. Another consequence of liberalization after many years of repression, was an extreme proliferation of newspapers, although many did not last beyond their day of first appearance.

In 1991–1993, the Congolese of all political persuasions, engaged in a national debate searching to reinstate democracy in the country. During this debate, which is known as *Conférence Nationale* (National Conference), Congolese newspapers came to be identified with three camps. One pro-democracy, supported the so-called Opposition Radicale, spearheaded by L'Union pour la Démocratie et le Progrès Social (UDPS) under the leadership of Etienne Tshisekedi wa Mulumba. The second camp included the supporters of the Mobutist party, the MPR. Finally, between the two extremes, stood the newspapers supporting those known as moderate opposition, to which belonged the Union des Fédéralistes et des Républicains Indépendants (UFERI), the party of Nguz Karl-I-Bond.[22] In 1997, Laurent Désiré Kabila replaced Joseph Désiré Mobutu as president of the Congo. Under his short-lived dictatorship (May 1997–January 2001), Kinshasa newspapers could still be classified as pro-opposition, progovernment or in-between.

The Congolese Press Today. More than ten general-audience newspapers appear in Kinshasa today. In peacetime, some provincial capitals had their own independent newspapers, also. Parts of the Congo have been in a state of war since the mid-1990s, others since the ongoing rebellions began in 1998. Today, the rebels and their Ugandan, Rwandan and Burundian allied troops control almost half the national territory. It is difficult to know how many newspapers actually operate in the provinces. Prior to the war, Bukavu, capital of South Kivu, had four newspapers, and Eastern Kasai had ten. All but one were created between 1991 and 1997, a period of a tentative return to democracy after twenty-six years of steady dictatorship. Similarly, Mbandaka published two irregular periodicals.[23]

Government Press. There are three additional types of publishers in the Congo: the government, the church-related press and the nongovernment organizations. The Agence Congolaise de Presse (the Congolese Press Agency) is the number one government press agency in the Congo. The agency distributes the information to subscribing newspapers, radio and television stations, state services, private businesses and nonprofit organizations. It is headquartered in Kinshasa and operates regional branches in the provincial capitals and some districts. Usually, due to the unavailability or extreme delapidation of local printing facilities, the role of the branches is limited to collecting information for the national station in Kinshasa.

NOTES

1. Mufita Kabemba has studied verbal competition in more than twenty-three Congolese societies. The following discussion is based in most part on his work in this field. These and other illustrations of verbal competition are from Kabemba's *Littérature oral et authenticité (II): Revue jiwe* (Lubumbashi, Zaire: MPR/UNAZA, 1974), 55–67.

2. Kabemba, *Littérature oral et authenticité*, 67–70.

3. Batukezanga Zamenga, "Le jeu favori," section of "Souvenirs du village," in *Literatures francophones d'Afrique centrale*, ed. Jean-Louis Joubert (Paris: Nathan, 1999), 210.

4. Leo Frobenius, "Lungonyonyo et Nkashama" in *Mythes et contes populaires des riverins du Kasai* (Bonn: Inter Nationes, 1983), 299–300.

5. Frobenius, "Aux pays des defunts" in *Mythes et contes populaires*, 48–50.

6. Clémentine Faik-Nzuji, "Essai de méthodologie pour l'étude des proverbes luba du Kasai" (BA Thesis, Ecole Normale Moyenne du Sacre-Coeur, Kinshasa, 1967), 200–207.

7. Clementine Nzuji, "Mwetu mundela," in *Kasala-poemes* (Kinshasa, Zaire: Edition Mandore, 1969), 13–15.

8. The National Dance Theater of Zaire, *Nkenge: An African Dance-Opera* (New York: The African American Institute Performing Arts Program, 1981).

9. Charles Lonta Ghenzi, "Je l'aime a la folie," in *Literatures Francophones d'Afrique Centrale*, ed. Jean-Louis Joubert (Paris: Nathan, 1999), 234–235.

10. Ghenzi, "Je l'aime a la folie," in Joubert, 235.

11. T.K. Biaya, "De l'aube des temps jusqu'alors: l'histoire contemporaine des Luluwa par Nyunyi wa Lwimba," *Revue Canadienne des Etudes Africaines/CJAS* 18, no. 1 (1984): 23–25.

12. Maliza Mwina Kintende, "Que cachez-vous dans ce sac?" in *Literatures Francophones d'Afrique Centrale*, ed. Joubert, 221.

13. Valentin Mudimbe, "Un pur cauchemar," in *"Literatures Francophones d'Afrique Centrale*, ed. Joubert, 203.

14. Biaya, "De l'aube des temps," 23–25.

15. Sangalayi, Inc., "Njanja wa lufwila, Le train de la mort," in *Du Zaire au Congo* (Bruxelles: privately printed, 1997), 1–5.

16. The information in this section is from Mbelolo ya Mpiku, *La Situation de l'Information et de la Communication en République Démocratique du Congo* (Kinshasa, Zaire: Institut Facultaire des Sciences de l'Information et de la Communication, 1999), 13–19, 25.

17. Georges Tshionza Mata, *Les Médias au Zaire* (Paris: Editions l'Harmattan, 1996), 22–23, 27.

18. ya Mpiku, *La Situation de l'Information et de la Communication en Republique Démocratique du Congo*, 61.

19. Tshionza Mata, *Les Médias au Zaire*, 37, includes this representative list of notable Congolese journalists and their newspapers: Antoine Roger Bolamba (*L'Essort du Congo*), Lomami Tshibamaba (*La Voie du Congolais*), Evariste Kimba (*L'Essort du Congo*), Gabriel Makosso (*Le Courier d'Afrique*), Joseph Mbungo (*Presénce Congolaise*), Denis Malingwendo (*Le Progrès*), Pascal Kapeta (*L'Etoile*) and Clement Vidibio, (*Hébdomadaire Zaire*).

20. The six surviving newspapers were: *Beto na Beto, Elima, Jua, l'Analiste, Mjumbe* and *Salongo*. Among the fatalities were *La Dépêche, Le Courier d'Afrique, L'Etoile du Congo* and *Le Progrès*. See Tshionza Mata, *Les Médias au Zaire*, 28, 33.

21. Among the few that continued to operate with some degree of independence were *Umoja* (1985), *Le Phare* (1987), *Le Potentiel* (1987) and *La Semaine* (1988). Tshionza Mata, in *Les Médias au Zaire*, 34–35, 40, alludes to a 1987 editorial conflict between *l'Analiste* and *Elima* and *Salongo*.

22. Newspapers such as *Umoja, Le Phare, Le Potentiel*, and, to a certain extent, *La Conscience* identified with the democrats. *Salongo, Le Soft de Finance and L'Evenement* aligned behind the Mobutists. *Temps Nouveaux* supported the centrists. See Thsionza Mata, *Les Médias au Zaire*, 57–58.

23. The number of general circulation newspapers headquartered in each province is as follows: Kinshasa (12), Eastern Kasai (9), South Kivu (4), Equateur (2), Eastern Province (5), Lower Congo (2), Western Kasai (2), North Kivu (3). See ya Mpiku, *La Situation de l'Information et de la Communication en République Démocratique du Congo*, 33, 50, 54.

4

Art and Architecture

HUMAN MOTIFS—ancestor statues, ceremonial masks, regalia for authority figures, decorative human faces—as expressions of values are overwhelmingly prevalent in Congolese traditional art. Likewise, paintings portraying life scenes and authority figures occupy a central place in modern popular art. Some life scenes portray activities taking place around houses or public buildings.

Housing in rural Congo reflects variations in the landscape (forest versus savannah), custom (circular houses in some cultures, rectangular in others), and sociopolitical status. For example, the impact of the sociopolitical status on housing was striking in the case of the contrast between the size of houses in a King's court and the houses in an ordinary man's compound. It still exists in the city between African sections and former white-only sections. In squatting zones (zones of spontaneous growth), cleavages exist between the walled villas of the well-off and the much more modest houses of the minimum-wage earners.

The first section of this chapter focuses on human motifs in selected artistic traditions and life scenes in modern popular art, particularly portraits of authority figures. The second section examines the traditional home of the Congolese in respect to the house's design and structure, ecological orientation, building materials and construction process. The second section also discusses housing and construction in Congolese cities, particularly in Kinshasa, the capital, in reference to residential types, land occupation processes, land distribution agents, the construction process and planned housing.

CONGOLESE ART YESTERDAY AND TODAY

Rich and long artistic traditions existed in the Congo prior to Belgian colonization. One of several elements that all had in common was the preeminence of human motifs. During colonization, two trends of popular art developed in two Congolese cities, Lubumbashi and Kinshasa. Life scenes and portraits of authority figures prevail in both trends.

Human Motifs in Congolese Traditional Art

Some of the best known Congolese artistic traditions are Kongo, Kuba, Luba (of Katanga), Hemba, Yaka and Mangbetu. Human motifs are pervasive in the art of these peoples and others discussed in this section.[1] They include ancestral figures; divination, initiation and healing spirits; human faces; authority regalia; and ceremonial masks.

Ancestor Figures. Artistic productions featuring ancestor figures have been found in all parts of the Congo. Statues occupy a preponderant place among ancestors' representations. Kongo funerary monuments are among the well-known ancestor figures. Some monuments date to the seventeenth century, but others are more recent. For example, a stone monument portraying a character identified as Malasa is dated 1921. Funerary monuments portray different characters. One, a thoughtful-looking man, sits with his left hand supporting his cheek and the right hand holding the hip. Another, a symbol of maternity, represents a seated mother holding her baby in her lap.

Kongo funerary monuments were made in stone. Elsewhere, statues featuring ancestor figures were made of wood instead. The Hemba people, a branch of the Luba of Katanga, who live in the Kongolo region, produced some of the most beautiful (classic) ancestor figures, as did the Suku of Bandundu. Suku artistic productions include an ancestor figure with a special hairdress dominated by a crest and the line of the stomach dominated by the navel. The Jaka, another ethnic group living in Bandundu, had wooden ancestor figures among their artistic productions. They were adorned with beads and cowries. Under the influence of Christianity, Kongo artists of the past have left behind in the Mbanza Ngungu area metal crucifixes dating from the seventeenth century.

Divination, Initiation and Healing Spirits. Some statues with human figures were inhabited by spirits other than the ancestors. These spirits were invoked for protection or divination. Such was the case among the Bayombe, a branch of the Kongo of Lower Congo. Among the Jaka, divination statues were covered with a bag except for the head and the feet. The Holo people, who live in Bandundu at the border of Angola, had a spirit called Nzambi, to whom they addressed their prayers.

In some productions, the human motif, statue or human face, is not an art piece in its own right but a part of another art object. For example, a Pende protective post had the form of a female statue. A Teke diviner's cane, featuring a human body with a long neck, houses the spirits. During divination, the medicine man consults these spirits about the nature of an illness and the recommended cure for it. Symbols on the cane represent supernatural powers. Double pupils in the eyes reflect clairvoyance. Feathers and a canoe show that the spirits can go anywhere, either by air or by water. The bottom part is the oar of the canoe. A trumpet from the Mayombe area in Lower-Congo contains a seated figure holding a plant in its mouth. This is a medicinal plant used for driving out evil spirits. A Leele instrument used ritualistically to cut fragments from sacred trees rested on a handle in human form.

Human Faces. Rather than whole bodies, some arts portray human faces only. Human faces are found on a variety of Congolese artistic productions, including stone bracelets, trumpets, fly whisks, knife handles and combs. The upper end of a Jaka slit drum used in divination and healing ceremonies consisted of a woman's head wearing earrings and necklaces. The Luba of Katanga had a rectangular wooden divination instrument with a human head. During divination, the instrument was seated on the ground or on a stool while both the diviner and the client held it. The oracle (revealed knowledge) was delivered when the instrument began to shake. Leele friction oracles had human heads, also.

Authority Regalia. The power symbols of the chiefs and kings often carried human motifs. For example, a Kongo king's power cane portrayed a whole person, sometimes two persons, at the top or one person at each end. The fly whisk of a Kongo woman of power was surmounted by a human head. A Teke village chief had a fly whisk terminating in Janus heads. Pende chiefs and important persons carried an ax on their shoulders. The ax's upper end was a woman's head and its blade formed her tongue. The Mbala people of Bandundu produced an authority cane surmounted by a female statue character remarkable by her high hairdress and the continuous line of her eyebrows.

Ceremonial Masks. The art of making masks was practiced throughout the Congo, where masks were employed in a variety of functions. Suku masks were used in circumcision ceremonies. Some of them took the form of a helmet topped by an animal, such as the antelope, a symbol of speed and the dancer's agility. The Holo, the Suku's neighbors, produced dance masks, including multifunctional masks used in the exorcism of children and in making hunting parties successful. Multifunctional masks were also found among the Jaka. Fertility and successful hunting were among the major services for which they solicited the intervention of the spirits residing in these masks. The Pende, too, were excellent mask producers. Some of their masks were three in one, including a large mask flanked between two smaller ones. Another type of Pende mask was reserved for notables and only used in selected solemn ceremonies. The Kuba people produced a type of mask employed in funerary and folk dances. Another mask, made of wood, metal and cloth, was worn during mourning rites for a woman. The Luba of Katanga were known for being mask producers also. Some of their masks belonged to secret societies. The Kumu people, who live in the southeastern part of Kisangani, had a diviner's mask made of painted wood, which they employed in initiation ceremonies and solemn divination sessions. They also used it at the death of an initiate. The Ngbaka of the Ubangi River had a type of mask that they wore in circumcision ceremonies. Their mask carried a scarification on the nose, a typical Ngbaka ethnic mark.

Some masks were only employed in ceremonies involving authority figures—chiefs, noblemen, kings. The Kuba of Mweka had a mask used only in initiation ceremonies and dances associated with the mythical origin of Kuba royalty. This mask's face was made of skin, with cowrie shells for eyes, a wooden nose and a mouth covered with beads. Another dance mask belonging to the Kuba royal family could only be worn by an older person during consultation and was identifiable by the small holes that surround the eyes.

Decorative Figures and Faces. Some human figures on art objects were primarily decorative. The Mangbetu of Ituri and their Azande neighbors were prolific producers of decorative arts. Both groups produced many items with human faces or complete human figures with artificially elongated heads, symbols of beauty in their culture. These items include gourds, knives, harps, boxes, whips, pots, pipes and bells, among others.

Trends in Modern Popular Art

Modern popular art is most developed in Congo's two leading cities: Kinshasa, the political, commercial and administrative capital, and Lubumbashi, the mining center.[2] Art in each center received an impetus from a European

Head sculpture. *Institut Des Beaux Arts.* Collection of
the author.

person living in the Congo, who served as a patron, coach or academic tutor.
Painting dominates modern popular art. Visual arts (painting and photog-
raphy) in the two cities play three major roles: image making, historical
narration and chronicling the present. In image making the artist portrays
individuals in an accouterment or in proximity of material possessions that
confer them a more admired identity, such as looking prosperous or powerful. The artist who is involved in historical narration retells and reshapes
past events to fit assumed or expressed expectations of the client. Chronicling
art creates pictorial records of current events as perceived by ordinary people
in the community.

   In portraying these roles, artists are not at all bound to rules of factual
accuracy. They seem to understand their mission as readjusting the events to
reflect popular understandings of them. The following is a brief overview of
the characteristics of the major visual arts in Lubumbashi and Kinshasa over

Portrait of Mary Magdalene: an example of modern popular art by a graduate of Kinshasa Ecole de Beaux Arts. Collection of the author.

various periods in Congolese history. Scenes portraying Patrice Lumumba as a national hero are also included.

Popular Art in Lubumbashi. In Lubumbashi, popular art owes its start, character and growth to the work of Pierre Romain-Desfosses, a Frenchman who came to live in Lubumbashi in the 1940s and who placed a particular emphasis on decorative art inspired by ethnic folklore and artifacts. It was later encouraged by Laurent Moonens, a Belgian artist who was active in Kinshasa in the 1940s, and moved to Lubumbashi in the late 1950s to train African students in applied and decorative arts at the Academie des Beaux Arts (Academy of the Fine Arts). The art was geared initially to responding to the tastes of the European consumer, and later, to those of the political institutions of Katanga. Serving as a medium of communication between the artist and the audience, paintings in the Lubumbashi popular art appeal to the public's shared memories of the city's history and to the memory of major ethnic groups having contributed to the making of this history. Paintings carry instructional messages addressed less to the individual than to the group.

Popular Art in Kinshasa. Just as in Lubumbashi, two foreigners stimulated popular art in Kinshasa. In the 1940s Maurice Alhadeff, a businessman and patron of popular art, sought from the very start to orient art production in the Congo toward both the local and international marketplace. In the same time frame Victor Walenda, a missionary and founder of the Kinshasa Academie des Beaux Arts, promoted Congolese art-making traditions first but then shifted to Western styles. Artistic production was first targeted at foreigners and later attempted to appeal to the local public. References to local history are practically absent from the Kinshasa painting tradition. Also, they often portray individuals rather than groups.

Portraying Life Scenes. Life scenes are attempts to re-create life events. Some scenes are documentary, dating from the time the events actually occurred. Others are re-creations of events as perceived and dramatized by the artist. Events alluded to in paintings of the latter category do have a historical base. However, the artistic medium used to represent them may not be historical. Thus, a painting depicting a life scene in a precolonial village may be the work of a contemporary artist attempting to reconstruct life experiences learned from the oral tradition or from written history. Lubumbashi popular art is known for having an abundance of scenes involving portraits of Patrice Lumumba as a national hero and martyr.[3]

Village Life in Precolonial Times. Paintings on this theme generally portray village life before the time of the slave trade and the colonial periods as peaceful and in harmony with nature. The scenery includes forests, water or both. Individuals are featured performing ordinary daily chores: coming from the fields, pounding corn, millet or cassava, and tending animals. The painting may totally be the product of the artist's imagination rather than an actual life scene that the artist experienced or observed.

Patrice Lumumba, a National Hero. Popular art in the Congo fulfills another major function: that of immortalizing the nation's heroes. Patrice Lumumba is the most glorified hero to date. During Lumumba's short tenure as a national leader, many events made him a hero in the public eye. Congolese artists have capitalized on those events to exercise their creative minds. In many respects they have portrayed Lumumba as an extraordinary human being, unique among Congolese leaders by his courage, powers and dedication to Congo's liberation.

For instance, Lumumba was in prison when a roundtable was convened in Brussels to discuss the independence of the Congo. Congolese delegates required Lumumba's presence as a condition for their participation. Artists have portrayed Lumumba with the Congolese delegation at the roundtable. In preparation for independence, Congolese leaders created political parties, most of which were ethnic based. Patrice Lumumba's party, the Mouvement National Congolais (MNC), was practically the only party that was truly nationalistic. Kinshasa and Kisangani were the party's major bastions, but it also had representatives elsewhere. One manifestation of political life following the formation of political parties and the roundtable was campaigning for election. In one scene, Lumumba is portrayed wearing signs that read: *Votez tous pour M.N.C./L. Liste No. 4 moi* (Everybody vote for M.N.C./L. List No. 4). In another, he is holding an electoral campaign meeting in a village, standing with his arms up, surrounded by men and women. In the election, Lumumba's party carried the majority which, in coalitions with a number of other parties, won him the position of prime minister of the new Republic of Congo. On independence day, King Beauduin of Belgium spoke, praising the grandeur of King Leopold II, founder of the Congo Free State, precursor of Belgian Congo. Joseph Kasa-Vubu, the person to become the first president of the independent Congo, spoke to the Belgians thanking them for their civilizing mission in the Congo. Lumumba, conscious of being the leader of the people and the incipient prime minister, spoke to the Congolese masses, exalting them for their fight for independence and dignity. Some paintings featuring events of Independence Day show Prime Minister Lumumba, King Beaudouin and President Joseph Kasa-Vubu addressing dignitaries and the public.

ARCHITECTURE AND HOUSING IN THE CONGO

The Congolese people live in three types of houses. They are distinguishable by differences in the building materials, which may be nondurable, semidurable or durable. In rural areas the house design and ecological orientation reflect cultural values and worldviews. In the cities, colonial history and postcolonial reactions produced three types of urban districts, La Ville, La Cité and squatting zones.

The Traditional Congolese House

House construction begins with a design in the mind of the builder. Traditionally, the design is transferred directly from the builder's idea to the structure without a blueprint or a paper drawing. The form and the structure of the house are custom bound. Some groups build round houses, and other groups build rectangular ones. The builder first traces the house's design as he conceives it on the ground with an instrument or with his heel. He measures the dimensions by placing his feet one in front of the other and moving forward until they reach the desired length. He sometimes measures

Small houses in a rural town built in nondurable materials. Foreground; shelter for relaxation, with woven walls and straw roof; background, small house with mud walls and straw roof.

the sizes with equal steps. Often, round houses have no verandas. Rectangular houses are built with a veranda in some regions and without one in others. Some peoples build their houses with a pointed roof; others make a gabled roof instead. The walls are made of poles planted into the ground and tied with a rope to a beam at the top. The roof is also built with vertical poles tied to the beam at the lower end and to pillars supporting the frame at the upper end. The pointed roof rests on one central pillar. Gabled roofs rest on three or more pillars aligned and equally distributed for balance. Next, they tie horizontal reeds to the vertical poles of the wall and to those of the roof. The walls are then plastered with wet mud. They cover the roof with grass, leaves or both, depending on the region. Kindu, in Maniema, is an example of a region where the houses are built of nondurable materials.[4]

Housing Structure and Environment. A house, as a living quarters, has a certain structure. For instance, a classic Luba house comprises three sections. First, the bed is always located to the right when entering the house, with the head always turned toward the door. The hearth is always at the foot of the bed in the right corner, away from the entrance. Over the hearth is a stand where items are laid out to dry. This is also where fish and game meat are dried. The left side of the house, opposite the bed, is empty except for the far-left corner, where a jug containing drinking water is kept. The remaining space is used for sitting on a chair, stool, mat or goatskin when it is raining outside. It is also used for sleeping quarters for close relatives when separate quarters were not available. Sometimes, out of respect for the guest, the host would give his or her bed to the guest and would sleep on a mat on the floor opposite the bed.

Four rivers water the Luba territory from south to north. Rivers are believed to be carriers of evil powers that unleash calamities and cause harm to entire villages. Ancestors protect a man's homestead from threats, including natural calamities. The shrines for sacrificing to the ancestors are located by the senior wife's house. The husband's other protective powers are located by her house as well. Her house plays the role of a spiritually fortified place. Traditionally, in Luba villages, the house of the senior wife faced south, in the opposite direction of the movement of the scourge-carrying rivers. The house orientation and empowerment enabled it to detect perilous forces and reroute them from the homestead, thus protecting its members from calamities.[5]

Architecture and House Design in Mangbetu Tradition. Mangbetu architectural technology has evolved over time.[6] The most standard traditional houses of ordinary people were simple. The houses built in the grassland were different from those in forest. Grassland houses were round and had thatched roofs. The walls were covered with mud, bark or woven mats. Forest houses were made of wooden frames stitched together and covered from top to bottom with a layer of palm leaves inside and a layer of plantain leaves outside supplemented by straw, grass or skin. Many layers of leaves sealed the structure to keep out water. Usually, forest houses were smaller and less resistant than those built in grasslands. Houses in both settings had a pitched roof. They also had a spacious door but no windows. An 1874 report by a visiting European states that the house walls were so strong that the structure offered "an astonishing power of resistance to the fury of elements." The interior was divided into a sleeping area near the entrance and a storage compartment farther down.[7]

This house building tradition changed gradually. By the late nineteenth century, leaf walls had largely given way to walls of poles rammed with mud. House doors had changed also. Doors of handmade boards or old shields had come to prominence. Shield doors were covered with artistic designs similar to those previously found on bark cloth. Thatched roofs offer the advantages of remaining dry and providing easy maintenance. Therefore, they continued to dominate in the grasslands. The construction of Mangbetu's houses has been characterized as a time-consuming and sometimes difficult undertaking. The following steps can be identified in the construction process: cut poles and dig holes in the hard ground; lash horizontal bamboos or vines inside and outside the poles; build a framework of poles for the roof; add a grid of smaller sticks to the framework; cover the roof with grass or leaves; leave space between the roof and the wall free of horizontal sticks and grass or leaves to allow light and ventilation; strip the vertical poles that are visible in the free space of bark to spot termite tunnels and remove them before they destroy the poles.[8]

The owner and possibly other men carry out these operations. Once these tasks are completed, women bring water and mix it with earth to make the mud needed for covering the walls. Both men and women participate in the actual work of plastering the walls with mud. This is group work executed by relatives and friends at the request of the house owner. It culminates in a feast that he offers in honor of the participants as compensation for their work. A homeowner's work does not end when the construction is complete. Mangbetu people take good care of their houses and other buildings, such as granaries, cooking houses and shelters. They are continually repairing, washing and beautifying them. House beautification includes mural paintings and sculpted house posts with geometric designs cut in them, sometimes with alternating white colors and darkened mud colors. Just as with the house posts, mural paintings represent animals, people, and geometric designs.

Mangbetu people surround their houses with large and well-maintained courtyards followed by vegetable gardens. They group houses into settlements made up of related extended families. In the past, settlements extended over one to two miles and were located uphill between dry land crops, such as yams, or downhill near streams and crops requiring moisture, such as plantains. Oil palm plantations separated village groups along a particular hill. Each village had an open-sided sitting area, which was shaded for protection from the sun and rain. This area was used as a gathering place for discussions, disputes, drinking and dancing gatherings. The gathering shelter stood by the houses of a man of high social status, such as an important elder. The residential settlement pertaining to a particular extended family consisted of many houses, a sheltered sitting area, a cooking shelter, granaries, chicken houses and a shelter for a signal drum.

The houses were toward the center of the settlement. Here lived fathers, brothers and sons with their wives. A few yards off stood the houses of clients and slaves. Some settlements were smaller. These were the residences of individuals who had recently broken away from a large unit or had suffered some misfortune. A number of settlements formed a village. Each village, big

Lubumbashi: building in La Ville—Théâtre de la Ville (City Theater).

or small, controlled large hunting and fishing ground and extensive lands for agriculture, including fields and lands left fallow for future cultivation. For these reasons, they built villages several miles apart. Because of the fallow system, they periodically moved the villages to new sites closer to the location of new fields. In time of war, they moved the houses closer together and surrounded them by a palisade.

Housing and Construction in Congolese Cities

Congolese cities have both a colonial history and a postcolonial history.[9] In colonial times, the section of the city occupied by the Europeans, including the main business district, was called La Ville, short for La Ville Européenne (European City). The various parts inhabited by Congolese were collectively called La Cité, short for La Cité Indigène (Native City). Employees of large companies were housed in work camps rather than with everybody else, in La Cité. The city of Leopoldville, which later became Kinshasa, was created in 1881, when Henry Morton Stanley founded a European station next to the indigenous village of Kintambo. Between World War I and World War II, a commercial district developed around another local village by the name of Kinshasa. Kintambo and the original European community and services

Kinshasa: building in La Ville—the Bata building in Kinshasa in the 1960s, including housing stores and a gallery (first floor), Congo-American Language Institute (second floor) and apartments (upper floors).

around it, today called Ngaliema, became Leopoldville West, whereas Kinshasa and the new European business district were called Leopoldville East. Between the two concentrations, another location, Kalina, became the headquarters of all colonial administration services and residences of high-ranking personalities of the colony. The combination of Ngaliema, Kalina and the business district became the core of La Ville. Kinshasa and the communities that later developed around it, Lingwana (Saint-Jean) and Barumbu, formed La Cité.

La Ville is located along the Congo River across from Brazzaville, capital of the former French Congo. Kinshasa, Barumbu, and Lingwana are south of La Ville. The rest of La Cité (areas inhabited by Congolese) developed south of these three communities. Following this development, the three nuclei and Kintambo became known as L'Ancienne Cité (Old City) and the new additions as La Nouvelle Cite (New City). Today's Dendale, to which was later added Ngiri-Ngiri, formed La Nouvelle Cité.

In the 1950s planned cities were built for the Congolese. In Kinshasa, they included Immocongo (Matonge), Bandalungwa, Matete, Lemba and Quartier Moulart. Parallel to the latter development was that of Ndjili, at the southeastern outskirt of the city, which was built on the Dendale and Ngiri-Ngiri model, that is, with unstandardized houses. Throughout the period of Belgian colonization, urban migration was restricted. However, Congo's independence brought an end to these restrictions. The country experienced an influx of migrants from the countryside into the city. This accompanied an intraurban movement from La Cité to suburban areas or unoccupied areas inside La Cité. With these movements was born a new type of residential area named Zones de Squatting (Squatting Zones), also called Cités Satéllites (Satellite Cities). Makala, Quartier Mombele, Kinsenso, Quartier Fonkobel, Masina and Kimbanseka are some Cités Satéllites born out of this movement. Zones de Squatting was also used to refer more specifically to settlements of illegal occupants on state-owned lands. Settlements legally built on state-owned lands were collectively called La Zone Annexe. Binza, Djelo-Binza, the central prison of Makala, Lovanium University and the Sanatorium (a medical center for treating tuberculosis) were part of La Zone Annexe.

Land Occupation Processes in Kinshasa. Some Congolese working for colonial companies lived in work camps controlled by the employing companies. Colonial government agencies or contracted services directly regulated urban life, including land occupation, in both La Ville and La Cité for the most part. For most of the colonial period, the Congolese were not legally permitted to own lands. They could only become renters or tolerated occupants of some other sort. Government agencies determined the lands to be zoned as residential for Congolese, the modalities of occupation and related fees or taxes. However, some wards inhabited by Congolese in metropolitan Kinshasa were not part of La Cité proper. For example, at the outskirts of the city proper were located entities pertaining to Bateke and Buhumbu ethnic chiefs, the precolonial owners of the lands on which Kinshasa is located. Administratively these entities formed the Secteur Bahumbu (Bahumbu Sector). The basic unit in the *secteur* was the village, which was headed by a village chief. When the village was settled on lands whose other inhabitants did not belong to the ethnic group of its occupants, land problems were turned over to the jurisdiction of an authorized member of the landowning group. Above the village was the *groupement*, an entity formed by a group of villages placed under common authority (the *groupement* chief), who was appointed by the colonial administration. At a still higher level was the *secteur*, an assemblage of *groupements* deemed too small to be viable autonomous administrative units. The colonial authority appointed the chief of the *secteur*, who might or might not be a traditional chief. The following *groupements* belonged to the Bahumbu Secteur: Kimpoko, Kinkole, Kinsielele, Lemba, Masina and Mikondo.

In 1960, prior to independence, traditional villages in the Kinshasa suburbs were invaded by the surplus population from Kinshasa's older communities and by new urban migrants. The influx brought complex problems that were beyond the competence of a traditional Teke or Humbu chief. Very soon, the population influx into suburban Kinshasa was aggravated by civil disobedience ordered against the colonial authorities by the leaders of the Association of Bakongo (ABAKO), which at the time was the most powerful ethnopolitical organization in the city of Kinshasa. ABAKO incited its members to illegally occupy state-owned lands. (At the time, the independence of the Congo was approaching.) In addition to defying the colonial authorities, ABAKO leaders relocated hundreds of their members in the city. They were positioning themselves for the anticipated national elections and for staffing the institutions of the future independent Republic of the Congo. Not long after, the Union des Bateke (UNIBAT), one of Bakongo's political rivals, requested 4,000 urban land plots. Facing the government's refusal, Pierre Mombele, UNIBAT president, ordered the Bateke people, in February 1960, to occupy lands in what became Quartiers Mombele, in Lime Commune. The Bayaka and other Kwango-Kwilu natives did likewise, occupying the ward called Camp Luka.

The squatting zones are one result of widespread waves of illegal occupation of urban lands. However, unlike in other countries, squatting zones in Congolese cities were not agglomerations of shacks. Therefore, they were more preferably called satellite cities. One satellite city, Kimbanseke, grew from a small village extension of Ndjili to become an impressive satellite city on its own. Nevertheless, illegal occupation did not even spare the environmentally risky zones, such as swampy valleys (Lemba, Makala and Yolo), slopes exposed to flooding during torrential rains (Makala, Kinsenso), areas under high tension lines and empty spots within preexisting cities (Quartiers Fonkobel, Camp Luka, Quartier Mombele). No squatters invaded former European zones. Perhaps the squatters knew that the Europeans considered La Ville their exclusive domain and would not tolerate squatting zones in their midst.

Land-Distributing Agents. Another outcome of widespread illegal land occupation was that many levels of authority became involved in land distribution. Some such authorities were improvised in response to issues generated by the squatting phenomenon. Individuals in this category performed functions in regard to the traditional lands that had traditionally been assumed by the traditional chiefs. Political leaders, leaders of ethnic associations and members of ethnic groups considered the first occupants of the land all became involved in one form or another of land distribution. For example, a certain M. Mayilu took the role of spokesman for the populations of Foncobel. Pierre Mombele, leader of Bateke, did likewise in an area near Limété, which ended up carrying his name (the Quartier Mombele). Mfwambomo oversaw the land and distributed plots in Ngaliema. He was a member of a group considered to be the first occupants of the land. There, Chief Gampani, after occupying the Masina squatting zone, put his son in charge of judicial and political functions. In other instances, temporary councils of elders were created to assume land-related functions. They sold plots and resolved land disputes as entitled members of a *groupement* or a traditional village. In Limete, for instance, municipal authorities appointed a council of clan representatives to oversee land issues in Quartiers Mombele.

Kinshasa is built on the lands of Bateke and Bahumbu. Traditionally, within each group, certain clans enjoyed the prerogative to provide leaders for the overall society. These leaders assumed the responsibility to organize communal life and exercised control over the lands, to the benefit of the entire community. Members of these two groups saw in land distribution more than a source of revenue. They found the power in land distribution to counter the political clout exercised over Kinshasa and its surroundings by the Bakongo, their political rivals, who outnumbered them.

Population influxes into the squatting zones, land scarcity and multiple, uncoordinated, land distribution agents produced fierce competition for land. They also generated countless and endless land conflicts, which became popularized in a song titled "Makambo ya Mabele" (Land disputes).

Construction in La Cité. Employers set the standards for planning and building houses in work camps. In La Cité, persons who could afford it acquired a plot from whatever public agency was in charge. The plots were drawn uniformly, but the houses were built to each owner's specifications; therefore, houses in La Cité and in the squatting zones were not standardized. Because of high unemployment and the underpayment of Congolese workers, the money for construction was often only available intermittently. Therefore, construction generally extended over long periods. To see people living in a house still under construction, sometimes over a considerable period, was usual.

Kintambo and Kinshasa were rural villages before incorporation into the

Mbuji-Mayi: large house in *La Cité*—house under construction using durable materials.

city. Houses in the first years of their incorporation were similar to those in Congolese villages. They had grass-thatched roofs, mud-rammed walls and unpaved floors. The builders extracted the soil for the mud from a pit dug in the yard where they were building the house. Usually, they brought in the water for construction from some distant creek, spring or river using jugs, buckets or barrels. They soaked the soil with water and mixed it with their feet to make the mud. Both the plastering and the smoothing of the wall surface were done by hand. They brought in the grass for the roof from wherever it was available. A special type of tall grass, called *masela* in the Luba language, is the most suitable for roofing. It is long enough to be tied to a transverse of the frame by the middle and still hang over. It is strong enough to withstand rains for an extended period. To increase resistance, the grass is separated into tied bundles. While roofing, the bundles are tied very close to the frame and overlapped to keep the rains out. They tie the grass to the frame in rows arranged from the bottom up, with each new row partially hanging over the previous one. The top row for a pitched roof is first tied by its top as firmly and neatly as possible. Then it is placed over the pitch of the frame, with the grass evenly scattered around the roof's summit. Finally they fasten the grass to the frame on all sides of the roof.

For a gable roof, the top grass row crosses the gable and hangs over on both sides.

With increased urbanization, Congolese neighborhoods received running water, first from public pumps in different wards. Later they built the pumps in individual plots of those who could afford to pay the required installation and monthly consumption fees. To date, residents who do not have running water in their yards sublet from those who do. Gradually they constructed the houses in La Cité with semidurable and durable materials. Sun-dried brick walls replaced rammed-mud walls. Later, cinder blocks replaced sun-dried bricks. Occasionally, builders used terra cotta bricks instead of cinder blocks. Roofing materials changed from grass to tiles or to corrugated iron. For example, red terra cotta bricks and corrugated iron roofs dominate the houses in La Cité of Boende, a town in the Equator province.

To build a house in La Cité, a plot owner contracts a skilled mason for the design and the foundation and a carpenter for the roof. The same contractor is both brick mason and carpenter. Owners and family members often participate in the building process. They may make the bricks, bring water to the construction site and help in any other way as needed. The bricks are made one by one, using square wooden boxes. Mud bricks are made with the soil from a pit dug in the yard and mixed with sand collected from the topsoil of the yard. Durable bricks are made of cement and commercial sand. The quality of the bricks requires specific proportions of cement, sand and water. Homeowners generally prefer that an experienced brickmaker perform this task. The bricks are left to dry for some days before building. Rain falling on the bricks while they are drying makes them stronger and resistant to future rains.

House building begins with the foundation. It should be as strong as possible. The walls are then erected on the foundation after it is dry. The correct proportions in the cement-sand-water mixture are necessary to make the house durable. An expert builder does the roofing.

For many, the completion of the family home is not the end of building activities on the plot. Income permitting, the homeowner will have an elongated structure with several rooms for renters built gradually over time and on the same plot, generally in the back, facing the street.

Planned Housing. Work camps and owner-financed homes and renter rooms were quickly outgrown by the demand for housing. In 1949, as a remedy, the colonial government created privately managed public construction companies in major cities and charged them to build and manage houses for Congolese. In 1952, these institutions were consolidated into a single agency, the Office des Cités Africaines (OCA). Kinshasa had most of the OCA-built townships. Elizabethville (Lubumbashi), the provincial capital of Katanga and Luluabourg (Kananga), capital of the Kasai province, also had their share. Houses in these planned neighborhoods were standardized to cut costs. Nevertheless, they were too few and too expensive to meet the demands and fit the budgets of most of the population.

In Kinshasa, houses in planned cities were multiple unit structures. Immocongo (renamed Matonge after independence) was an exception. Immocongo was destined for high-level civil service employees and Congolese professionals, such as medical assistants and registered nurses. Housing here consisted of individual houses. A few neighborhoods in some planned cities consisted of one-level, multiple-unit apartments. Such was the case in one part of Matete. The dominant housing type in the rest of Matete and in other planned cities, such as Lemba, Bandalungwa and Moulart, consisted of two-story apartments. All were built in a row facing the main street, with just a small space separating them. Uniformly, the sitting room and the kitchen were on the first floor. A little yard on the front separated the building from the street. The kitchen opened on a small backyard connecting the apartment to a narrow walking alley running between neighboring apartment rows facing in opposite directions. The bathroom was an integral part of the building, next to the kitchen but facing toward the backyard. Two small bedrooms and one larger master bedroom were upstairs. Apartments in some later developments such as Lemba were larger than the first ones.

In Kinshasa, a section of each planned neighborhood was zoned commercial. The commercial zone in a planned neighborhood consisted of a group of apartment buildings surrounding the local marketplace. Each apartment was divided into four small rooms, a kitchen and a bathroom, just like the rest of the neighborhood. The room facing the marketplace was reserved for business. The others were for the trader and his family to live in. Following Congo's independence (June 30, 1960), planned neighborhoods were subjected to real estate speculation. Wealthy individuals with powerful political connections rented OCA houses and sublet them at exorbitant prices. Many others transformed their apartment by building additional rooms in their back yard. Many others walled in their front yard for more privacy. Others, particularly in the commercial zone, transformed the front yard into a bar or an extended boutique.

***Housing in* La Ville.** Houses in the wards once reserved for Europeans were built of durable materials, large and well maintained. They generally called the houses here villas. In the early years of colonization, a smaller house for servants was located behind the main house. They colloquially called it a *boyerie* because the Europeans called the African servants "boy." After independence, wealthy Congolese kept the habit of building *boyeries*, but using them for dependent relatives. Many houses were surrounded by a walled enclosure with a large wire gate. By the entrance or in a corner there was usually a smaller house for the guard who controlled the gate. Villas of public authorities had larger gates and more than one guard. La Ville was generally urbanized. It had paved roads, and every home had running water and electricity.

The business district had two distinct looks. Small retailing businesses accessible to the Congolese were always situated toward the borderline of La Ville, in the direction of La Cité. They were often owned by Jews, Greeks, or Portugese, all of whom the Belgians called *les étrangers* (foreigners). Some of the shops looked clean, but others smelled of spoiling food and were crowded with flour bags, stocks of salted fish and palm oil jugs. Stores were lined up facing the roads the Congolese took to the city's main marketplace. The main business district in Kinshasa had wide streets and many tall buildings, particularly after independence. They called the streets here "avenues" or "boulevards" to distinguish them from the small streets in La Cité, which they call *rues* (streets).

NOTES

1. The discussion of the art of these and other groups in this chapter is based primarily on Joseph Cornet's *Art from Zaire: 100 Masterworks from the National Collection*, translation and Introduction by Irwin Hersey (New York: The African American Institute, 1975). See also Robin Poynor, "The Western Congo Basin" and "The Eastern Congo Basin," in *A History of Art in Africa*, ed. Monica Blackmun Visonà, Robin Poynor, Herbert M. Cole, and Michael D. Harris (Upper Saddle River, NJ: Prentice-Hall, 2000), 366–411 and 412–437. On Mangbetu architecture and art, see Enid Schildkrout and Curtis A. Keim, *African Reflections: Art from Northeastern Zaire* (Washington, DC: American Museum of Natural History, 1990).

2. Jewsiewcki, ed., *A Congo Chronicle: Patrice Lumumba in Urban Art* (New York: The Museum for African Art, 1999), is a recent comprehensive study of modern popular art in the Congo.

3. The principal sources for this section are: Jewsiewcki, *A Congo Chronicle*, and Schildkrout and Keim, *African Reflections*.

4. Siradiou Diallo, *Le Zaire aujourd'hui*, 3rd ed. (Paris: Les Éditions j.a., 1989), 150.

5. Leonard (Tshilemalema) Mukenge, "Croyances religieuses et structures sociofamiliales en société luba," *Cahiers Economiques et Sociaux* 5, no. 1 (1967):15–17.

6. Schildkrout and Keim, *African Reflections*, 101–106.

7. Schildkrout and Keim, *African Reflections*, 102.

8. Schildkrout and Keim, *African Reflections*, 103.

9. The information on housing and construction in Congolese cities is based on the author's personal experiences and the following studies: Etienne Kayitenkore, "La construction dans les zones de squatting de Kinshasa," *Cahiers Economiques et Sociaux* 5, no. 3 (1967): 327–353; Honoré Mpinga, "Ville de Kinshasa: Organization Administrative et Politique" (Memoire, Institut d'Etudes Politiques de Bordeaux, 1967); Honoré Mpinga, "La Coexistence des pouvoirs 'traditionnel et moderne' dans la ville de Kinshasa," *Cahiers Economiques et Sociaux* 7, no. 1 (1969):67–90; and Honoré Mpinga, "Les Mécanismes de croissance urbaine en République Démocratique du Congo," *Etudes Congolaises* 11, no. 3 (1968), 95–103.

5

Cuisine and Dress

THE CONGOLESE PEOPLE grow a vast range of food crops, including grains such as corn, rice, millet and sorghum; tubers like cassava, sweet potatoes, yam, taro and, in Kivu, the white potato; different varieties of beans—red, white and green; black-eyed peas; groundnuts; pumpkin; banana, including plantain, oranges and mangoes. Practically all food crops are consumed everywhere, but different staples dominate in different regions or among some ethnic groups wherever they live. Some foods are consumed as meals, others as snacks. Cuisines and eating habits differ as well. Overall, a full meal includes a staple, some vegetable, and some fish or meat when available. Various types of insects, including caterpillars, accompany, or substitute for, meat or fish. Kinshasa, the capital, is the meeting place of cuisines from all over the country, as exemplified by *nganda* restaurants (eateries serving ethnic dishes).

The Congolese dress has evolved from bark clothes and raffia clothes to the present day women's wrap and men's European-style dress. During the Mobutu dictatorship, men were forced to dress like Chinese. They wore the *abacos*, which was modeled after Chairman Mao Tse Tung. During the same period, those who could not afford the *abacos* resorted to *dashiki*, a West African style shirt generally worn hanging over the pants.

The first part of this chapter discusses three aspects of food in the Congo, notably, starchy foods, foods to eat with starches, and *nganda* restaurants. The second section discusses the Congolese dress and types of adornment.

CONGOLESE DIET AND CUISINE

Every complete meal served in a Congolese family contains a starch and something to go along with it. Both components reflect regional and ethnic preferences, although some starches and some vegetables are found almost everywhere.

Starchy Foods

Different starchy foods dominate among different peoples. For a typical Luba man or woman, for example, to eat is to eat some *nshima*, a paste made out of a mixture of corn flour and cassava flour. Some other groups have their equivalent of *nshima* under different names: *bidia* in Western Kasai; *fufu* in the Bandundu, Equator and Lower-Congo provinces and in the City of Kinshasa; and *ugali* in Katanga, Kivu and Upper Congo provinces.[1] The cassava-based *kwanga* bread is another starchy food consumed in different parts of the Congo, of which Kinshasa, and Lower Congo are the most known. There are also plantain-based dishes (*makemba*), of which the most celebrated is *lituma*, a baked plantain dish, speciality of people from Kisangani and other parts of the Upper Congo province. Rice, beans and sweet potatoes are other major sources of starchy foods. Wherever a particular starchy food is highly valued, they serve it with green vegetables, insects, fish or meat. Cassava leaves are the most popular green vegetable. Preparation and cooking processes for the starches and the dishes that go with them are described next.

Nshima. This starchy food prevails in the Luba/Kasai territory. It is a paste made of corn flour and cassava flour. The ideal here is a balanced combination of the two kinds of flour. Elsewhere in Kasai they call *nshima bidia*. The relative importance of corn flour and cassava flour in the *bidia* varies with their respective availability. Corn is a seasonal crop, but cassava is more perennial. Therefore, they serve cassava-based bidia throughout the year. The equivalent of *nshima* or *bidia* in other regions of the Congo are *fufu* and *ugali*. *Fufu* is the term used in Kinshasa, in other Lingala-speaking parts of the country and in Lower Congo and Bandundu. The dominant tendency in these regions is to use cassava flour exclusively. The term *ugali* is used in Swahili-speaking provinces, for example, Katanga where they use only corn flour.

Corn for making *nshima* is dried and then hulled and pounded with a pestle in a large, wooden mortar. It can also be ground using a small flat stone on a large concave stone. The grinder, traditionally a woman, first places on the concave stone enough corn grains to fit in the hollow space. Then, while kneeling behind the grinding stone, she holds a smaller stone or another pestle with both hands and pushes it back and forth, pressing it against the big stone. By so doing she smashes and pulverizes the corn grains. She carries out this operation repeatedly until the load is completed. Each time, she collects the pulverized corn in a large basin or closely knit basket.

Cassava is generally pounded rather than ground. Nowadays, they have replaced these traditional methods of making flour by a small engine-powered corn mill. In the village, dried cassava is kept in the attic of the kitchen. The exterior of dried cassava becomes dark and dusty. Therefore, scrubbing it before cooking is necessary. They feed the residue from scrubbing to goats and sheep. After scrubbing, cassava for *nshima* is sliced and pounded or ground. In the city, the need for scrubbing is minimal since storage time is generally short.

After the corn or the cassava has been pounded or ground, the product is sifted to separate the refined flour from the unfinished pieces. The leftover pieces of corn are cooked to make a porridge for human consumption in time of famine. Leftover cassava pieces are thrown to goats and sheep. Only the refined flour is used to make the staple *nshima*.

To cook the *nshima*, you heat the water first, then slowly pour a small quantity of corn flour into the water while stirring with a wooden spoon. When the mix comes back to a boil, cassava flour and more corn flour are added and stirred up to a full consistency. In this stage, the mix has become *nshima*. It is then put into a wooden bowl or calabash and arranged with a wet wooden spoon. In city, imported porcelain dishes have replaced calabash and wooden bowls. Finally, the *nshima* is served with greens, insects, caterpillars, fish or meat if available.

Kwanga. This is a fermented bread made out of cassava. It is the most common starchy food in Lower Congo, Bandundu and Equator. *Kwanga* is perhaps the most commercialized manufactured indigenous food item in the Congo. *Kwanga* manufacturing is a long process. It begins with harvesting cassava roots from the fields. Harvest is followed by three to four days of soaking. Soaking softens the roots and removes the bitterness from certain cassava varieties. Cassava is soaked in a pond, preferably by damming a freshwater creek.

On the third or fourth day, when cassava roots have softened, they are taken out of the water, peeled, rinsed and inspected to remove strings. After draining the water from the cassava, the soft, clean pulp is pressed by hand

and placed on a flat board to be ground with a roller. Also by hand, the cassava is molded into balls. Then the balls are cooked in boiling water until the color turns brown. The balls are drawn from the water, drained and pounded once again. Finally, the balls are formed and wrapped in banana leaves. The packages are then placed in a large cooking pot and boiled for about two hours. The packages are taken out of the water and dried to the sun. In this stage the *kwanga* is ready to eat.

Variations in the *kwanga* manufacturing process include soaking, removing strings, grinding or pounding, forming balls and boiling the balls wrapped in the leaves of some plant. Differences relate to size of the *kwanga*, duration and number of times cooked, draining and drying. In some Lower Congo areas, *kwanga* packages for baking are placed in a pit and covered with earth; they are then cooked with a fire built on top of the pit.

Lituma. This is the most celebrated plantain dish in Kinshasa, and a speciality of people from Kisangani. *Lituma* is made with baked plantains. The generic name for baked plantains is *makemba ya kotumba*. Plantains for *lituma* or for any other cooking styles are first washed in water in their skins and then placed whole into boiling water. Plantains for *lituma* are boiled for a short period and then drained. Next, they are peeled, cut into small pieces, mixed with cassava flour and mashed with a wooden roller on a board or a grinding stone. They may also be pounded in a wooden mortar. The mashed plantains are then formed into balls, wrapped in banana or reed leaves and tied. They are baked slowly under warm ashes, charcoal or a wood fire, or sometimes on a metal grill.

Plantains can also be eaten fried or simply boiled. Plantains for frying, *makemba ya kukalinga*, are boiled for a very short time and drained on a grill or on banana leaves, just as for baking. They are then cut into halves, or into more pieces in case of long plantains. Meanwhile, the oil is heating in a metal or clay pot. Palm oil is heated longer than peanut oil or any other imported oil to allow the oil to separate from the residue. The oil turns darker, and then pieces of plantains are placed in the open pot and fried, being turned at intervals to avoid burning and allow for even cooking. When the plantains' color turns brown on both sides, they are taken out of the pot and placed on a plate or a grill to drain before being served. Boiled plantains, *makemba ya kotokisa*, are the most basic form of cooking plantains. As with the previous forms, the plantains are washed before boiling. However, they are boiled longer, until they are soft enough for immediate consumption.

Loso na Madesu. This dish is rice combined with beans. Rice is dominant in the diet of some Congolese groups, such as the Atetela. Beans dominate the diet of the Bashi. In Kinshasa and other cities, they still eat each as a separate dish. Increasingly, however, the two are eaten together, as a single dish. In either case, the rice and beans are prepared and cooked separately. In villages, both preparations involve pounding and hulling. In the city, they sell rice and beans ready to cook. The first operation for both is washing and cleaning them. Clean rice can be cooked right away. Usually, after the first boiling, the fire is reduced gradually to allow for slow cooking. Beans require several hours of soaking and slow cooking. After cooking, they are mixed, either in the pot or on the serving plate. In this case, the beans serve as sauce to accompany the rice. Beans may also be mixed with a sauce before being added to the rice.

Mbala. Sweet potatoes are cooked in ways similar to those for plantains, that is, boiled, fried or baked. Of these methods of cooking potatoes, boiling is the most widespread. For this method, as for the others, the sweet potatoes are washed in cold water. Then, the potatoes are peeled with a knife, and boiled or fried to satisfaction. Sweet potatoes for baking are left in the skin and baked individually, unwrapped or wrapped in banana or reed leaves.

Bitoto. This dish is a mixture of several kinds of food: bananas, cassava, butter beans, corn, squash, fish, cassava leaves, onions and tomatoes. Ethnically, *bitoto* is associated with the Bayombe, a branch of the Kongo ethnic group.

Tshimuku. Women in Luba villages once manufactured a cake called *tshimuku* by mixing mashed sweet potatoes with dry roasted peanuts. The processing of *tshimuku* begins by rubbing roasted peanuts with the fingers to remove the chaff from the nuts. After placing them in a basin or a tightly woven, lightweight, round basket, the next step is shake the basket to separate the nuts from the chaff and blow it away. Then the women pound the nuts in a wooden mortar or grind them with a grinding stone. The paste is mixed with potatoes in a basin and stirred with a wooden spoon after adding some water to it. To complete the processing you form balls of potato-peanut mix, wrap them individually in banana or reed leaves and bake the packages for a short period.

Foods to Accompany Starches

The starchy foods, particularly *nshima (bidia), kwanga* and *lituma*, are not meant to be eaten alone. They are always accompanied by some other type of food, usually green vegetables, but also insects, fish or meat.

Cassava Leaves. Cassava leaves preparation begins with washing, pounding and soaking. Soaking lasts an hour or more and is done in a pot. Sometimes, cassava leaves are boiled, and then prepared, pounded and cooked without soaking. The Luba have the reputation of being cassava leaf lovers. The Luba name for the cassava leaf vegetable is *matamba* or *kaleji*. The high frequency of *matamba* consumption in Luba families is romanticized as a measure for the manifestation of love: "Blessed is the one who is loved like *matamba*, more *matamba* are picked even if there is still some in the pot."

Tshitekuteku. This green, spinach-like vegetable is probably the most frequently consumed vegetable after cassava leaves. Its plural form (*bitekuteku*) and the plural form of the second Luba word for cassava leaves (*tuleji*) are often used in the generic sense of greens. Sometimes, these terms are used to refer to a meal offered to an honored guest even if the meal contains neither vegetable. The plural forms *bitekuteku* and *tuleji* denote abundance, saturation or humbleness to a host of mark.

Mfumbwa. Some of the vegetables that enrich the Congolese cuisine are plants that grow wild. *Mfumbwa*, one of the most popular greens in Kinshasa, grows widely in the Lower-Congo and other regions. It is eaten fresh or dried. *Mfumbwa* preparations for cooking include washing fresh leaves in cool or warm water and cutting them in very small pieces. *Mfumbwa* for future consumption is sun dried and stored in dry bags or clay pots. That for immediate consumption is cooked in a pot with tomatoes, salt, onions, celery and pepper.

Mushrooms. Although they are not cultivated, wild mushrooms are eaten throughout the Congo. Luba people consider mushrooms a bit more special than the other vegetables, perhaps because they are less available and because meat is rare. Sometimes, children are told that mushrooms are a kind of meat. Mushrooms are picked during the rainy season in areas where the grass has been burned. Sometimes, one may come across a patch of mushrooms on the way to somewhere else and take the opportunity to pick them. However, seeing mushrooms, especially seeing just one mushroom, on the way to the traps, fishing or hunting is considered a bad omen by some. In Luba families, all the vegetables mentioned here and others are served with the starch staple *nshima*. Elsewhere, they accompany other Congolese staples such as *kwanga, lituma* or *loso*. They are never served without a starch staple.

Other Greens. Other major green vegetables in the Congolese diet include *muteta* (bitter leaf), *mudibu* (pumpkin leaves) and *bilungalunga* (sweet potato leaves). *Mupala, njilu* (eggplant), *mulembwa* (okra) and *busa* (a special variety of okra) are in second place. Luba people consider okra as a vegetable for women and children, although many adult men eat it also. *Muteta* is bitter, so it is generally mixed with any of the other vegetables listed here except for cassava leaves, *mupala* and okra. Eggplant is cooked separately or mixed with cassava leaves or another vegetable. Sometimes, it is also eaten raw or baked. Only rarely will it be the only vegetable in a meal.

Insects. Only certain species of insects are edible. They include certain varieties of ants, crickets, grasshoppers and caterpillars. Two varieties of edible flying ants, one white (*bintunta*) and one brown (*nswa*), develop in a particular type of mound. The white ants develop in slim and cone-shaped mounds, and the brown ones develop in larger, dome-shaped mounds. White ants are eaten raw or grilled and the brown ones are eaten broiled, grilled or dried. A third variety of edible ants (*mankenene*), called soldiers in English, does not fly. They, too, develop in mounds. The most widespread variety of edible crickets, *mintuntu* or *likelele*, live in individual holes in the ground. Edible grasshoppers include the varieties called *minkese, malala* or *mbedi* and *kamanyimanyi*. The latter variety is perhaps the smallest of all edible grasshoppers. Ants of the soldier type, crickets and grasshoppers are usually eaten grilled or broiled.

Caterpillars occupy an important place in Congolese diet. They, too, are gathered rather than farmed. Edible caterpillars are called *meshi* as opposed to those that are not, which are called *bishishi*. *Meshi* are named after the trees in which they grow. Close to these are the grubs (*mposa*) that develop in the heart of the palm tree. The most commercialized of all caterpillars (*mansamba*) in the Congo are from Tshikapa, in the Western Kasai province. The last species of edible caterpillars worth mentioning develops in the young grass that grows in a field that has been burned. These caterpillars are much smaller than the others.

Fish and Meat. Naturally, fish is more abundant in regions near waterways. The Congo River, its major tributaries and their own feeders, and the lakes are important reservoirs of fish. Fish is cooked in various ways, including baked, boiled and fried. Fish for future consumption is generally smoked for better preservation. Salted fish, called *makayabo*, preserves itself even better. People living in rural areas have greater access to game meat than do urban dwellers. In contrast, commercialized beef and pork are more associated with urban life. Fresh meat is mostly served stewed. Kinshasa marketplaces, front courtyards of bars and some spots along major arteries are famous for the sale of *maboke* (highly peppered fresh fish baked in banana leaves) and *kamundele* (small pieces of barbecued goat or beef sold on skewers as shish kabob). There is also *likobe*, a boneless game meat mixed with oil, onion and spices and baked in banana leaves.

Mwambe. *Mwambe* is chicken cooked in a sauce made out of dried cassava leaves and peanut paste. The paste is made with dry peanuts. The first step is to roast the peanuts optimally, that is, until and no later than the moment when the inner covering of chaff can be removed gently. After roasting, the peanuts are placed in a wide-mouthed container such as a calabash bowl or a close-knit basket. The next step is the removal of the chaff. This operation is carried out by hand after the roasted peanuts have cooled down. Then comes the winnowing, which in turn is followed by the pounding of the peanuts in a small mortar or grinding on a board. Presently, some individuals own a small grinding machine. Peanut paste is to be added to boiling cassava leaves near completion of the cooking process. After the mixture has cooked some more, cassava leaves and peanut paste have become *mwamba*. Chicken for the *mwambe* is prepared and cooked separately as well. When it is done, then it is mixed with the *mwamba*. The two are then cooked together for a short period and then served with *kwanga* or *loso*. Sometimes palm oil or commercial peanut butter substitutes for peanut paste.

Nteta. The generic term for seeds is *nteta*. Pumpkin seeds are the most common seeds used in Congolese recipes. *Nteta* preparation and cooking are performed by women. The woman in charge of this task first removes pumpkin seeds from the fruit by hand or with the help of a spoon into a basin or a calabash bowl. She washes them in this container and picks them up by hand one by one. Then, she dries them to the sun on top of a stand generally used to dry cassava, on a mat placed on the ground or even on a well-swept spot on the ground. When the seeds are dried to satisfaction, she shells them by hand. Then, she mixes the *nteta* with fresh tomato and fresh-cut onion and grinds them with a pestle in a mortar. After collecting the mashed product in a basin or a pot, she forms balls of *nteta* with the palm of her right hand and places them on a plate or in a calabash bowl.

Nteta ne Mishipa. In most cases, *nteta* are cooked with dried fish. The cook prepares *nteta* and then fish. To prepare dried fish, she starts with heating some water, which she pours into a basin; she then places dried fish in the water. By hand, she separates the fish from the bones. After this operation is completed, she rinses the fish and cooks it in water.

Nteta ne Meshi. There exist some other ways to cook *nteta*. One is *nteta ne meshi*. This is *nteta* cooked with caterpillars. Caterpillars are generally treated in some way before cooking. Caterpillars that are hairy or have tough skin are burned and washed before frying. Bitter caterpillars are soaked for a couple of hours before cooking. Other caterpillar preparation techniques include drying or coating with flour, depending on variety and taste. When mixed with pumpkin seeds (*nteta*), both caterpillars and *nteta* are mixed together after preparing the seeds. Whether cooked alone or mixed with *nteta*, caterpillars are served with one or the other of the following staples: *nshima, loso, kwanga,* or *makemba*.

Nteta ne Munyinyi. Another common way to cook *nteta* is with fresh meat, called *munyinyi*. Goat meat is the most commonly consumed fresh meat in the Congo. Beef can be used as a substitute when available and affordable. The meat for *nteta* is stewed and seasoned with an aromatic herb called *tshikota*.

Sauces and Condiments. The most common cooking style in the Congo is the stew. The juice from cooking greens, fish or meat serves as sauce for dipping the *nshima* or for sprinkling over rice. Tomatoes and onions are grown in the Congo. However, tomato consumption is more associated with urban life than with village life. Tomatoes are added to meat or to vegetables to form the sauce. Onions are equally available throughout the Congo. They are practically absent from some areas, so many villagers season their food with various aromatic herbs. For example, rather than onions, Luba villagers season their vegetables or meat, especially chicken, with the leaves of an aromatic herb called *tshikota* or with those of two other aromatic plants called *lwenyi* and *tshidibulwenyi*. The latter two plants are very close to each other. In fact, *tshidibulwenyi*, the name for the second plant, means "that which is like *lwenyi*."

Of course, the Congolese, do cook their vegetables or meat with salt and oil. However, some, such as the Luba of Kasai, prefer their cassava leaves with very little salt. They season their meat or vegetables with sweet green pepper and hot red pepper. Ethnic groups also differ as to how heavily they spice their food. For example, Luba people do not heavily spice their food, whereas the Songye and many other groups do.

Nganda Restaurants

The urban diet is more cosmopolitan. It combines starches and cuisines from different regions. It also incorporates European imports and European-style, locally manufactured foods, such as bread and beer. This coexistence is manifest in the Kinshasa small restaurants called *nganda*, which serve ethnic dishes.

Nganda *Restaurants*. The *nganda* flourished in the 1970s and 1980s. They were one of the few typical women's businesses in Kinshasa. (The word *nganda* is used for both the singular and plural forms.) *Nganda* were eateries functionally standing between bars and restaurants. On the one hand, like bars, *nganda* were places where more drinking than eating took place. On the other hand, they resembled restaurants in that they served real meals, not snacks. Found throughout Kinshasa, the *nganda* featured the dishes of different ethnic groups.

Kongo People's **Nganda.** The Kongo people originate from Bas-Congo (Lower Congo), the country surrounding the lower part of the Congo River, from the neighborhood of Kinshasa downstream. Their *nganda* served primarily dishes of fish cooked in a special vegetable sauce called *fumbwa* and eaten with *kwanga*, the typical Kongo starchy food.

Riverside People's **Nganda.** The *nganda* of the people who come from areas along the Congo River, from Mai-Ndombe up-river, serve fish dishes called *maboke*. *Maboke* are dishes of fresh fish baked in reed leaves and served with *makemba* (cooked plantains).

Kasai People's **Nganda.** The *nganda* of the people from Kasai feature goat meat and cassava leave greens served with *nshima* starch or rice (*losa*). Also served in the *nganda* of Kasai people is *mutu wa mbuji*, a soup made of parts from goat head.

The *nganda* of a particular ethnic dominance were mostly found where ethnic consumers of the particular dishes they serve lived. In week days these facilities were mostly frequented late afternoon and evenings. More cosmopolitan *nganda* of the Ngombe business district opened during the day and reached their highest popularity during the lunch hour.

Nganda were more than eating and drinking facilities; they were also meeting places for persons who shared certain affinities. *Nganda* customers could be classified in three social strata. The first stratum consisted of the least fortunate customers. They generally came in groups and began by contributing money on the spot to pay for the meal and beer. Contributing money enabled them to afford some of the foods of their youth that the high cost of living had prohibited for most of them. Also, meeting at the *nganda* offered them an opportunity to share information and comments on current news.

The next stratum of *nganda* goers comprised individuals who were relatively well-to-do. They disposed of quite sizable sums of money obtained through speculative businesses or trafficking in precious stones. They, too, took advantage of the *nganda* to share information and debate issues. Unlike groups of the preceding category which generally sat outside, the latter groups, as a rule, sought to be seated inside the *nganda* where higher prices were charged.

Another category of *nganda* goers comprised professionals, such as physicians, university professors, chief executive officers (CEOs) of banks or political figures. They were treated with much respect. *Nganda* were practically the only places where they could relax in discretion. Also, they only frequented select *nganda*.

Many *nganda* were operated in places of residence. As a rule, *nganda* operators were single women, divorced people, widows or women living together as an unmarried cross-sexual couple with men. *Nganda* stayed open until late in the night. The individuals who frequented were sometimes disreputable, and for this reason, *nganda* were not operated by married women.

DRESS AND ADORNMENTS

Congolese Dress

Older persons in Congolese villages speak of times where people used to dress in bark clothes or raffia clothes. Nowadays, the wrap dominates among women and European-style clothes among men. During the Mobutu regime men dressed in *abacos* or in *boubou*. The *abacos* is a men's four-button or six-button single-breasted unlined suit with a notched collar and narrow lapel. It can also be made with a mandarin-type collar. A West African import, the *boubou*, or *dashiki*, is a shirt generally in multicolored printed material that men wear over their pants. It is often part of a suit. President Mobutu had large groups of male and female cheerleaders (*animateurs*) trained to sing and dance to his glory. They wore green *kikwembe* and *libaya* (women) or green pants and *le boubou* (men). Members of various organizations wore uniforms.

Women's Dress. The most common women's dress in ancient times consisted of a raffia or bead skirt (*tshivunga*). The torso was generally uncovered. Gradually, the raffia or bead skirt was replaced by a wrap covering the entire body from the waist down to the ankles. The wrap has remained the distinctive dress of the Congolese woman to date. The wrap (*kikwembe*) is worn with a top of the same material sewn the African way (*libaya*) or a Western-style blouse. In rural areas, the wrap is often simply tied at the waist by a cloth belt with the upper edge of the wrap hanging over the belt. On special, or festive occasions, the upper part of the wrap is generally rolled over. Some-

Woman of moderate means: items of dress include: a long wrap and a *libaya* (African-style top) of the same material, a simple head tie and a necklace but no earrings.

times women wear two wraps rather than one. In this case, the first (*kikwembe*), a longer wrap, hangs over a belt. The second (*liputa*), generally a smaller wrap, is worn around the hips and rolled over several times at the waist. The bra is not part of a rural woman's typical dress. Slippers, sandals and thongs are typical footwear for those who can afford them. Those who cannot go barefoot.

Well-off women, mostly urban, wear more beautiful and more expensive wraps, tops and shoes. The preferred material for quality wraps is called *wax*. The Congo had a *wax* print textile factory at Maluku. Nevertheless, women of distinction prefer imported *wax*, particularly the one from Holland. It is believed to be of better quality. It preserves its texture and look over a longer period and lasts longer. The Congolese woman often substitutes an imported blouse for a *wax* top. For a more satisfactory dress she wears a kerchief tied around her head with the ends hanging down in the back. The head kerchief can be of a different material or the same as the other wraps. *La Congolaise moderne* (the modern Congolese woman) enjoys complementing her festive dress with some jewelry, such as a bracelet, a necklace and earrings. However, conspicuous wearing of jewelry is not a common practice among Congolese women.

Men's Dress. Congolese men, just like women, once wore one or two pieces of raffia cloth around their waist. Later, printed material replaced the raffia. Until the 1940s and early 1950s, men in some countryside villages dressed in a cloth material (*kikwembe*) wrapped around the hips with the upper edge pulled through a belt at the waist and turned over several times to form a roll (*tshifunda*). The shirt was tucked inside the *kikwembe*. The men's *kikwembe* was comparable to today's most common African women's dress, with the exception that the color was either all white or *nzobanzoba*, that is, an alternation of white and blue stripes descending vertically. Sometimes, the *kikwembe* was wrapped around the body under the left arm and knotted over the right shoulder. In this form the dress was called *mupalala*. The *mupalala* could be worn without a shirt but, since the right side remained open, it was worn with shorts or long pants. The men's *kikwembe*, just like women's, descended from the waist to the ankles; the *mupalala* from the shoulder to the knees.

In the 1950s, long and short pants replaced the *tshifunda* completely. The *mupalala* could still be seen in some regions. Long or short pants were worn with a shirt (*muteelu*). At first the shirt was mostly a short-sleeve one (*tshijika*). Gradually, the long-sleeve shirt (*nshimishi*) became popular. To date, the tie (*nkolu*) and the dress jacket (*nkotshi*) are more urban than rural attire. Today, as in the past, during ceremonial dances, particularly those executed in the waist, men wear a women's wrap rolled in *tshifunda* around their waist.

Citizenship Dress. Dress has never been exclusively an expression of personal taste. It has always had multiple functions. Among other functions, dress may be an expression of political will imposed by a person of power. During the Mobutu dictatorship (1965–1997), Congolese men's dress un-

derwent two revolutions. The first revolution came out of China. President
Mobutu adopted Chairman Mao Tse-Tung's *abacos* for himself and imposed
it on all the citizens as the national dress for men. Ties and jackets were
banned. *Abacoses*, imported ready-made or sewn locally with imported material, flooded Kinshasa stores. In fact, local tailors, Congolese and foreigners,
became makers of long-sleeve and short-sleeve *abacoses*. However, the *abacos*
was too expensive for the ordinary citizen. This condition favored the second
revolution, the popularization of the classic multicolored clothing material
for women, *le wax*, among men. At first, *le wax* became valued more than
ever before. Congolese women of high socioeconomic status became unof-
ficial fashion models. A variety of *wax* materials were imported from Holland.
The local factory followed up with imitations. From being exclusively a
women's clothing, the *wax* became men's clothing as well. Wearing *wax* shirts
became acceptable to men. Along with the *wax*, men adopted *le boubou*, the
Congolese version of the West African *dashiki*. *Boubous* in multicolored *wax*
material became part of a man's normal clothing choices.

Special Attire. President Mobutu created large groups of supporters, men
and women, whose role was to sing and dance to his glory. Dressed in party's
colors, these specific groups, called *animateurs*, held public cheerleading celebrations, singing, dancing, praising Mobutu as father of the nation and
guide of the Zairean revolution. The *animateurs* were dressed in a uniform
carrying the president's image in his official attire. When the president's attire
changed, the *animateurs'* uniform changed to reflect his image and colors in
the new attire.

Many other groups in uniform participated in manifestations of support
to the Mobutu regime on festive occasions. Before Mobutu's November 24,
1965, coup d'état, June 30 (Congo's Independence Day) was celebrated with
pump. After the coup, November 24 came to prominence instead, as did
Mobutu's political party, the Mouvement Populaire de la Revolution (MPR),
and its youth branch, the Jeunesse du Mouvement Populaire de la Revolution
(JMPR). The JMPR was preceded by the Corps des Volontaires de la Republique (CVR), which started in 1966. From supporting the creation of
two parties in replacement of the tribal-influenced parties of 1960, CVR
became an integral part of Mobutu's single party, MPR, when the latter came
into existence in April 1967. Thus CVR became the prefiguration of the
JMPR, the perennial youth movement of the MPR. CVR's colors were green
and white. JMPR members wore a khaki uniform with a Mao collar (round
collar similar to the collar made popular by Mao Tse Tung, China's president
at the time).

The various sections of the military forces had different colors. The army had a khaki and camouflage uniform. Paratroops had a khaki uniform and a helmet surrounded by a red strip. The gendarmes (military police) also had khaki uniforms, but their helmet had a white strip. The commandos wore camouflage with green berets. The land forces had khaki uniform and berets. The navy wore all blue, and Navy officers wore blue shirts.

Several civilian groups wore uniforms as well. Kimbanguist Church members wore green bottoms (men's pants and women's skirts) and white tops (shirts and blouses, respectively). Women wore green head kerchiefs also. Students had school uniforms. Local branches of the Red Cross and the Salvation Army participated in the parades. They wore their classic colors, that is, the American khaki and the white, respectively.

Adornments

The search for esthetics permeates artistic productions throughout the Congo. Body adornment, elaborate coiffure, stylistic wall painting and esthetically sculpted royal implements are only a few from among the many types of esthetic expressions found in Congolese art. The Mangbetu are among the groups whose keen sense of beauty is most acclaimed. Illustrative cases follow.[2]

Esthetic Decorations. Scarification was practiced almost everywhere in the Congo. It conveyed more than the message of ethnic identity or bravery. Typically, scarification, especially on a woman's abdomen, was meant to accentuate beauty, attractiveness and eroticism. A statue of a female Yaka ancestor wore a skirt of esthetically arranged beads. She also wore a coiffure carrying beautifully sculpted designs. A Hemba female statuette was sculpted with a design singling out the center of the abdomen in the form of a lozenge. Among other impressive decorations, she had long eyebrows, a large face, and a coiffure demarcated from the face by a chain-like design. Concern with esthetics was not limited to the human body. In Nsundi Sese, a locality in Tshela, in Lower Congo, extensive decorations were found on powder boxes. The Nkanu of Bandudu decorated their masks with a polychrome hairdress corresponding to the high reliefs found on their circumcision huts. The Lele people's pipe bowls were head-shaped and surmounted by a zigzag decoration reminiscent of the one generally found on Lele's own palm wine cups. The Kuba, Lele's neighbors, drank palm wine from a horn beautifully decorated with a lizard and with motifs similar to female tatoos. In the Kuba country, even therapeutic enema implements were beautifully decorated. The Kuba

Statuary: Decorated   Human
Body. Collection of the author.

people make the famous raffia velour from Kasai. Kuba royal drums were admirably decorated with pearls, shells and grains. The Binji made elephant statues fully covered with interlaced designs comparable to those of the Kuba.

The Mangbetu Culture of Adornment. The Mangbetu have a rich artistic tradition. The vast range of their artistic productions includes ivory horns, harps of hide, plant fibers, wood and brass; ceramic pots, calabash gourds and iron knives in the form of an ivory hand. Besides richness and variety, Mangbetu art is remarkable for its preoccupation with beauty.[3] Many Mangbetu utilitarian instruments served as ornaments when they were first made and as tools after they aged. As an example, brooms were first used in dances, where they were held in the air as wands, and only later were they used for sweeping.

One aspect of aesthetics is adornment of the body. From birth, a Mang-

Utilitarian Art: Carved Ebony Chair. Collection of the author.

betu child bore around the waist a belt carrying amulets and charms made of animal skins, claws, bones, teeth and shells. These objects were intended to transfer to the child the strengths and swiftness of the animals from which they were made. They were also expected to protect the child from diseases and witches and bring good fortune. In the past, children also wore a cord made of human hair or plant fibers bound around the head to elongate it. Around the age of puberty, after circumcision for a boy, the child underwent scarification. A girl's scarifications were supposed to enhance her beauty.

Both men and women were preoccupied with the shape of their heads, the hairstyle and the adornment of the head. Rich people's hairstyles were more elaborated than those of persons of modest socioeconomic condition. Well-off women supplemented their hair with hair taken from prisoners of war or purchased from other women. The turn of the century brought on new hairstyles. By the beginning of the twentieth century, the zeal to make the head look overelongated had faded among men, whereas it had become

Woman's hair styled with thread.

common for a woman to add a halo-shaped basketry frame covered with hair to her own hair.

The care for the head was extended to combs, hairpins, hat pins and hats. Mangbetu men and women wore combs made of palm fiber, porcupine quills, wood and metal as adornments for their hair. Men wore hats attached to their hair with pins. Women wore hats occasionally, such as for dances. Ordinarily, women wore hairpins and combs made of metal, bone or ivory.

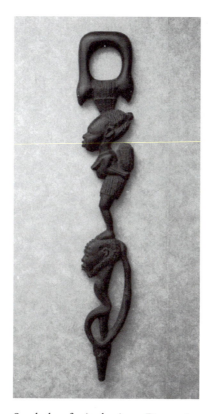

Symbol of Authority: Decorative Walking Stick. Handle: two-headed snake wrapping down and around the shaft. Shaft: woman carrying baby on her back and standing on a man's head. Collection of the author.

Mangbetu weavers combined several techniques to enhance beauty in the hats. For example, most hats were woven of palm fiber strips plaited in various patterns combining natural and dyed colors. Patterns of fiber strips on the hats alternated inward-looking and outward-looking layers to create surfaces reflecting light differently. Strips of sorghum were sometimes woven into the hat, adding beauty from their bright, buff color. Bundles of many kinds of feathers were tied together and attached to the hats.

Marshal Mobutu Adornments. President Mobutu himself first converted to the abacos. He developed the cult of personality (self-promotion) to its highest. In fact, he had the citizens call him "Supreme Guide, Father of the

Nation." During the national news his photo was presented descending from the skies like a god in human form. He also wore made-to-taste multicolored, *boubou*-like shirts. An artistically sculpted mace and a leopard-skin hat accompanied *le boubou* (*dashiki*). In 1982, Mobutu proclaimed himself marshal and adopted the green, gold and red as the official colors of both his political party, the MPR, and his insignia of power. His official attire included several ornaments, all in the same three colors. He wore a sash across his chest and over the right shoulder, two medallions on his chest (the bigger one to the left and the smaller one to the right), a mandarin-like collar, an insignia on the crest of his cap featuring a leopard as his main authority symbol, a mace in his right hand as another permanent authority symbol and a bandolier hanging over his left shoulder and descending in front almost to the waist.

NOTES

1. Besides the author's personal experiences, this section was inspired by the observations of several Congolese men and women residing in Atlanta, Georgia, or visiting Atlanta from the Congo. In year 2000, during the preparation of this book, the author had interviews or conversations with the following individuals on various aspects of Congolese cuisine and eating habits: Papa Simon Ilunga, Mama Mwa-Tshitambwa, Reverend Lucien Luntandila, Mama Jeanne Lukibouwo Luntandila, Dr. Mabiengwa Naniuzeyi and Mrs. Constance Naniuzeyi, Mr. Shimata Tshinanga and Mrs. Ngoya Tshinanga, Mama Wakuteka, and Mr. Stephane Mabika Ilunga.

2. On Congolese esthetics, see Enid Schildkrout and Curtis A. Keim, *African Reflections: Art from Northeastern Zaire* (Washington, DC: American Museum of Natural History, 1990). See also Monica Blackmun Visonà, Robin Poyner, Herbert M. Cole, and Michael D. Harris, eds., *History of Art in Africa* (New York: Prentice-Hall, and Harry N. Abrams, Publishers, 2001), 366–437.

3. On the Mangbetu art of adornment, see Schildkrout and Keim, *African Reflections*, 123–141.

6

Marriage, Family, and Gender Roles

TRADITIONAL MARRIAGE in the Congo is more than a union between two individuals. It is, above all, an alliance between two families. The sealing of the marriage alliance involves a transfer of some wealth (bridewealth) from the groom's family to the bride's family. To this traditional alliance, colonization has added the Christian marriage and marriage registration in the official records of the state. The conjugal family that results from such a union can be monogamous (involving one man and one woman) or polygamous (involving one man and two or more women). In either case, it is never the complete family. It is a subunit of the extended family, which traditionally translates to the full notion of family. Nuclear family members of a particular extended family are interrelated in a web of rights and obligations designed to foster unity among them.[1] In marriage, the Congolese woman is expected to become a mother, to take care of her children and, along with her husband, to provide for the household. Spouse, mother, caretaker and provider, the Congolese woman commands the respect of both men and other women. The loss of any of these statuses jeopardizes her dignity, as with unmarried women, especially those who involve themselves in extramarital affairs. This chapter contains three sections, which examine marriage, the family and the Congolese woman.

MARRIAGE

Marriage Preparation

In a traditional setting, marriage preparation begins informally in early childhood and is stressed in puberty rites. In the past, marriage was the essence of the betrothal system.

Long-term Marriage Preparation. Marriage preparation begins in the early years, when children play "husband and wife" or "mother and child." Girls play "mother" by holding sticks in folded arms or on their laps in the manner adult mothers hold their babies. Consequently, Congolese children grow up expecting to get married when they reach the appropriate age. Maturity for marriage is both a physical and a social criterion. Physical maturity is marked by the body changes that occur at puberty. Puberty for girls is manifested in the appearance of first menstruation and the development of the breasts and the pelvis. For boys, puberty manifests itself in such features as the growing of a beard and deepening of the voice. Physical maturity alone does not qualify one for marriage, however. Marriage requires social maturity, also. It is measured by one's ability to assume gender roles and responsibilities associated with the status of husband and father or wife and mother. Physical maturity and social maturity are interrelated. In the countryside, a young man shows his physical suitability for marriage by building himself a house and tilling a field of his own. In the past, he was sometimes asked to perform these tasks for the future in-laws, sometimes for up to two years. Such was the case with the Ngbaka of Ubangi. A young woman was considered fit for marriage when she could carry out the chores of an adult woman, including cooking, participating in farming activities, fetching water and gathering cooking wood. Usually, girls mastered these tasks around puberty. Boys became marriageable later. Sometimes, Ngbandi young men remained unmarried until the age of thirty years.

By the time young persons reach the age of marriage, they already know the categories of people who are potential marriage partners and those who are excluded for reasons of kinship ties, custom differences or particular historical events. The circle of individuals who are ineligible for marriage because of close kinship ties varies in size. Many Congolese societies prohibit marriage with any member of the mother's or the father's clan. For example, among the Hema of Ituri, individuals who bear the same totemic name (identifying them with a particular clan) cannot marry. Other societies practice cross-cousin marriage. This is the marriage of a man with the daughter of his paternal aunt. Cousins who are potential marriage partners are alerted of this eventuality throughout infancy. With such long-term preparation, actual marriage is the consummation of a union already in existence in their minds.

Immediate Preparations. Because marriage is important for society as a whole, mutual agreement between a man and a woman is not enough to make them husband and wife. Their union must be approved by society for it to become legitimate. In Congolese tradition, marriage is an alliance between the groom's family and the bride's family. In the past, the two families intervened quite early in the marriage process. Mental preparation, as described for cross-cousin marriage, was not the only form of parental involvement in the premarital stage. Family reputation and personal character were subject to scrutiny on both sides, especially when the two families lived in different villages and did not have enough prior knowledge of each other. Marriage would not be authorized until certain questions were satisfactorily answered. These included whether members of either family treated their spouses well and showed respect to their in-laws. They also asked about hereditary diseases. Depending on the ethnic group, concern for family reputation was extended to whether women in the bride's clan were known for being faithful to their husbands. Men of the groom's family were scrutinized for instances of spousal abuse. Men and women were also questioned about being quarrelsome, drunkards or thieves. Mutual investigation by the two families continued throughout the betrothal period.

Betrothal began with marriage proposition and presentation of the groom's family to the bride's family. It ended with the actual marriage. The duration of this period, that is, of the bride's stay in the groom's family prior to marriage and in preparation of the latter, varied by ethnic group. It could be stopped by negative reports from either side. In such a case, the marriage was called off, even if the future spouses wanted to try it. By so doing, the community refused to take responsibility for moral, health or social damages that might have resulted from the anticipated union. The well-being of the community as a whole prevailed over personal feelings of individual members.

On the positive side, the two families' mutual investigation was designed to ensure the marriage's stability and prosperity. Each family was concerned about the entering spouse's ability to work and to provide for the household according the established patterns of division of labor between sexes. The woman's future in-laws examined her physical build, particularly her legs, to ensure that they were strong enough to enable her to carry out the duties expected of a wife. During the betrothal, she was tested on actual tasks associated with her imminent status. However, no matter how highly positive the reports from both sides were, in addition, the parents generally asked the two candidates solemnly if they consented to their marriage. Only when each had publically given his or her consent did they transfer the bridewealth that sealed the marriage alliance between the two families.

Sometimes, the desire to entrust one's daughter or to have one's son marry into a good family led to arranged marriages by parents without the children's consent. Also, through some parental arrangements, such as among the Ngbandi, a girl could be married to an older man before reaching physical maturity. In this event, the marriage was not consumated until she began menstruating. Before this time, the bride would live with the groom's mother, who would thus assume the responsibility of completing her rearing.

Sometimes the groom or the bride rejected the candidate proposed by the parents in favor of one of his or her own choosing. Long periods of grooming were designed to reduce such an eventuality. However, the parents were not always successful in trying to convince the two youngsters to enter the proposed union. Sometimes, the children dropped their rejection of the arranged marriage. Other times, they persisted. This could lead to the young man or woman running away with the candidate of his or her choice. This generally left the parents with no choice but to accept the accomplished fact when the two lovers returned to the village after consumating the union.

Concluding Marriage

The Bridewealth. The sealing of the marriage alliance involves a transfer of some valuables (bridewealth) from the groom's family to the bride's family. Rarely, the marriage payment consisted of a dowry rather than a bridewealth. The dowry is provided by the bride's family rather than the groom's family. Sometimes marriage payments were repeated throughout the husband's life. Such was the practice among the Boas, who live in the Itimbiri-Ngiri region in Upper Congo province.[2]

The bridewealth or the dowry was usually paid in kind. In-kind valuables represented the wealth of the area. For instance, the goat is the animal of honor among the Luba of Kasai. The Luba paid the bridewealth in goats. Among the Bashi of Kivu, owning many cows is a sign of high status. Thus, they paid the bridewealth in cows. In regions where metalworking tools were most valued, people paid the bridewealth in metal tools. For example, the bridewealth among the Kote of the Congo Basin consisted of an arrow, a knife and copper rings.

Animals and metal tools were often combined. For instance, the Ngbandi paid the bridewealth in metal goods and goats. Some groups in the Balese-Komo region of Upper Congo paid theirs in iron objects, domestic animals (hunting dogs and chickens) or hunting tools such as arrows. Other groups added currency rather than tools to domestic animals. Among the Luba of Kasai, a variable amount of currency accompanied the goats, which made up the bulk of the bridewealth.

Sealing the Marriage Alliance. Marriage is customarily concluded at the residence of the bride's family. Prior to the date agreed upon for the event, information is sent out to all interested parties. The elders of the host family preside over the meeting. One of them serves as the group's principal spokesperson. The guest family delegation is headed by an elder who serves as a spokesperson also. Each party includes a witness who is not a family member.

Emissaries of the guest family are welcomed according to the hospitality customs of the host family. Usually they are treated to a special meal prior to the business encounter. The gathering takes place in a house or outside in the shade of a large tree, in the courtyard of an elder. An elder who is the spokesperson of the host family opens the meeting by asking the elder of the guest delegation to tell the assembly what is on his mind. The latter responds by declaring his identity, the family and the clan he represents and who the other members of his delegation are, including the groom. He ends by expressing the desire of his entire delegation and the larger family community at home to see the groom and the bride become husband and wife and the two families united through the couple's marriage.

At this moment, the bride's family spokesperson tells the groom's family representatives the amount and composition of the bridewealth. His counterpart from the groom's family hands the bridewealth that he and his companions have brought along to their witness. The witness counts the bridewealth aloud piece by piece and then, after proclaiming the total amount, passes it over to the bride's family witness. This witness counts the elements of the bridewealth aloud, one by one, and declares the total. If the bridewealth is lower than the asked-for amount, the witness also declares the missing parts. At this point, the groom's family spokesperson tells the assembly how the latter family intends to pay the rest of the bridewealth. The promise was generally accepted because paying the entire bridewealth on the spot was resented as an ostentatious show of wealth and an attempt to revile marriage to the rank of a commercial transaction among strangers.

If the bridewealth and other conditions for marriage are met, the elder representing the bride's family, before touching the bridewealth, asks the bride if he should accept it. If the response is positive, he asks the groom if he, too, really wants this marriage. Quite often, a question is also raised to the public asking if anyone is aware of any condition that would prohibit the marriage. If nothing militates against the marriage, the bride's family receives the bridewealth from the hands of the groom's family witness. From now on, the groom and the bride are husband and wife. To confirm the alliance thus established, the host family treats the guest family to a grand feast. They will slaughter a goat or another animal of honor according to the custom in the bride's society. Etiquette in Congolese traditional society pro-hibits members of the host family to partake of the meals cooked specifically for guests of honor. The expectation is that the guests would carry home a sizable portion of the meat as a testimony of the good treatment received from the host family.

The Sacrament and Marriage Registration. To marriage involving the payment of the bridewealth, the Belgian colonizers added the Christian wed-ding and the recording of marriage in the civil register.[3] Christian marriage is a sacrament administered by a religious person. It presupposes baptism. During colonization, Christianity was imposed on the Congolese people as a strategy to force them to abandon their cultural ways and adopt those of the colonizer.

Missionaries came to the Congo early during the Congo Free State period with the mandate to convert the Congolese to Christianity and to teach them respect for the colonizers and subordination to their values. They conducted the first experiments for this scheme on orphans and abandoned children whose parents had been taken away into slavery in the Americas or killed in enslaving wars. Through these children, the missionaries hoped to implant the European family model. The children, nicknamed "children of the state," were kept in some newly created Christian mission stations. Around the mission stations with such children, the missionaries established villages of adults from diverse ethnic groups who had been rescued from enslavement. These villages became known as "White Man's villages." They were in Boma, Lusambo, Makanza (Nouvelle Anvers), Mikalayi, and Moba (Beaudoinville). Couples in these villages were forcibly married in defiance of African customs. Men and women were aligned separately, facing each other across an empty space. The women were asked to select a man, then the couples were baptized and united in matrimony by the missionaries. This practice gave the name "Christian villages" to these communities.

State children were the first to be exposed to Western-type education. At maturity, they were married in the Christian way. They became the first auxiliaries to the Europeans in the colonial administration, the colonial army and the missionary work of evangelization. The imposed European model of family is Christian, monogamous and limited to the couple and their children, who are identified by a common, family name.

Another novelty brought to the Congo through colonization was the civilian marriage, which is enacted by an authorized government official. Throughout the colonial period in the Congo (1885–1960), this type of marriage remained inaccessible to most Congolese people. The Congolese did not enjoy the legal status the civilian marriage entailed. Nevertheless, they were required to have their indigenous or Christian marriage registered with the Office of Civil Affairs. Thus, a tradition was created by which a couple who was married in church would go through three steps: a traditional marriage performed between the families through the transfer of the bride-wealth from the groom's family to the bride's family; a Christian sacrament administered in church by a member of the clergy; and marriage registration before a government official. Non-Christians went directly from traditional marriage to marriage registration.

THE FAMILY

The Congolese family is a multidimensional reality. As a rule, the conjugal family of a man and a woman, or a man and many women, is a subunit of the much larger, extended family.

The Conjugal Family

Types of Residence. In most parts of rural Congo, a newlywed couple settles in the husband's parents' community. This practice is called *patrilocal residence*. They may settle in a new locality, generally of the groom's choice, a pattern known as *virilocal residence*. In some traditions, the couple resides in the wife's home village. *Matrilocal residence* is the name given to this arrangement. Actual living arrangements vary as well. Sometimes the bride spends the day at the husband's mother's house, participating in all the women's activities there and going to her husband's house only to sleep. Usually, however, the husband has his own homestead. His wife or wives live in there, interacting with the in-laws daily. Among some Congolese ethnic groups, the polygamous husband (a man with two or more wives) lives in a house with several bedrooms. The wives share living spaces during the day and retire to different bedrooms at night. In other groups, each wife has her own house.

In urban centers, the residence is chosen by the man in normal circumstances. Men became urbanized before women. In colonial times, single men were recruited to labor in work camps or administrative stations, some of which later became towns or cities. Much later, the colonial authority decided to stabilize African labor. Only then did they authorize the Congolese men to bring their wives and to have a family in the work camp. Women first became urbanized as wives joining their husbands. The man generally had arranged for housing by the time the wife arrived, so the residence belonged to her husband. This situation has continued today, even among unmarried adult women who are called "free women" (*femmes libres*). Free women rent individual rooms or apartments. If they cannot afford to rent, they live with relatives or share with friends. Free women receive their lovers in their own quarters. If the relationship becomes serious, the man usually moves the woman into a different living structure under his control, unless he cannot afford one.

The Mandate to Procreate. Marriage is expected of every normal man or woman. First marriage represents the passage from youth to adulthood. Being adult and single is treated as an abnormality. Among other things, it deprives one of descendants and interrupts the chain of generations. Likewise, in marriage procreation is a moral imperative unless serious attenuating circumstances preclude having children.

The desire to procreate, to take good care of the children and to successfully raise them to maturity helps explain, in part at least, certain marriage situations. Marriage at puberty was often prompted by a desire to protect young people from bringing forth children out of the wedlock. When such a birth occurred, the man was often forced to marry the woman, whether he liked it or not. Among some ethnic groups (the Luba, for example), in the absence of marriage, the woman was ostracized. Polygamy was perceived as an opportunity for having more children. Many women refrained from sexual intercourse during the breast-feeding period because they were preoccupied with the health of their babies. Some would go live with their parents during this time. A more traditional woman would encourage her husband to take on a second wife or tolerate his decision to do so although she might have otherwise opposed it. The marriage of a widower with children to his wife's sister or of a widow with children to her husband's brother was seen as necessary to assure that the children grow up with two parents. Marriage counseling for a couple with children is always oriented toward preserving the marriage in the greatest interest of the children. The parents from both sides take a leading role in counseling the couple to stay together for the

Young father with children.

welfare of the children. They may make such a move at their own initiative or in response to a request from either spouse.

Birth Control. Early marriage and polygamy address two important issues related to birth control: neglected children and improperly spaced children. Traditional birth control methods focused on birth spacing. They included such techniques as: virginity, abstinence, polygamy, withdrawal, medicinal plants, contraceptive rites and abortion.[4] These techniques were practiced to various degrees by different ethnic groups. Virginity before marriage was enforced where children born out of the wedlock were not welcomed. The Luba of Eastern Kasai belong to this category. It was ignored where they were. This was so among the Atetela ethnic group.

Total abstinence by nursing mothers was the most commonly practiced birth control method. Abstinence usually lasted one or two years, but in some places it could continue for three or four. Women who conceived in a short period after giving birth were ridiculed in songs. A man accused of trying to break his nursing wife's abstinence was reprimanded publically. As with virginity, withdrawal before ejaculation (coitus interruptus) was practiced by some and rejected by others. For the Luba, withdrawal was consid-

Large two-parent family: Mr. Illunga Mwene-Mbondo and his wife and children.

ered a moral violation. Before conception a child exists as a spirit, usually of a past relative. The sperm is the vehicle that carries the spirit, now a soul, into the mother's womb. Withdrawal interrupts the process of incorporation already begun, thus cutting off a human life in the making.

Such embarrassing or morally disturbing situations could be precluded by sending the wife to live with her parents until the end of the nursing period. Also her mother could come to stay with her in her house, thus forcing the husband to sleep elsewhere. Ritual taboos were used to reinforce abstinence. They would rub the mother's body and the baby's body with a reddish substance and white clay to make them unattractive. During the nursing period, the mother, particularly the mother of a special birth child (twins or a premature child) devoted herself to the needs of her baby. She neglected her own care, making herself unattractive to the husband.

Some birth control practices had a supernatural connotation. Sometimes, a woman would wear a special belt around her waist or keep a snail in a corner of her house. In other cases, family members would gather in a woman's house and conjure away pregnancy by proffering special words. In still others, a woman would drink a mixture of filings from the blacksmith's forge and water. All these practices were intended to prevent pregnancy by causing temporary sterility in the woman.

Abortion was the ultimate measure for those who had not used other methods or when other methods had failed to prevent pregnancy. Abortion was not widely practiced in rural areas. It was limited to those cases where an unwanted pregnancy threatened the life of a nursing mother or her baby. Now, abortion is more frequent in urban centers, particularly among unmarried adult women and school age adolescents. Abortion is induced by swallowing a liquid from an infusion of herbs or the bark from certain trees. In cities it is also performed by medical personnel.

Gender Roles in Marriage. Productive activities in rural Congo and domestic chores everywhere in the country are divided along gender lines. Men hunt big game and women gather herbs and insects. Both men and women fish, but with a different material and techniques. Men tend cattle and goats, and women raise chickens. In agriculture, men fell trees but both men and women till the soil and seed to various degrees. Harvesting is primarily done by women. House building is often considered a man's duty, but women's contribution is not negligible. In most regions, men build the frame and the roof. Both men and women cut and transport the straws, and men put them on the roof. Women then cover the walls with mud. Brick houses are built by men. Men also engage in long distance trade, traveling on foot or by bicycle. Both men and women ride in trucks driven by men. In most part, women sell at the marketplace while men work in factories, shops or offices. In the home, the women cook and clean the house and the men do the repairs.

Mutual Responsibilities. Man and woman are responsible for each other's welfare. In Congolese villages, women look forward to marrying men who can support them. Husbands are expected to take charge of their wives' shelter, food, clothing and medical care and even to help their parents. Other than by cultural predisposition, very few women in Congolese cities could live independently. The August 1, 1988, Family Code lists nine mutual obligations of the spouses: cohabitation, husband's authority over wife and obligation to protect her; cooperation in maintaining the household; sharing the expenses for running the household according to their respective means; mutual commitment to living together; caring for each other; being faithful, respectful and affectionate for each other; for the wife, the obligation to follow the husband to where he lives; and both spouses' obligation to provide food for each other.[5]

Female-centered, extended family: Mrs. Kabedi Mwa-Mujinga of Kolwezi with her children and grandchildren.

The Extended Family

Traditional Congolese communities are based on kinship and common descent. Descent determines succession and inheritance. Biologically, every person descends from both parents' families. Socially, however, depending on the prevailing traditions, a person may be counted as belonging more to one group than the other. Despite the descent system in force, the Congolese man or woman, adult and married, participates in several kinship networks.

Descent Systems. Four types of descent and kinship can be identified among the Congolese people: bilateral, patrilineal, matrilineal and double. In the bilateral system, the person recognizes kinship ties and interacts in kinship terms with as many individuals from both descent lines as he or she wishes and can. Thus, the size of the active kin group varies within the same family. The Lunda, the Tio and the Twa ethnic groups practice bilateral kinship. A Lunda person may choose to live in a particular extended family or in a group of extended families.

In a patrilineal system, the individual traces descent in, and is recognized as a member of, groups founded by the ascendants of the father. Where this system exists, the children belong to the father's descent groups. In the case of the parents' divorce, the children are automatically assigned to the father and his relatives. Residence in this system is patrilocal as well: the married couple resides among the relatives of the husband. The Luba of Kasai recognize patrilineal descent and live in patrilocal villages.

Luba nuclear families, whether monogamous or polygamous, were imbedded in a hierarchy of larger groups connected at different levels of descent. The most immediate descent level was the extended family. Luba extended families included seven generations of relatives identifiable by special kinship terms. These were siblings (brothers and sisters), parents, grandparents, great-grandparents, children, grandchildren and great-grandchildren. In each generation, cousins were treated as siblings.

Male descendants of the same paternal grandfather were at the core of Luba extended families. These individuals had common responsibilities to the grandfather and to each other based on their fathers' position within the grandfather's household. Obligations were sanctioned by the ancestors, with rewards or punishments affecting the individual, his children or grandchildren. Extended families that were descended from a common ancestor, collectively sharing ownership rights over ancestral lands, formed the next descent level. Communal ownership of ancestral lands was the most significant feature of this level of common descent. Being a legitimate offspring of a Luba father gave a child automatic access to these lands. The Ngbandi who live in Ubangi are one of the many other ethnic groups tracing descent through the paternal line.

In the matrilineal system, descent is traced through the mother. In this system, individuals belong to groups descended from common maternal ancestors. The Kongo of Lower Congo are matrilineal.[6] The Kongo were organized in clans and clan sections. The clan sections were divided into "houses," and the houses were divided into lineages. Clan sections were exogamous; their members were not permitted to marry individuals from houses of the same clan section. The house was the landowning unit. It was composed of two or more lineages. It had the responsibility of allocating land tracts to its constitutive lineages. Lineage members exploited the same track of land. Individuals owned their own plots within the lands allocated to the lineage. The trees growing on theses plots remained the collective property of the lineage. The lineage was also the level of movable property inheritance. Lineage members inherit from one another.

Where double descent was practiced, individuals claimed patrilineal descent for certain functions and matrilineal descent for others. Some Mongo groups practiced double descent. They inherited nobility titles and positions through the maternal line. Power was passed from a man to his daughter's son. Inheritance and the cult of the dead followed the patrilineal model.

Kinship Networks. Other than rights and obligations inherent in common descent groups, family relations are expressed in kinship terms. Every married person is involved in three kinship networks: one with relatives from the father's side, one with those from the mother's side, and a third one with the in-laws. A common characteristic of triple nexus kinship relations is the practice of applying the terms for close relatives to distant relatives and even acquaintances. Most typical are the terms for *father, mother* and *siblings*. In Tshiluba, the language of the Luba of Kasai, a person calls many individuals father (*tatu*): the biological father, the father's brother or cousin; the husband of the father's sister or cousin; the mother's sister's husband; and any person of the father's generation. Even the father's sister is called *tatu mukaji* ("female father"). Many individuals are also called *mamu* ("mother"): the biological mother, the father's other wives; the mother's sister or female cousin, the father's brother's wife; and the mother's brother's wife. The mother's brother or male cousin is *manseba* ("male mother"). Any older woman is addressed as "mother." Motherhood is a very respected status. By respect, the term *mother* is extended even to one's own daughter after she becomes a mother or when is old enough to become a mother and behaves with the dignity of one. Many Congolese languages do not have a word for "cousin." Cousins and any relatives of the same generation are designated by the same term used for "brother" or "sister."

Multiple Family Allegiances. In these various scenarios, the individual is integrated into several family-related groups, whose members are expected to care for each other. A married adult man with children maintains family relations and obligations to his wife (or wives) and children, relatives from his father's side; relatives from his mother's side; and in-laws. For a city dweller who has a concubine (a girlfriend living with him) besides his legitimate wife, the relationship may involve her parents, at least indirectly. It extends to her children both from him and from her previous unions, especially if the children live with the mother.

Together, the individuals to whom a person is related through these categories of kin constitute that person's extended family. This is latent kinship. Among them are those who form the active kinship. These are the individuals with whom a person interacts frequently or intensively at some focal points. Active kinship plays many vital roles for its members. They socialize the person through teaching, involvement in activities, praising good behaviors and disapproving bad ones. They contribute to meeting material needs by sharing food and offering free hospitality. Government-funded public assistance does not exist in the Congo. Rural Congo does not have inns or lodges for travelers. Relatives are often the only support for the indigent, the unemployed or travelers in need for temporary lodgings. (Urban hotels are for foreigners and for Congolese who want to step out of the tradition.) Relatives also provide the bridewealth for marriage. They take care of the sick and those who are otherwise incapacitated. Without life insurance, adequate pension plans or social security, family members and friends provide care for the elderly and funeral and burial expenses.

Not all relations within the extended family are based on mutual interests as defined by the individuals who participate in them. Some are religious in nature, that is, mandated by supernatural forces believed to regulate human lives. To start with, the active extended family includes the ancestors as departed elders, who continue to regulate and share life with their earthly descendants in a spiritual form. The ancestors bless the obedient descendants who perform their familial obligations to one another well and punish those who do not. Beliefs in ancestral interventions in human lives are expressed through incantations, libations, sacrifices and other forms of veneration.

Communal Living and Resource Sharing. Sharing living quarters with relatives from different nuclear families is a common practice in the Congo. A typical homestead in a rural area contains several houses. Young people usually sleep with siblings and cousins of the same sex at a brother's or uncle's home. Urban dwellers used to send their children to the village to live with grandparents, uncles and aunts. This enabled the children to know their relatives and to learn about family history and norms. Practically all city residents house relatives, including in-laws, who have come in search of better opportunities in education, employment, business or health care. They hope the guest relatives will become independent and move out to their own quarters. However, the stay at the host relative's house may become permanent because of the shortage of jobs and affordable housing. Most people live in overcrowded homes. In these conditions, the burden of supporting many relatives is very high. Palliatives do exist. Petty trade is the most common practice. Women also engage in prostitution, a disgrace to the family that has become unavoidable for many.

THE CONGOLESE WOMAN

The Mother

The Congolese woman born and raised in ancestral traditions is above all a mother. Her motherhood responsibilities—caring and providing for her children—typically rank higher in her heart than any other.

The Dream of Motherhood. It is the dream of most Congolese girls to get married and have children. Boys and girls rehearse for their future roles as parents by playing husband and wife. Adolescents go through initiation to mark off the passage from childhood to maturity, that is, to the age of marriage and parenthood. Remaining single for a long time after puberty, especially for a young woman, is considered unfortunate. The Congolese woman finds dignity and fulfillment in marriage and in motherhood. Man's sexual potency and woman's fertility are major considerations for marriage to take place. Both the ethnic groups that tolerate sexual activity before marriage and those that discourage it are concerned about young people's future parenthood role. The former consider it an apprenticeship conducive to good performance in marriage. The latter see in it a risk of contracting habits or diseases that might jeopardize procreation and marriage stability. The night following the conclusion of marriage, adults place spies around the new couple's house to ensure that the young man has fulfilled his duties. His success that night is saluted early the next morning with songs of jubilation by the groom's mother and other women. If several months pass following marriage without the wife becoming pregnant, everyone begins to worry about the man's virility and the woman's fertility. The two will be confronted about what is going on in their bedroom, and appropriate steps will be taken to correct the situation.

The Caretaker. The Congolese mother is, above all, a caretaker. In rural areas, a woman's care for her baby begins before pregnancy, as she avoids practices that are likely to jeopardize her ability to conceive and bring forth a healthy child. Children are believed to be returning spirits. In some villages, a woman who wished to become pregnant would befriend infants and little children in the hope that their spirits would convince some of their former playmate spirits to select her as a mother. During the last months of a pregnancy the traditional Luba woman abstains from sexual intercourse because she believes that the sperm could damage her baby's vision.

After giving birth, the Congolese woman is totally dedicated to her baby. She keeps the baby in her arms during most of the day, and she sleeps with the baby close to her chest throughout the night. She nurses whenever she feels the baby needs nourishment. She eats lots of cassava leaves and other fresh greens to increase the milk in her breasts. When she wakes up every morning, she wakes up her baby also. She sits on a mat or on the bed with her legs extended and lays the baby on the stomach on her lap to give the baby a massage and stretch his or her legs and arms. Then she takes the baby outside or to the front veranda for a bath.

Traditionally, the bath was given in a clay pot containing leaves, roots or lianas of plants known for their strengthening power. The mother would stand up bent forward, with the baby seated on her feet. First, she would fetch some water from the pot with her right hand and give it to the baby to drink. As she washed the baby, she paid particular attention to the baby's eyes, nostrils and ears. At the end she would blow into the baby's ears to clear out the water from the bath. She would dry up the baby and rub the baby's body with some paste-like cream to keep the skin smooth. She would breast-feed and then give the baby to a baby-sitter to take care of other family needs.

The mother is constantly concerned with her children's health. If she has special birth children, such as twins or a premature child, she observes the taboos and ensures that rituals for keeping such children alive and strong are performed. She checks the baby's temperature variations by touching his or her body with the back of her right hand. She looks in the baby's mouth for irritations and in the ears to detect infections. She observes the color and consistency of the baby's stool. She presses the baby's stomach down with her hand to diagnose constipation. She checks the color of the baby's eyes. If she has had a child before, she already knows some herbs for treating common children's diseases. If she, the husband or a medicine man brings in some medicinal roots or leaves, she will be the one to administer the cure and monitor the progress.

Adult women and girls carry out household chores. In the morning, having taken care of her baby, the Congolese mother sweeps her house and the courtyard around it. She tells the baby-sitter how to care for the baby during her absence and then leaves for the fields. Before returning home, she passes by the river to bathe and then by the spring to fetch the water for the home. Back at home, she breast-feeds the baby again and then cooks the midday meal. Men and women eat separately. She serves the men first and then the women. Children eat with the adults of their sex, except when they are very young. Infants eat with the mother, who feeds them either before or while she is eating.

After the meal, the Congolese mother attempts to take some rest in the veranda of her house or the shade of a tree nearby. Very often, she has little time to do so because before long she must prepare to cook the evening meal. Already while attempting to rest, she may be watching over pieces of steeped cassava spread on a reed mat to dry, trying to keep goats away. She may be protecting drying beans or peanuts from chickens. Preparations for the evening meal may involve grinding corn or cassava and sifting the flour. It may, in addition, include plucking and washing cassava leaves or other fresh vegetables. Cassava leaves must be steeped and ground in a mortar before cooking. While preparing the food or cooking the meal, she may be breast-feeding the baby as well. Again, when the cooking is completed, she will serve the men and then the women. When the meal is over, she washes and breast-feeds the baby before putting him or her to bed. She may have to wash older small children as well if no other woman is available to help her with this task.

In the village, between the evening meal and bedtime, adults and children assemble around the family fire, where the adults entertain and educate children with animal stories, riddles and family histories. Children of all age attend. Normally, the youngest ones fall asleep very early. The mother takes them to bed unless she has an older daughter to help her. As a rule, it is only after serving the others that the Congolese mother retires for the evening. Even then, she continues to take care of the baby throughout the night.

An urban Congolese mother continues to be the main caretaker in the family. She feeds her baby at the breast or otherwise. She tries to supplement breast-feeding with canned food, if she can afford it, or with adult food after softening it in the sauce or some other way. She still sleeps with her baby close to her chest, or in a crib, placed next to her bed if she can afford one. She washes her baby in a basin rather than a clay pot. She gets the food supplies from the marketplace rather than from the family fields. If she is fortunate enough to be able to hire a housekeeper, she still has to supervise the work. She is the one to notice if a child is sick, to take the child to the dispensary or otherwise treat the child.

The Provider. Not only is the Congolese mother the number one caretaker in the household, she is also a major provider. Even where the man is supposed to be the primary provider for the family, the woman still plays a vital role in supplying the household in necessities. Dominant economic activities differ from region to region, but women's participation is considerable in all regions. It is even considered greater to men's in many respects. Where agriculture is practiced in the forest, as in the Ubangi area, men cut the trees and till the soil; women sow, weed, dress the ground and harvest the crops.

Woman of modest means: items of dress include thongs, a long wrap, a smaller wrap ending in a bumper around the waist, a blouse and a head-tie, with no jewelry.

Fishing is important in this region. Fishing by intoxication is the most important form in the area. Men build the dams to contain the water upstream; the women then spread intoxicating substances over the water downstream and then catch the floating fish. In Uele, the work on Zande rulers' fields, which contributed to their wealth and prestige, was performed by their wives and clients. Gathering, a woman's chief activity among the Mbuti, supplied 70 percent of foods used in their diet. In the Congo Basin, Mongo men's participation in the agricultural process was limited to clearing the land. Women did the rest. A similar situation existed among the Lega and other groups in Maniema. In Lower Kasai, Leele women carried an overload of agricultural tasks due to scarcity of married men. Leele men only participated in agricultural activities when they reached the age of maturity, which co-incided with marriage. However, marriage was generally delayed due to wide-spread polygamy. Most men therefore remained single until their thirties and women had to assume most agricultural chores.

Most Congolese women who migrated to cities during Belgian coloniza-tion did so as housewives joining their working husbands. At the time, mar-ried workers received some family allowance. Those with children received a little bit more, proportionate to the number of children. Nonetheless, work-ers' earnings were generally too small to cover their survival needs from payday to payday. The workers developed various strategies for economic survival. One quite common strategy consisted in splitting the household income for the period into two portions: one to buy the necessities for im-mediate consumption, the other to purchase some commodity with rapid turnover for sale. Ideally the small amount invested in the first purchase would continue to roll over. The surplus incomes gained from frequent op-erations would serve to cover daily needs. Such on-the-side business, when it only involved buying and selling operations, was carried out by the wife.

Sideline businesses involved food items purchased in bulk and resold in smaller quantities. A bag of flour was divided into small packages or bowls, for example. Handling food items was a woman's apanage. Workers' wives developed the habit of retailing local produce such as cassava, corn, beans and fresh vegetables bought from peddlers from neighboring villages. In Con-golese neighborhoods they also resold import goods such as sugar, salt, pow-der milk or stock fish from Portuguese, Greek or Jewish merchants whose stores were on the border of the European district facing in the direction of African quarters. With the passing of time, the providing role of urban women increased. After independence, it became a generalized absolute ne-cessity, as wages and salaries dwindled and paid jobs became increasingly unavailable for men and women.

The Wage Earner

Paid jobs for women were scarce during Belgian colonization. For the most part, they were limited to housekeeping and to crop-planting and harvesting

Contemporary woman wage earner: items of dress include a fancy *libaya* (African-style top), head scarf, necklace and earrings.

campaigns. These activities were temporary or seasonal. The scope expanded and more permanent jobs appeared gradually as education for women was slowly introduced.[7] Little by little, women became catechists, midwives, elementary school teachers and nurses. Income from these activities belonged to the women who had worked for it. At the time, they were not expected to contribute to the conjugal household budget. Procuring the necessary resources for feeding and maintaining the household was the responsibility of the husband. Women undertook these activities to be able to help their own parents. The parents expected this assistance. The more educated the women, the greater the compensation the parents expected for having contributed to their upbringing and education. After independence, educational opportunities for women expanded. More men became more open to the idea of their wives working away from home, in their absence, under the control of another man. The ever-increasing cost of living and the insufficiency of their own income forced some husbands to change their mentality in this direction. Women also wanted more economic independence from their husbands. These changes accelerated the acceptance of women's participation in the labor market.

The private sector and the public sector had different wage standards. In both sectors, men and women received equal pay for equal work. Both men and women received premiums when they were offered. Private sector employees were covered by collective agreements, which were more difficult to obtain for public sector employees. Therefore, workers in the private sector, particularly at the higher levels, were better paid than workers in the public sector. They enjoyed better benefits, such as year-end bonuses, school fees for children, cost-of-living allowances and vacation pay. These benefits outweighed the family allowance and the housing allowance received by public sector employees.

Married women in either sector, except the few who had reached management levels, did not receive a family allowance or a housing allowance. By law, these benefits were allocated to men, a holdover from the time when men worked outside the home and women worked at home. A married woman's paid job was considered a supplement to the husband's. Under the same logic, at equal rank, married women paid higher taxes than men. In these respects, the married woman was disadvantaged even in relation to the unmarried woman in a similar situation. The latter enjoyed a family allowance for her children and a medical care allowance in her own name.

As was the case before independence, women's income from a paid job continued to be considered a supplement to the husband's. Women whose husbands' incomes met the household's needs did not feel compelled to work for an employer outside the home. When they did work, they did so to be able to procure some luxuries for themselves or to support their parents. Occasionally, such as at birthdays, they purchased presents for their husbands and children. These they considered benevolent gestures rather than obligatory contributions to the household. For a woman of modest condition whose husband did not make enough money to maintain the household, finding a paid job became a necessity. Sometimes household needs were so great that she would accept work to obtain benefits, even if her work made no difference in real household income. For instance, in the 1970s and early 1980s, employers took charge of school registration fees for employees' children. Sometimes, employees could buy items at discount prices from the company store. Salaried work also offers the possibility to join the company's employees' mutual aid association. In these associations, members contribute money for a different participant at regular intervals. When one round ends, another begins. For many women, becoming the beneficiary of a round was the only occasion they could afford to buy some clothes, contribute, along with the husband, to the purchase of some household appliance or pay school fees and materials for their children. Participation in mutual aid associations fosters a spirit of solidarity, which is activated in times of family trials such as death.

In Congolese cities, as in the villages, households are responsible for the survival of many people. For example, a study conducted in Kinshasa in the 1980s reported that 1,131 persons lived in the 150 households investigated, that is, an average of close to 7.6 persons per household. This number included 886 (78 percent) children and 245 (22 percent) adults. Of the 886 dependent children, 441 were children of the householders, 445 were not, that is, there was almost a fifty-fifty distribution. The large number of dependents placed an additional burden on the woman to find ways of contributing to the family budget.[8]

The Single Woman

In the Congo, living single is an urban phenomenon. Modern Congolese cities developed outside tradition, in locations selected by colonial authorities to become administrative posts, ports or mining fields. Initially, only Congolese men recruited for their labor were brought to these sites for a specific period. After the term, the recruits were returned to the village and replaced by others. Life was very hard in these transplanted centers due to lack of accommodations and steady supplies of food. Gradually, the urban population became stabilized as more permanent dwellings were made available. Men began bringing their wives to cities, but for many people this remained a very difficult goal to achieve. Their wages were too low to enable them to maintain a family, let alone to procure the necessary bridewealth for marriage. They continued to rely on their parents who remained in the countryside for the bridewealth. Now, in many rural areas, parents themselves had become incapable of procuring wives for their sons with revenues from their farming activities. They were subjected to all kinds of corvees and forced to sell their crops at prices below subsistence levels. In some areas, parents had to wait for a daughter to get married in order to obtain the needed bridewealth to procure a wife for a son.

Women therefore became scarce in developing Congolese cities. As the time went by, women from surrounding areas and from regions where transportation by road or waterways was easier, including some fleeing hardship in the villages, began to abound in cities. Nevertheless, women continued to be scarce. Exposed to the cultural melting-pot characteristic of urbanism as a way of life, and taking advantage of the availability of brothels and makeshift rooms for rent, some women opted for a life of pleasure and short-lived love. They were later joined by city-born teenagers, some of whom had become mothers out of wedlock, including those expelled from home by their parents. Other women joined the singles' ranks following a divorce.

After Congo's independence (June 30, 1960) restrictions to rural-to-urban migration were lifted. More men and women flooded into the cities. Nevertheless, the status of single women continued to be depreciated. In fact, despite the motives for living single, "free women" are not highly regarded at all in the Congolese society. Single women who engage in temporary sexual unions are considered to have low moral standards. Congolese languages use the term *ndumba* for prostitutes and free women because both are considered socially unacceptable.

Prostitutes typically live marginally even in periods of abundance. Above all their lives are very unstable. This is a recurrent situation that prostitutes try to remedy by joining mutual aid associations, or by forming cooking and eating partnerships, or else by regularly contributing taxi money for group members to use on those nights when they leave the bar or the night club without a client. A widespread perception is that prostitutes are undernourished. They live on minuscule quantities of food that they purchase day by day. In contrast, they spend too much money on clothing and beauty.

Prostitutes sometimes suffer from venereal diseases, another stigma. They are required to receive regular medical evaluations and carry a card with a record of appointments, test results, and treatments if tested positive. Money pressures prevent many from keeping regular appointments. They are afraid of testing positive. Had this to happen they would lose clients during the treatment period. This would mean having no income at all. Consequently they become permanent incubators and carriers of sexually transmitted diseases. Of the 50,783 prostitutes subject to medical check-ups living in Lubumbashi in 1971, only 9,089 (18 percent) had honored the required check-ups. Of the latter number, 1,471 individuals (16 percent) were carriers of some sexually transmitted disease. The largest majority, 7,618 (84 percent) had tested negative.[9]

NOTES

1. This section draws particularly from Leonard (Tshilemalema) Mukenge, "Croyances religieuses et structures socio-familiales en société luba," *Cahiers Economiques et Sociaux* 5, no. 1 (1967): 3–97, and Jan Vansina, *Introduction à l'ethnographie du Congo* (Kinshasa, Zaire: Editions Universitaires du Congo, 1966).

2. Vansina, *Introduction à l'ethnographie du Congo*, 68.

3. Mabika Kalanda, *Le code de la famille à l'épreuve de l'authenticité* (Kinshasa, Zaire: Laboratoires d'Analyses Sociales, 1990), 14–16.

4. Ronald S. Waife, *Traditional Methods of Birth Control in Zaire*, Pathpapers Series Number 4 (The Pathfinder Fund, December 1978), investigates traditional birth control techniques among various ethnic groups in the Kasai and in Katanga.

5. Kalanda, *Le code de la famille à l'épreuve de l'authenticité*, 53–54. The highly negative picture of the prostitutes is commensurate with the high value that most Congolese traditional societies place on marriage and legitimate procreation. However, although still disapproved, prostitution in Congolese cities is becoming gradually more tolerated as a necessary evil. Today, stories are being told of an increasing number of destitute parents who close their eyes on their daughters' sexual life and sources of revenues.

6. On the Kongo, see Wyatt MacGaffey, "Lineage Structure, Marriage and the Family amongst the Central Bantu," *Journal of African History*, 24 (1983): 173–187.

7. A classic work on Congolese urban women is Suzanne Comhaire-Sylvain, *Femmes de Kinshasa, hier et aujourd'hui* (Paris: Mouton, 1968).

8. Muadi Muamba, "Contribution de la femme kinoise aux dépenses du ménage" (B. A. Thesis, Institut Supérieur d' Etudes Syndicales, Kinshasa, 1983), 21–23.

9. Nzengi-Amalo, "La femme célibataire dans la sous-region de Lubumbashi" (Thesis, Université Nationale du Zaire, Lubumbashi, 1974), 21.

7

Social Customs and Lifestyles

MAKING A LIVING on a daily basis and celebrating special events are two coterminous aspects of human life. Most Congolese live in rural areas and draw their subsistence from agriculture, gathering, hunting and fishing. These activities are seasonal. Natural phenomena—ecological conditions and atmospheric changes—modify their nature, rhythm and productivity. People carry out these activities individually or in teams. If extractive activities characterize living in rural areas, trade is what sustains life most in the urban settings. Of particular relevance to most urban dwellers is buying and selling in the informal market, where they often ignore official rules.

Other than routine activities, there are special events that punctuate the life cycle and enhance the quality of living. Special ceremonies celebrate birth, puberty and death. They also prepare the individual for success in the next stage of the life cycle. To these traditional life-cycle ceremonial moments, colonization has added baptism, graduation, and Christian wedding, along with new holidays, such as Easter, Christmas and New Year. Other celebrations mark international observances such as Labor Day, or national holidays like Martyrs Day and Independence Day.

This chapter discusses three ways of making a living: (1) following a natural calendar, (2) combining independent work and teamwork and (3) trading in the informal economy. The chapter also reviews celebrations of life-cycle events at birth, puberty and death, and religious and civic observances.

MAKING A LIVING

People who live in rural areas pattern their productive activities on the rhythm of natural phenomena, ecological or atmospheric. They seek to maximize their production in farming, hunting or fishing by integrating independent and team work strategies. City dwellers turn to trading in the informal economy to make a living or to prosper financially.

A Natural Calendar

Agricultural activities and related subsistence activities vary in response to monthly and seasonal changes in the climate. The names of months reflect variations both in productive activities and in atmospheric conditions. The Luba agricultural calendar illustrates this fact.

The Luba Agricultural Calendar. The Luba people have a twelve-month calendar.[1] The names of months evoke the productive activities of the region and natural phenomena associated with them. No one knows what month was considered first in their calendar before the coming of the Europeans. September was probably first because many important events in the life of the Luba take place in September.

The major agricultural season in Luba society extends from September to December. It coincides with the first part of the rainy season. The rains start at the end of August and the beginning of September. This precise period of the year is called *mvul'a mbedi*, a contracted form for *mvula wa mbedi* ("first rains"). September is more significant than August in the life of the Luba people because their activities resume after the dry season that runs from May to August. Among other things, the insects (*ntongolo*) start to buzz and drone anew. The month has the name of these insects and the noises they make (*Mudila-Ntongolo*). Young people go out into the wilderness to catch them. Edible caterpillars come back and mushrooms grow. Besides this natural abundance in September, people plant corn and peanuts. Corn is a predominant crop in the Luba diet.

October, November and December are named after two varieties of winged ants. One is white (*bitenda* or *bintuntu*) and the other is brown (*nswa*). Both varieties are edible delicacies. October is called *Kabitenda* or *Kaswa Bitenda* because the white ants come out of their mounds during this month. In November, small numbers of the brown ants start to come out. This month is *Kaswa Banga*. In this context, it means "the little insect that can be seen here and there." December is *Tshiswa Munene* ("the month of large and abundant brown ants") because the brown ants (*nswa*) actually swarm. They are much more abundant and more commercialized than the white ants. The brown ant is so important in the life of the Luba that the color brown is named after them. Brown things and brown-skinned persons are described as having *mubidi wa luswa*, which means having the color of *luswa* (singular for *nswa*).

January is hot and dry. It is called *Tshiongo wa Minanga*, an expression that means "month of drought." The January drought reminds people of the long dry season (*mushipu*), which extends from May to August. They also call it *Kashipushipu*, or "small dry season." In January, corn and peanuts are harvested and dried in the sun.

February, March and April are associated with the second term of corn production. Corn is planted in February. Once planted, however, the grain is vulnerable to the insects that swarm during this month. *Luishi*, a derivative of *tuishi* (insects), is the name for February. March, *Lumungulu*, is simply an extension of February. In this month, people are still planting. April is the weeding month. Men, women and children are mobilized because the work is abundant and they need many hands to complete it. The husband/father has the responsibility to give everyone a hoe, the most important farm instrument. This month is *Luabanya-Nkasu*, or "hoe distributor."

An additional reason for mobilizing labor in April is to free the husband/father. He can then devote his time to clearing the river bank in May to plant dry season corn. The dry season begins in May, and they can plant nothing in the savannah. The only moisture for crops is along the river banks. The machete (*mwele*) is used to work along the river banks. Hoes are unsuitable, so they are put away during this period. *Tshisanga nkasu* (assembling hoes) is the name given to the month of May.

June, July, and August are months of the dry season. This is also the cold season. In June, both the cold weather and the drought are only starting. This month's name is *Kashipu-Nkenza* ("the first cold, dry air"). In July, both the cold weather and the drought intensify. Life dies out. The rivers are dried out. Trees have lost all their leaves, but clouds are often in the sky. In August, the cold weather decreases gradually as clouds become thicker and more frequent. The last part of the month marks the beginning of the rainy season and life starts to come back. July is *Tshibungu Mulume* and August is *Tshibungu Mukaji*. Literally, the words *mulume* and *mukaji* used in the names of these two months mean "male" and "female," respectively. In the Luba language, male and female are often opposed to each other as strong and weak. *Tshibungu* is probably derived from *mabungi* ("clouds"). If this is the case, then *Tshibungu Mulume* (July) means "the cloudy month with a strong cold" and *Tshibungu Mukaji* (August) means "the cloudy month with a weak cold."

Independent Production and Teamwork

In farming, as in other subsistence activities, individual and collective methods of production co-exist. Individual production reflects the philosophy of self-help, which is widespread among the Congolese people. Collective methods increase short-term productivity and foster the spirit of community and sharing. The nuclear family, whether monogamous (one wife) or polygamous (many wives), is the most widespread unit of collective production. Childless widows and widowed parents whose adult children have left work alone. Young men preparing for marriage may also have individual fields. The extended family functions more as a unit of consumption than a unit of production.[2]

Two other forms of collective production in farming the land are based on friendship and good neighborhood relationships. One is occasional, and the other is essentially permanent. In the occasional form, a farmer who wanted to advance more quickly in clearing the land, tilling the field, or weeding would visit his friends, acquaintances and relatives, preferably in the evening. He would invite them to help him a specified day. After the work, he would treat them to a nice meal of *nshima*, a starch staple in the Luba diet, served with meat or fish and accompanied with local beer (*tshibuku*). Harvesting crops and plastering walls of a house with wet mud, are women's duties in many societies. When they needed several helpers for either activity, women rather than men were invited to the party.

One name for the more permanent form of collective work is *tshinkudimba*, literally "like a pigeon" (*nkudimba*). This alludes to the pigeon's habit of turning around in a circle, with its head bent down while producing sounds similar to singing and dancing. The members of a *tshinkudimba* rotate working their fields together once a week on a selected day. A treat at the beneficiary's home follows each work party. In many parts of the Congo, this method was transferred to the city, where they still practice it. The difference is that urban dwellers contribute money rather than labor and rotate withdrawals from the pool.

The third method is to establish a producers' cooperative. Here, the field and the crops belong to the members collectively. They share the products according to preestablished criteria of equity.

Hunting is another domain of activity where individual and collective methods of work are practiced. The hunter knows the location of various species of game animals, thanks to his knowledge of their habits and habitat. He identifies their sounds and footprints. He knows the styles of their trails and the devastation they cause to plants or crops. Individuals usually practice trap hunting. Sometimes the trap is a pit dug on a particular game's habitual passage. It is covered with the kind of grass preferred by the targeted animal or a type common to the area. Sometimes a spear is planted in the pit. Usually the hunter hides near the pit ready to finish the fallen animal with a powder gun, spears or javelins.

Hunting by fire setting was common in some regions. To practice this form of hunting, men set a fire around a large area suspected of containing game animals. They then move behind the fire, picking up the small game killed by the blaze or the smoke. The hunters are essentially getting ready to use their spears or bows for the large game that will try to escape from the blazing grass. While men are doing this, women and children follow, at a distance, picking up the rodents killed by the fire and digging out those that have managed to hide in holes or mounds. When the encircled area has been consumed by the fire and the large game brought down, the men join the women and the children in picking up birds and small animals.

The Congolese also hunt by stalking and hounding. They generally practice stalking individually. The animal is shot with a gun. Hounding is practiced in a party. At the beginning, they hold the dogs on a leash, each hunter being pulled by his dogs as they track the animal's smell. Once they sight the game, the hunter releases the dog and both begin to chase the animal. Since dogs are faster runners than men, they wear bells around their waist so that the hunters may identify their location and direction at every moment.

A collective hunt of rodents begins with identifying their trail and possibly tracing it to the burrows where they live. Then a coned trap made of netting is set on the rodent's trail with its back toward the rodent's burrow. The hunt takes place at a time when the hunters sense that the animals are away from their burrow. Starting from a point behind the animals, the hunting team advances in a row, making noises, and beating the bushy grass and the shrubs with clubs. The purpose is to frighten the animal and drive it into the trap as it tries to rush toward the hole. Once in the trap, the captive has little room to move around and to try to turn back out. In addition, it will not be long before a member of the hunting team approaches and kills it with a club.

A last form of hunting rodents that is worth mentioning consists of digging into the mounds where animals live. It takes place in a clearing after the grass has been set afire. They usually practice it collectively. It involves three sorts of cooperation. First, the work of digging is often too much for one individual to complete it in an optimum time, so digging is usually a team effort. Second, rodents' burrows have several exit holes distributed in different directions and at different distances from the mound. There is a need for some team members to stand in alert at different potential exit holes, while others are digging. Finally, at the end of the digging operation, when the burrow is open, they need several persons to kill the animals before they can run away.

Fishing. The Congolese practice different types of fishing, individually or collectively. They practice angling individually most of the time. Generally, angling from a hand-manned canoe requires the cooperation of at least two persons so one can control the canoe while the other is busy with a heavy fish, for instance. Fishing with a net in high waters requires even more people because of greater possibility for heavy catches and greater risks for capsizing. The Wagenia of Upper Congo near Kisangani extend their cooperative fishing methods to net making and repairing. They build scaffolds and make and repair their nets while standing at different levels of the scaffold.

A particular form of fishing practiced by women is collective in nature. It takes place in the heart of the dry season, when the creeks are at their lowest. The women dam the creek, intoxicate the fish with a substance called *bubawu* made out of certain wild leaves, and catch the fish as they float over the water. Downstream of the dam, the women also erect makeshift fences of wood and stones around spots of water, bail them out with a wooden bowl (*lupu*), and capture the entrapped fish.

Trading in the Informal Economy

Economic reports on the Congo generally include sections or comments on the informal economy or informal sector.[3] This concept stands for various kinds of economic transactions carried out regularly and openly in defiance of official rules that everyone is aware of. Although large informal transactions do take place, in large part the informal sector consists of marginal survival activities, nicknamed *"Debrouileez-vous"* ("Fend for yourself"), or "Article 15."[4] Peddling, artisanal activities and selling in the market belong to this category.

Peddling. The first form of independent activities practiced by Congolese people in urban centers was peddling or petty trading. During colonization, urban migration was controlled. The Congolese entered the modern market economy as temporary contract workers whom they sent back to the village at the end of the contract. During the contract, the workers depended on neighboring villages for food supplies. Several formulas developed. They arranged to walk to the villages. Or the villagers brought the food to the camp. Some developed friendly relations with particular families in the close-by villages, allowing them to eat and pay later when pay day came.

Of all these practices food peddling by sellers from surrounding villages was the most successful in the first years of urban development in the Congo. At first, many products brought in by villagers interested the Europeans as well: fresh corn, sweet potatoes, fruits, vegetables, fresh fish and game meat. They tolerated peddling in European neighborhoods otherwise closed to the Africans who were not domestic workers. Peddlers went from house to house, loudly announcing the kinds of produce they carried. The interested buyer would come out of the house, stop the seller and buy what he or she wanted. As time went by and communications improved, the Europeans began to receive imports more easily and developed their own ways of supplying themselves with local produce. They then put pressure on the colonial government to curtail peddling in their neighborhoods. The government prohibited peddling anything in the European wards except for selected items such as fresh fruits.

Through government regulations, peddling decreased in African neighborhoods as well in favor of selling at marketplaces and at home. Peddled products included basic staples such as cassava, corn and beans. In times of scarcity for these products, workers' wives would go out to wait for the food peddlers at some point along their route. Some points became marketplaces. The Pont Gabu market and the Ngiri-Ngiri market are among those which developed in this way. A different regulation favored the development of business practiced at places of residence. They required the Congolese to carry a work passbook or a temporary unemployment card. To avoid trouble with the police, individuals who did not have these documents learned to do things in their own neighborhood as much as they could. Those with articles for sale would place them on a chair, a stool, a table or a mat at some place in the yard where they could be seen from the street. Gradually, more individuals built a wooden shelter at this location in their yard. Thus, the boutique notion was born. They also developed the practice of selling bread, peanuts, cigarettes, bananas, biscuits and matches along the street, particularly at bus stations and in front of bars. Overall, these activities are so minuscule that attempting to levy taxes on them would be malicious.

Artisanal Activities. Artisanal activities in the Congo are another typical category of informal activities. They are often unregistered and not subjected to any particular location, production or commercialization standards. The crafts involved included shoe repairmen, plumbers, photographers, mechanical repairmen and carpenters among others. These activities were minuscule because of the inferior quality and size of the locations, the staffing and the kind of equipment. The operation usually consisted of the owner and six apprentices or less working out of one or two small rented rooms. Their equipment consisted of a few basic rudimentary tools.

The sales volume and available supplies were insignificant as well. Craftsmen were adult individuals who had worked in a similar capacity for an employer. The apprentices were young adult school leavers. Young boys and adult men worked as shoeshiners along the street as well. In more recent years, more numerous and much younger school dropouts have joined the ranks of the minuscule self-employed. Hairdressers fit into this category. They practice along the street, recruiting their clients on the spot from among the women who pass by. Tailoring is another such trade. In some parts of the city, young boys dominate it. They, too, are school dropouts.

Selling at the Marketplace. Selling at the marketplace belongs to the informal sector as well. Market vendors often do their business without respecting the official rules. Most are marginal in size as well. Price bargaining in the marketplace is a typical old informal operation. Food shortages and price-gouging were frequent in Congolese cities even long before the current permanent economic crisis. To control them, the government periodically set price maximums, which unfortunately were never respected. Also, Congolese traders customarily used unstandardized measurements such as piles, packages, or cans with concave bottoms. The imprecision of such measurements was such that, after the transactions, customers were often left with a feeling of having been cheated. The government instituted standards of measurement such as kilograms, meters and liters to make changes that would benefit consumers. Again, however, it never enforced official measurements.

The absence of effective price ceilings and standardized measurements favored the classic African practice of price bargaining. Everyone practices price bargaining at the marketplace, so merchandise prices at Congolese markets may not be marked. When the price is marked, the asking price is always higher than what the seller expects to get. Practically nobody, except some uninformed foreigners, buys at that price. On the other hand, only the insincere buyer walks away because the asked price is too high. The serious buyer is supposed to propose the price he or she is willing to pay. Ideally, the sellers expect that even an individual who is not buying but asks the price would make an offer. Failure to do so is to wish bad luck on the seller. The buyer deliberately sets a price lower than what he or she expects to pay. After each party has quoted a price, the negotiation begins. As a rule, the seller rejects the buyer's proposition and sets a second price lower than the first one. The buyer makes a second proposition, a little bit higher than the first one. After a game of alternating price and counteroffer, they reach a point where the seller says that this is the lowest he or she can go. Then the buyer, if he or she is serious, pays the price and takes the merchandise.

CELEBRATING LIFE EVENTS

Men and women in Congolese villages used to carry out birth rites and initiation rites designed to strengthen their children and prepare them for success in adult life. At the occasion of a death, relatives perform funerary rites designed to prepare the spirit of the dead for acceptance into the world of the spirits. Since Belgian colonization, Congolese Christians celebrate baptism, Easter and Christmas, among other new holidays. Christians and non-Christians alike celebrate graduation, wedding, Labor Day and New Year.

Traditional Rites of Passage

Birth Rites. Birth rites were practiced in all Congolese cultural traditions under different forms, such as adornment of the child and the mother with certain colors, performing songs and dances, making animal sacrifices and partaking of the ritual meal and treating the child and the mother with certain medicinal herbs or concoctions. Some rituals were renewed periodically, such as at every new moon. Others coincided with babies' development stages, such as the appearance of the first teeth and taking of the first steps. Still others marked the end of the breast-feeding period, when the parents were about to resume sexual relations (generally a year or more after birth). The following illustrations come from the Yansi society.[5]

Yansi Birth Rites. The Yansi live in the Kwango region. After giving birth, a Yansi mother separated herself from society to be in exclusive contact with her baby. She and the baby lived in her own mother's house. They terminated the separation in two stages. First, after a month of separation following delivery, the mother would undergo a ritual allowing her to come out of the house, sit on the same mat as her husband, and greet men. To this effect, she would take the child to a knowledgeable medicine man. The latter would prepare a concoction of grilled egg shells mixed with other substances. He would give some of it to the baby to eat on the spot, put the rest in a bag and instruct the mother to feed the baby a little bit of the substance every day until exhaustion. He would also instruct the mother to attach the bag to the legs of the bed in which she and the baby slept and to discontinue the treatment if for some reason the bag fell to the floor. When the cure was complete, or when the bag had touched the soil, the mother returned to the medicine man for a second ritual treatment. After this, she resumed her normal conjugal activities. They designed the separation and the treatment to strengthen the child before exposure to the outside world and to allow the mother to devote herself totally to her baby's care. The time spent in seclusion enabled her also to gradually build up her own strengths and cleanse herself of the impurities associated with birth giving.

Among the Yansi, as among other groups, not all babies were born equal. Some babies were considered extraordinary and more delicate to handle than others. Twins and triplets are extraordinary by their number at birth. Ordinary children are conceived one at a time. Two children from a single act of copulation is a special event. Triplets are even more extraordinary. Yansi parents of twins maintained a pot filled with special type of clay, which they used as ointment for the babies when the latter had fever. Each time the parents had to leave the twins by themselves, they would give them presents and explain to them that they would be absent temporarily, and that their being away was not an abandonment of their beloved babies. The presents often consisted of coins. Neighbors who met a parent of twins for the first time would greet him or her with a present for the babies, generally some money also. The money given to the twins by the parents, neighbors or any other person was kept in the babies' medicine pot for expenses on special occasions such as sickness, marriage or death.

Other Yansi children were considered special by the nature of the position in which they were born or a particular condition of their bodies at birth. Babies born with the umbilical cord around their neck were considered special. Special also were babies born with six fingers on one hand. Even more special were those born with their feet first. Some special ritual treatment of the baby generally followed these births. The mother observed the necessary taboos.

Puberty Rites. Puberty rites marked the transition from childhood to adulthood. Women performed girls' initiation rituals around the time of first menstruations. Boys' initiation rituals could or could not involve circumcision. Not all ethnic groups held collective circumcision ceremonies for their youth. Some had their boys circumcised in their early months or years of age. Likewise, girls' initiation did not necessarily involve genital mutilation. Many ethnic groups do not practice it. Preparation for sex roles during initiation involved the teaching of hygiene before and after sexual intercourse and proper position and comportment during the intercourse. They taught gender functions as well, such as proper attitudes toward reproduction, responsibilities and types of comportment associated with the status of husband or wife.

Lendu Initiation. The Walendu live in Ituri, in Upper Congo province.[6] Boys' initiation dramatized the kinds of leadership positions the society expected them to assume in their adult life. The initiation of young Lendu emphasized the function of village chief. Congolese societies had different traditions for passing over the power to rule from the incumbent to the successor. Whatever the actual method employed by a particular candidate to assume power, there were always some rituals designed to legitimize a new incumbent. Universally, a chief's inauguration in the Congo always includes some rituals designed to elevate him to the supernatural status of the spirits of former rulers. The chief's spiritual powers enabled him to protect the village and the subjects from hazards. The village chief also assumed the responsibility to initiate the young boys.

A Lendu village chief is the pillar that sustains the village community. A fig tree planted in the center of the village symbolized his pillar role. Village elders met around this tree to debate issues concerning life and destiny of the village. The members of the village community, as subjects, brought the tributes they owed the chief to the tree. It was also at the foot of the village fig tree that they handed over game from hunting to the chief. They performed popular dances around the tree. Through inauguration, the Lendu chief became the great sacrificer for the village. The altar for carrying out sacrifices to the spirits was at the foot of the tree.

The village chief performed the Lendu initiation. It was designed to motivate the youngsters to aspire to become chief, the highest post in the village. It began with an act of submission to the authority, through the paying of tributes to the incumbent chief. Candidates to initiation provided the sacrificial animals for the ceremony. The ceremonies included a symbolic transfer of the chief's function as the center toward which the tributes converged. To dramatize the transfer of this function, the chief loudly asks the candidates, "What do you bring to me in exchange for the position of chief?" "We bring you animals," they respond. "Where are they?" he asks again. "Here they are, Chief," the candidates answer. The Walendu raise goats, sheep and chickens. Each species was represented among the sacrificial animals. They tied and placed the animals on the altar. To symbolize the transfer of the chief's function as the great sacrificer for his people, the candidates for initiation held the chief's right hand with their right hands as the chief slaughtered the animals one after the other. The youths' sense of unity as members of the village was also stressed during initiation. Thus, after slaughtering the first goat or the first sheep, the chief ordered the youngsters to stand in a circle with each one holding with his right hand the left hand little finger of the person placed to his right. Then he stands before them, handling the sacrificial knife in his right hand and a flute in his left hand. He would blow into the flute and speak as he sprinkled the neophytes and the audience with the sacrificial blood. As the one in charge of the sacrifice, the chief cooked the meat and the blood in separate pots. All initiates present, old and new, eat the sacrificial meal.

Funeral Rites. The human is body and spirit simultaneously. When bodily life on earth ends, the spiritual life continues in the invisible world of the spirits. Funerary rites mark the transition from one to the other. Funerary rites are the most sacred of all rituals. In rural areas, they must be performed in conformity with the taboos and prescriptions inherited from the ancestors. An improper funeral causes ancestral dissatisfaction and can be repealed on ancestral request and replaced by a more dignified one. The practice of a second funeral existed among the Kongo people as a festival.[7]

Kongo Festival of the Dead. The ancestors often express their discontent with their earthly descendants by sending them a disease or other misfortune. In Kongo villages, sometimes diviners attributed some misfortunes to an ancestor's discontent with the burial they had given him at death, and who requested a second, more dignified, burial. In compliance, the clan chief, after conferring over the matter with other elders, would set the date for a more appropriate funeral. Prior to the date, he would go to the cemetery accompanied by members of his lineage, carrying five basins filled with fresh palm wine, to announce the big news to the ancestors. To this effect, he would squat in front of his predecessor's tomb and pray to all ancestors stressing the danger faced by the clan and imploring their powerful intervention. In the end he would offer them the basins and the wine as presents.

If, meanwhile, the deplored condition improved and the animals purchased for the feast remained in good shape, the chief would invite in-laws and all adult clan members. On the set date, all would go to the cemetery, bringing along all the animals for the feast. Squatting in the front of the tomb of his predecessor, the clan elder would say a prayer to the ancestors, present the animals to them, pour two wine calabashes on the tombs and distribute pieces of cola nuts to the ancestors. Upon returning to the village, the elder would offer a small party for the in-laws and the clan members. The guests would return home promising to come back for the big feast.

By the eighth week following the preceding ritual, in-laws began to come with drums. Dances began with the arrival of the first drum. By the tenth day, they had assembled all the drums. The Bakongo had a four-day week. The festivities lasted three sets of four days, that is, twelve days. At the very beginning, upon the arrival of the last important expected guest, the elder in charge set rules and regulations for the festive period. In particular, he would bar fighting, sexual advances to married women, sorcery, and roaming the streets at night. Eight days, one after the other, were passed in music, dance, eating and drinking. Day after day, groups of in-laws and relatives would bring their contributions to the feast. In return they received meat, palm wine and *kwanga*, the main staple food in Kongo people's diet. After all groups had processed, an account was made of expenses and assets. The next step would be buying dishes and boxes of gun powder, culminating in the washing of the cemetery.

The eve of the major jubilation day was sensational. Volleys of gunshots started early and resonated until late. All along, ivory trumpets blew and drums resounded endlessly. The following morning began in excitement. The cortege would parade to the cemetery for a libation and gifts to the dead. First, the officiating elder would pour palm wine on all the tombs one after the other. The in-laws would follow up by displaying plates, including brand-new sets, on the tomb mounds or on forked tree branches planted all around the tombs. Following the latter ritual, the elder would address the ancestors in an impromptu closing prayer of supplication, reviewing daily activities, lamenting the ills afflicting the village community and imploring ancestral support and protection. The prayer marked the end of the festive period.

New Rites of Passage and Holidays

Baptism. Where Christianity has implanted itself, baptism has replaced birth rites. Baptism takes place in a church in presence of parents and invited friends. Usually, an ordained minister (a Catholic priest or a Protestant pastor) administers the baptism. To the extent possible, they dress the candidates for baptism in white. They generally have their heads shaved before the event to allow the water to touch the scalp. Grown-up candidates participate in religious instructions several months before. On the previous evening they confess their sins and spend a holy night in anticipation of a day full of grace marking a new beginning in their lives. After the ceremonies the parents offer a chicken dinner at their home. As baptism is a family event, individuals of all ages partake of the meal.

Graduation. Under the impact of colonization and Christian missionaries, traditional initiation ceremonies have become outdated in many regions. Schools have replaced secret societies. Now children spend many years in school instead of weeks or months in the initiation forest. In many respect graduation is a real victory. For some it is traumatic. The ritual of announcing the results of the year's work takes place at school. In the past, only the students, the teachers and the school administrators attended. Elementary school graduates were ranked in decreasing order by their scores. The person with the lowest mark was announced last and booed. High school graduates are ranked by category beginning with *La Plus Grande Distinction* (summa cum laude), *Grande Distinction* (magna cum laude), *Distinction* (cum laude) and *Satisfaction* (passing). Those failing are not mentioned. The celebration takes place at the parent's home. Friends and relatives bring presents. Some give their gifts before the event as a part of the preparation. The graduate and the guests eat, drink and dance. In the city, graduates organize parties by school or by associations.

Wedding. The Congolese law recognizes three types of marriage: the traditional marriage, the Christian marriage and the official marriage. The traditional marriage is a family business, an alliance between two families, concretized by transferring the bridewealth from the groom's family to the bride's family. When the marriage alliance was concluded at the bride's family's, the bride transfer could take place then or sometime later. In the morning after the couple had successfully consumated the marriage, they held special nuptial dances to announce or consecrate the happy event. More specifically, nuptial dances salute the groom's masculinity, which is critical for procreation and, through it, the continuity of the family line. Christianity added a new dimension to marriage—a sacrament administered to a couple by an ordained minister in a church. Because of Christian missionaries' endeavors to supplant African culture, Christian marriage became more publicized and more enthusiastically celebrated. Marriage registration is generally attended by the couple, a witness for each party, and a relative of the bride to attest to the fact that the bridewealth has been paid as prescribed by the appropriate custom.

Most Christians in the Congo are Catholic. Catholic candidates for marriage generally go through a prescribed orientation at church before the sacrament is administered. Non-Christian candidates must attend training for baptism as well and receive baptism before marriage. The wedding is announced weeks ahead. The ceremony takes place in a church. A virgin bride dresses in white. Others dress in attractive clothes of any color of their choice. Parents, witnesses and guests assemble at the church at the scheduled day and time. A reception follows the wedding at the couple's residence or at the residence of a relative of either spouse who stands as a sponsor. Celebrations generally extend into the night with music and dances of jubilation mixing ethnic and national songs and melodies.

Christian Holidays. The most celebrated Christian holidays in the Congo are Easter and Christmas. The Easter season begins with Palm Sunday. On this day, churches generally fill with worshipers. Most impressive in rural churches are the palm branches or young trees that Christians bring to the service. Throughout the Catholic mass, people pray while holding their palms and awaiting the finale, a special time reserved for blessing the palms. The worshipers shake their branches or trees while the priest pronounces the benediction words in Latin. The Easter week is a busy one. It includes the Last Supper on Maundy Thursday and the Stations of the Cross procession on Good Friday. Saturday is for confession. On Easter Sunday, people wear white clothes if they can. Christmas is a purely religious holiday. Believers go to church dressed in their nicest clothes; afterwards they either return to their homes or go visit relatives or friends.

Popular Holidays. Two popular holidays deserve special mention: May 1, International Labor Day and January 1, New Year's Day. Trade unions were introduced into the Belgian Congo for white employees after world War II. They were extended to Congolese workers in the late 1950s, particularly after 1957. Congolese participation became more effective in the first years of independence. May 1 became known to the Congolese as a special day set aside world wide to celebrate the working class struggle for economic justice. The struggle includes decent wages, promotions, pensions and the overall humane treatment of workers. Trade union leaders organized and led marches attended by members and sympathizers. They sang and chanted slogans of encouragement for demanding justice and dignity for the worker. The appropriate attire included wearing something red as a symbol of the struggle. Under Mobutu's dictatorship, trade unions became organs of his unique political party, the Mouvement Populaire de la Revolution (MPR). They abandoned their fighting mission to become propagandists for the regime's ideology of unity behind the Head of State, the "Enlightened Guide."

The other international holiday celebrated in the Congo is the New Year. People prepare for the New Year by buying new clothes or making sure their old ones are in good repair and clean. They also want to ensure that some good meat—beef, goat or chicken—will be available for the New Year meal. Most city people buy beer and soft drinks. The aristocracy and the nouveaux riche procure imported wines and liqueurs. In villages men arrange with the women known for brewing the strongest indigenous beer. Early on New Year's morning, they go to the brewer's house to pick up their purchase. Those who have not planned go from brewer to brewer, tasting and choosing.

In the village, around 10:00 or 11:00 A.M., men begin to congregate under a tree or in a shelter in the courtyard. As they drink, some of them begin to sing and play the thumb piano or a modern guitar. By noon and early afternoon the food begins to come from the participating neighbor's houses to the host's house. After they have assembled all the food, including that from the hosting home, the host announces the eating time. Generally, men and women eat separately. Girls eat with the women and boys with the men. Sometimes, children are served separately. After the meal the music resumes. People sing and dance. Men and women, old and young, participate in the singing and dancing as they wish. Generally by late afternoon the beer runs out and some people get tired and start to leave. As the last one goes, the feast ends.

Civic Holidays. During colonial rule the Congolese did not have any holiday of their own. Toward the end, January 4, 1959, brought the Martyrs' Day in memory of the Congolese who perished on this day under the colonial bullet. Joseph Kasa-Vubu, then president of the Bakongo Alliance, a powerful ethnico-political organization in Kinshasa and the Lower Congo, was scheduled to hold a public meeting at the YMCA, on Prince Beaudoin Avenue, which later became Kasa-Vubu Avenue. At the last minute the colonial administration canceled the meeting. The masses revolted, throwing stones on Europeans' cars and looting and burning stores. The colonial army responded with gunfire. More than 300 persons lost their lives. In the early years of independence January 4 became commemorated as the Martyrs' Day. Congo independence brought another holiday. June 30, Independence Day, became a major civic holiday. On this day people would congregate in some public locations, some leaders would give speeches appealing to their nationalism and patriotism. All went well until Mobutu, the late former president, undermined Martyrs' Day and Independence Day to the benefit of November 24, the day of his military takeover. As his regime weakened in the wake of the democratization movement of the early 1990s people became disinterested in his regime, his party and his holiday. His successor, the late President Laurent Désiré Kabila, proclaimed June 30 a national holiday again. However, the ongoing state of war and people's extreme poverty and daily suffering preclude any meaningful celebrations.

NOTES

1. Joseph D. Katanga-Tshitenge, *Grandes périodes éducatives chez les Baluba* (Kinshasa, Zaire: Editions Imprideco, 1968), 82–85.

2. This section is drawn from the author's personal experiences, which resulted in familiarity with Luba culture.

3. Researchers at the University of Kinshasa have published several studies on this topic, for example, Tom De Herdt and Steefaan Marysse, *L'économie informelle au Zaire: (Sur)vie et pauvreté dans la période de transition* (Bruxelles: Institut Africain-CEDAF, 1996), and V.O. Ekanga, "Le secteur informel: Une approache globale du concept et son poids dans l'économie zairoise," *Notes de Conjoncture*, 22 (April–May 1995): 8–12.

4. Expressions such as "disguised unemployment" have also been used to designate insignificant petty business activities practiced by the Congolese. The slogan "Article 15" was popularized by the short-lived *Etat Fedéré du Sud-Kasai* (1960–1963). There were fourteen articles in the general dispositions of the constitution defining the state's responsibilities to citizens. Citizens who made requests not provided for in the constitution were encouraged to use "Article 15," meaning their own resourcefulness, to find solutions to their problems rather than count on the government for what they could do for themselves.

5. See Guy De Plaen, "Rôle social de la magie et de la sorcelerie chez les Bayansi," *Cahiers Economiques et Sociaux* 6, no. 2 (1968): 203–235, on Yansi birth rites.

6. See Lobbo Lwa Djugudjugu, *Société et politique en Afrique traditionnelle: Bahema et Walendu du Zaire* (Kinshasa, Zaire: Presses Universitaires du Zaire, 1980), on Walendu customs.

7. See Mulago gwa Cicala Musharimana, *La religion traditionnelle des bantu et leur vision du monde* (Kinshasa, Zaire: Presses Universitaires du Zaire, 1973), 38–41, on the festival of the dead among the Bakongo.

8

Music and Dance

MUSIC AND DANCE are mirrors of society. In the Congo they reflect, among other social realities, the coexistence of tradition and modernity, on the one hand, and the multiethnic structure of the country, on the other hand. However, in many respects, interethnic differences are in the form rather than in the substance because of a considerable cultural overlap supported by many shared values, worldviews and practices. In either setting, music and dance fulfill many functions. This chapter examines four broad categories of traditional music based on the functions that music plays in human life: (1) activity-related music, such as that played by a working team while hoeing rhythmically; (2) ceremonial music, such as that accompanying an initiation procession; (3) praise music played at the court of a king or a paramount chief to exalt his accomplishments; and (4) entertaining music played by young people while dancing in the moonlight. Modern popular music in the Congo developed independently of domestic musical traditions. It owes its initial developments to West Indian and West African influences. Angolan influences marked its growth years followed by the giants of the golden age in Congolese music—Joseph Kabasela and Lwambo Makiadi (Franco). The proliferation of bands with none dominating, the ascent of professional women singers and the commercialization and intercontinental spread of Congolese music characterize the current phase. Dominant themes include love, male-female relationship, politics and history, satire/diatribe, death and mourning. Modern Congolese music is discussed in this chapter from two perspectives: developmental stages and dominant themes.[1]

TRADITIONAL CONGOLESE MUSIC AND DANCE

Music is omnipresent in the lives of the Congolese people. It accompanies many activities, ceremonies and entertainment events. Mothers sing cradle songs in an attempt to put their babies to sleep. Farmers sing while working rhythmically in teams. In birth rite performances, music, and dance speak to the baby's spirit. The purpose of these performances is to befriend the spirit, to make it feel wanted and to prepare the child for success in adult life. In initiation celebrations, they convey to the candidates the social duties and responsibilities awaiting them in their imminent new status as adults. In lamentations, they express feelings of sorrow and affliction for the loss of the departed while reciting in loud praises their social accomplishments and those of their ancestors. Music and dance are powerful media for expressing reverence and praise toward persons of power. They are first-class entertainment devices in various social gatherings.

Activity-Related Songs

Africans in the Congo, as elsewhere in the continent, often sing while involved in various daily activities. For example, mothers sing to put their babies to sleep. Men sing while working in teams or carrying an authority figure on their shoulders.

Cradle Songs. Cradle songs are melodies sung to very little babies to induce them to sleep. Cradle songs are chosen for their meanings. The people believe that these meanings become part of the baby's subconscious value kit. Their efficacy resides in the melody. Along with the melody, they gently rock the baby back and forth while caressing certain parts of the body. The deep philosophical messages in these songs are illustrated by a translation of a Yaka cradle song:

> Whether one is seated or one is standing up, one is subject to the same fate. I enter the basket. When I think I am out of it, I realize I am still in it. What mystery is this? God responded, what is the animal whose feet hang in the brushwood while it continues to lie on the ground? Be quiet like Bird Ngundu.[2]

Collective Work Songs. Men often sing while collectively involved in some cumbersome activity to alleviate the burden of the latter.[3] One such activity is tilling the land. The participants at some pick moments synchronize the movements of the hoes to produce a common sound and then harmonize the sounds of songs with the sound of the hoes. The following song is one song often executed in a cadence by Luba farmers while hoeing in a team to the rhythm: *"Tuayi tshinamina. Wakubanduluka, tuamudia tshibawu"* ("Let us stick to the task while bent to the ground. He who straightens up his body will pay us fines").

During colonial rule, the Congolese were often summoned to haul heavy trees or stones attached to a long chain or a strong rope. The haulers, distributed evenly along the chain, would pull the load to the rhythm of their singing. The Congolese from Bandundu had a popular dance called *lunkamba*. They performed it while singing and moving their bodies as if pulling a heavy load by a rope.

Singing While Carrying an Authority Figure. When tradition was respected, customary chiefs were carried in a *kipoyi*, a chair/stretcher with two persons in front and two in the rear. The porters often sang while executing this task. In Luba tradition, traveling throughout the chiefdom to visit the land and the people was customary for a chief. A traveling chief could be set down only at the residence of the subchief *Tshikala*. Providing hospitality for the chief and his delegation was the assigned function of the person occupying the seat of subchief *Tshikala*. The porters used three strategies to alleviate the burden on their shoulders. One was the walk/run (*kusesa*), which was performed rhythmically. The second was a back-and-forth movement. The porters would stop, and move backward and forward several times before resuming the steady walk/run. The third strategy was to add a song to both the walk/run and the back-and-forth movement. The usual song for carrying a chief referred to the subchief's hospitality function:

Mukalenge e	The chief (on our shoulders),
Tumutula penyi?	Where will we set him down?
Anu mwa Tshikala,	Only at Tshikala's residence,
Tshikala Mmutupu	Unless Tshikala is not at home

When President Mobutu was still popular in the 1960s, he was often carried in a *kipoyi* during his visits to provincial capitals. In Bandundu, the carriers and the crowd behind them used to sing rhythmically and repeatedly, "Mobutu, we love you, yes we do" (*"Mobutu beto kuzola nge, nge"*). They tell a story that he stopped being carried when some voices from the crowd

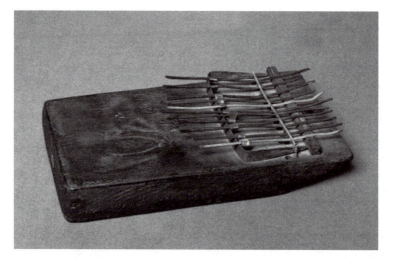

Kasanji: Thumb piano played by rural men. Collection of the author.

changed one word in the chant to say, "Mobutu, we love you, not" (*"Mobutu beto kuzola nge, ve"*).

Ceremonial Dances and Music

Throughout the Congo, men and women celebrate major events with rituals and dances. Big hunting expeditions, birth, initiation, and death are such occasions.

Hunting Rituals. Some activity-related music and dances had a supernatural connotation. The Kanyok of Kasai had a hunting song called *buyanga* that they performed while imitating the walk of big game. The performances celebrated past successes; if they did not sing them before a hunt, it could jeopardize future expeditions. The Mangbetu who live south of the Bomokandi River in Upper Congo had ritual dances and music designed to bring good luck to hunting expeditions. An oracle consultant who could communicate with the ancestors through visions and predict the future performed some of these dances.[4]

Birth Rite Dances. Babies are believed to be returning spirits. They react to their parents' actions more as spirits than humans. Consequently, they are generally welcomed with special ceremonies designed to make them feel wanted, to strengthen them physically and to ensure their future success in adult life. Mothers perform baby welcoming ceremonies. Part of the ceremonies performed by Luba mothers involves going from house to house collecting gifts of food items (*nsawu*) from neighbors. They announce the collection (*kusawula*) with a loud prolonged "oh oh oh" sound (*mukobololo*). Opening the mouth wide and pulling the skin forward between the jaws with the right thumb and middle finger makes this sound. Repeatedly thumping the open mouth with the palm can produce the same sound. Rather than making the sound, one woman participating in the collection would ring one bell for a single birth or a double bell for twins.

Women also sang and danced in front of the house of the ceremonial baby's mother. The most common instrument accompanying these ceremonial dances is the *disaka*, or maraca. The songs performed during the ceremonies carry messages about certain truths or the behaviors of certain human or animal characters as the following stanzas from a song illustrate:

Tshikololo nyunyi wa nsambasamba,	*Tshikololo* is a bird that flies in stages
Usambila wasabuka Lubilanji.	He does so even to the point of crossing the Lubilanji River.
Ndelela penyi,	Where would I give birth to my child,
Ntambwa wa ba Nkashama?	I the lion, fellow of the leopards?
Ndelela penyi,	Where would I give birth to my child,
Bena buloba babenga?	If land owners prohibited it?

Youth Initiation Mottoes and Songs. Many Congolese ethnic groups had formal initiation rites for boys and girls. Formal initiation included a period of isolation during which the candidates received intensive instructions about their responsibilities as men or women. The Kongo ethnic group had an elaborate initiation system that dates from the sixteenth century. The schools bore distinctive names that the Congolese scholar K. Bunseki Fu Kiau has translated into English by expressions that suggest their purpose such as: "Institutes for Life," "Eye-Enlightening Institutes."[5]

One purpose of this school system was to teach young people the value of living in harmony with nature. They learned the importance of the land, plants and farming for human survival and prosperity. Another objective was to teach the candidates the significance of their given names and the circumstances in which these names were chosen. At initiation, the candidates took on new names reminding them of their social and spiritual responsibilities toward the communities of the living and of the dead. Initiation-related training was designed to empower them morally and spiritually to carry out these responsibilities. Empowerment strategies for the initiation candidates included a new language. They had to rehearse mottoes, proverbs, songs and iconographic writings. One truth the candidates had to master through repetitions and songs was the importance of water to life on earth. As the trainer recited one by one the activities and species to which water is indispensable, the candidates responded, "water" in unison. The trainers also stressed the importance of marriage and healthy reproduction to the human survival and community life. They reminded the young people that in marriage, as in farming, "You reap what you sow." Therefore, the idea of seed was central to both and songs repeated during initiation include allusions to both meanings.[6]

Mourning. Dancing as a part of mourning is common to African societies. By custom the Luba buried their dead the morning following death. They played no music before the burial. The wake started on the day of death and lasted two weeks. The mourners, except widows and close relatives, tended to their activities during the day and returned to the wake in the evening. They devoted the wake to lamentation and presentation of condolences, some of which took the form of the *kasala* lyric song. This is a praise song for the dead person and his or her lineage. On the day after the wake there was intensive dancing and singing of *kasala* and other songs. They served large quantities of food and drink. Widows remained in the state of mourning for a year. When the mourning period ended, they would hold a grand feast with even more food, drinks, music and dances.

Praise and Entertainment Music and Dance

Kings and chiefs are set apart as rulers. Often the music to entertain them includes songs of praise, musical ensembles and instruments reserved for them, as illustrated below by Mangbetu court music. Music and dance are present in practically all Congolese cultural events, joyful and sorrowful. They add an entertainment dimension to whatever situations people must confront. At some occasions musical performances are only for entertainment. The *lutuku*, a Luba dance, is such a performance.

Court Music. Musical styles in rural Congo varied with political and social styles. For example, where there existed strong kingdoms or large chiefdoms, praise music for the king or the paramount chief was more complex and more elaborate. Such was the case among the Mangbetu people who live between the Uele and Bomokandi rivers in Upper Congo. Court music reflected the power and the splendor of the king. King Mbunza, who reigned in the nineteenth century, was a great king. Huge musical instruments were found at the king's court. Instruments symbolizing his power could not be found anywhere else. The iron double bell, large ivory horns and certain types of slit drums are in this category. Numerous and imposing musical ensembles performed for the king. Some were famous musicians personally invited by the king to live at the court while making a living from land provided by the sovereign.[7]

They played certain musical instruments for particular purposes. The double bell announced the king's departure for a battle, his visit to a subchief or his return to the court. Some types of slit drums, played individually or in combination, served many purposes: praising the king's power, enhancing the subchiefs' authority as the king's representatives. Slit drums transmitted messages concerning major life events such as birth, death, a grand feast, a major hunting expedition or war. During dancing feasts, slit drums could be used to request drinks for the musicians or to invite a spectator to dance. Whistles were widely used by court musicians and commoners for a variety of purposes.

Social Critic Songs. Some entertainment songs had a social critic connotation. In traditional Congolese societies, people often composed songs to express their satisfaction or dissatisfaction toward particular conditions. Luba women had a song in which they expressed dissatisfaction to possessive men:

Uvua kandelela anyi' ee,	Were you born just for me,
Tatu Kasomboyi wanyi?	Dear Mister Kasomboyi?
Uvua kandamika any' ee,	Did you think you were glued to me,
Tatu Kasomboyi wanyi?	Dear Mister Kasomboyi?
Ukavu wa kashidi anyi' ee,	Who told you you would be with me forever
Tatu Kasomboyi wanyi?	Dear Mister Kasomboyi?

Unpopular chiefs were also the object of songs expressing their subjects' dissatisfaction. Women used to sing these songs in the courtyard while grinding corn or cassava in mortars, on their way to, or when they gathered around water springs. In Kongo villages, during the colonial regime, songs of discontent toward the colonial authority contained coded messages inviting the population to secret locations (*ku Nenga*), where they exposed and debated the causes of discontent and strategies for dealing with it.[8]

Lutuku. A once typical adolescent and young adult dance in Luba villages is called *lutuku*. On a moonlit night, the male and female dancers stand in a loose circle. They sing and clap hands. One by one, they step into the center to execute a few personal steps and gestures before inviting the next person to move into the center. The invitation is done by performing certain dance gestures in front of the person, and by backing up as the latter moves forward into the circle. After executing a few further steps with the entering dancer, the exiting dancer takes over his or her place in the circle.

The *lutuku* includes songs with romantic connotations. These songs alluded to sexual relationships or to male-female relations and attitudes in general. *Lutuku* has a synonym, *mbenga*. One particular movement of *mbenga*, called *mbenga wa tshiadi* (*mbenga* by the chest), was considered special. This is the part of the dance where romantic connotations were made explicit. The shift to the *mbenga wa tshiadi* generally occurred after the dance had lasted for a while and the dancers had become very excited. Its coming was generally announced as a warning against married women. Whence its nickname of *mbega wa bana balela*, which means *mbenga*, "dance for singles." The warning was made by enunciating this expression followed by another: *mukaji mubaka kabwedi* ("married women are advised to abstain.")

In an ordinary *mbenga*, the dancer in the center can, and often does, transfer the dance indiscriminately to a male or a female dancer of his or her choice. In *mbenga wa tshiadi*, however, the transfer is made to a dancer of the opposite sex. At the time the two players are in the center, they slow down and rub their chests against each other or else the male dancer bumps into the female's chest as if by accident.

Kamulangu. This is another Luba musical performance whose major role is to entertain. It may be held at the end of the mourning period, at a graduation or wedding, or to salute an incarcerated relative's return to freedom. This circle dance is perhaps the most popular Luba dance to survive in the cities. The dance appeals to middle-age individuals and younger. The dancers stand side-by-side, looking toward the center of the circle. They move from left to right, each time two steps to the right, followed by a number of steps in the same position. At some point, one individual goes into the center to dance alone.

Kamulangu, like most other Luba dances, is executed in the waist. Before leaving the center of the circle the dancer invites another in by dancing in front of him or her. As the latter moves inward toward the center, the two dance facing each other for a moment before the person going out rejoins the circle in the spot of the one going in. The Luba people call waist dances *maja a mu tshimono* or *maja a mu tshifuka*, which means "dances executed in the waist." In Kinshasa, however, non-Luba people think the name of the dance is *mutuash* because during the time a man and a woman dance in their waist in the center facing each other often the male dancer would say *mutwash* or *mutwas*, particularly if the female partner was unmarried. Literally either word means "punch her," alluding to sexual intercourse.

Tulombo and Tshikuna. These two are additional Luba entertainment dances. Xylophones dominate in *tulombo* performances, hence *tulombo's* other name, *madimba* ("xylophones"). Other instruments played in *tulombo* include the skin drum (*ngoma wa ditumba*) and thumb pianos (*bisanji*). *Tshikuna* is another popular dance. Thumb pianos are the dominant musical instruments in playing *tshikuna*. The skin drum is played here, too. Still another entertainment dance was the *nsonso malengela*. It was accompanied with many thumb pianos and skin drums. Its players were dressed in pleated-wraps (*nsonso*), hence their name. Sometimes *nsonso* girls performed with male partners (*majina*).

All these dances are executed in the waist with the exception of *lutuku*, which is executed by throwing the legs in the air while turning around in a fast movement. *Tulombo* dances interest individuals of all ages. The majority of *tsikuna* dancers are young adults and teenagers. *Tshikuna* means "planting." The name refers to the fact that the dancer sticks the right heel into the ground periodically in a movement similar to the one made by the farmer to plant seeds in a field. This is the dance that young Congolese are now adapting to rap music.

MODERN POPULAR MUSIC

Modern music in the Congo developed in four stages reflecting dominant influences on musical trends, production intensity and quality.[9] The four stages coincided with the following influences, respectively: West African and West Indian, Angolan, the Congolese golden age of Joseph Kabasele's African Jazz and Franco Lwambo Makiadi's O.K. Jazz; and finally, the current phase of super-commercialization. Five themes stand out in this music: love, male-female relationships, politics and social life, satire/diatribe, and death and mourning.[10]

Developmental Stages

The history of modern Congolese music may be divided into four distinctive phases: (1) 1930–late 1940s, (2) late 1940s/early 1950s–mid-1960s, (3) 1960s–late 1970s, and (4) late 1970s–present.

1930s–1940s. The period between the 1930s and the 1940s was marked
by the dominance of West African and other foreign influences in Kinshasa/
Leopoldville. Africans from all over the continent gathered in Brazzaville,
Boma, Leopoldville, Pointe Noire and a few other places. Most importantly,
in the 1940s, Brazzaville, the capital of French Equatorial Africa, became the
center of French colonial politics in Africa. The Congo River, for all practical
purposes, served as a cultural transmission belt between the two colonies
(Belgian Congo and French Equatorial Africa). On both sides of the Congo
River, West Africans (Dohomeans, Senegalese, Cameroonians, Togolese and
many more) introduced their cultures especially in the areas of high-life music, cultural associations to their central African audience. They popularized
certain musical instruments (harmonica, accordion, acoustic guitar, talking
drums and the like).

The period brought over other foreign influences, particularly Afro-
Cuban, Afro-Brazilian. World War II brought additional nationalities to Africa. West Indians—specifically those from Martinique—brought with them
their music as well as their French colonial inheritance. European, Afro-
Cuban and West Indian dances were in vogue: tango Argentina, waltz,
rumba, bolero, meringue and *la Martiniquaise* or *matiniki/maringa*. This
initiation marked the break with the traditional *ngoma* (drum) and the beginning of the new era: the modern music phase. Some of the Congolese of
this period who left their imprint in music were Henri Bowane (guitarist),
Paul Kamba, founder of Victoria Brazza band, Antoine Wendo Kolosoy, and
Antoine Mundanda.

Late 1940s to 1950s. In the early years, the Bana-Angola, also known as
Bansansala or San Salvador emerged as a dominant voice in Kinshasa. These
musicians were the offsprings of Angolan immigrants. Even though many of
them were born and grew up in the Belgian Congo, the colonial reality forced
them to always identify themselves with mother Angola. Singing mostly in
Kikongo about social life and daily events, their artistic creation was dominated by ballads and serenades. The best known artists in this group were
Manuel Freitas, d'Oliveira, and Tino Baroza, whom many believed to be the
man who schooled the late Nicolas Kasanda (Dr. Nico).

1953 to mid-1970s. In the early 1950s, two major bands—African Jazz
and O.K. Jazz (Orchestre Kinois de Jazz)—gradually took over and transformed Congolese modern music for good. Joseph Kabasele, also called Kalle
Jeff or Grand Kalle, founder and CEO of African Jazz, was a talented com-
poser and singer often compared to Tino Rossi. Borrowing originally from
such Latin American musicians as Tito Puente, Johnny Pacheco, Mongito,
and others, African Jazz and the duo Kalle-Nico Africanized the classical

rumba, samba, bolero, tango and cha-cha-cha. The cha-cha-cha of Kalle is different from the one from Havana.

Kalle, a towering figure on the musical scene, championed the cause of national unity and Pan-Africanism in the 1960s. His songs, such as "Kimpwanza" (Independence), "Africa Mokili Mobimba," "Ebale ya Congo" and "Matanga ya Modibo," are a testimony to his internationalism. The presence of many international and talented musicians such as Manu Dibango and Gonzalez, coupled with Kabasele's close relations with the then-ascending petty bourgeois class in Kinshasa, made African Jazz the band of choice for the well-to-do and the sophisticated. Toward the end of the decade, the original African Jazz—through several splits—gave birth to many bands: African-Jazz Kalle, African Jazz/Jeanot, Bombenga, African Jazz Sukisa (Dr. Nico), African Fiesta National, also known as Afrisa National (Tabu Ley Rochereau), The Maquisards (Guy Vano) and many more.

Alongside African Jazz, the Orchestre Kinois de Jazz (1955 to present) was established at the initiative of a European. Very soon, the names of Daniel Lubelo (Ya Louna/De La Lune), Essous Jean-Serge, both from Brazzaville, and especially Francois Luambo Makiadi (Maitre Franco) became synonymous with O.K. Jazz. Their upbeat rhythm and lyrics were so appealing to young "Kinois" that in less than four years of existence, O.K. Jazz stood as a major rival to African Jazz. While the world may only identify Luambo Mokiadi with this band, its success rests on the shoulders of many unsung heroes: De la Lune, Jean-Serge Essous, Isaac Musekiwa (saxophonist), Joseph Kuami, Mujos, Vicky Longomba, Lutumba, Youlou Mabiala, Sam Mangwana, and many more.

Under Luambo's leadership, O.K. Jazz brought the Kongo culture together. They modernized songs and dances from Angola, Congo Kinshasa, and Congo-Brazzaville and injected them into classical rumba, bolero, and cha-cha-cha. Like African Jazz, the Tout Puissaint O.K. Jazz (T.P.O.K. Jazz) as it became known in the late 1980s, had its share of breakups. Thus, from the original band, one may count about two dozen offshoots.

Late 1970s to the present. Today, the Congo counts more than one hundred bands, most of them based in Kinshasa. One finds many of them overseas and all over Africa. Only two schools of modern Congolese Music exist today: African Jazz and O.K. Jazz, or Kalle Jeff and Maitre Franco/Luambo Makiadi. The absence of super-bands characterizes this fourth phase. Neither an African Jazz nor an O.K. Jazz is dominating the musical scene, although plenty of good musicians remain in the Congo. The other characteristic of this phase has been the rise of women as lead singers and entertainers: Mpongo Love, Abeti, Tshiala Muana, Mbilia Bel, Faya Tess.

The Congo is known throughout the world for its modern music, which has become a source of national pride for every Congolese person. From the 1960s to present, the Congolese music dominates the national broadcasts of many African countries from Burkina Faso to Tanzania and Kenya. Congolese musicians are in Conakry, Abidjan, Yaoundé, Douala, Libreville, Brazzaville, Harare, Kampala and many other major African cities. They occupy center stage in the entertainment world throughout the continent. Young men and women in these cities like to imitate, as best they can, the moves of famous Congolese musicians-dancers such as Nioka Longo, Mbilia Bel and Tshiala Muana. Music producers in France, Belgium, Japan and many other countries have capitalized on this phenomenal success to the maximum. For instance, to boost its musical productions, the Japanese giant Sony teamed up with Wenge Muzika. On the other hand, banking on the Congolese artists' ignorance and lack of legal protection, pirates have made a fortune by illegally copying and distributing Congolese music around the world.

Finally, commercial motives drive Congolese music more than ever. With the infusion of new technology and new equipment (keyboard, synthesizers, mixers), many unemployed, uneducated young men, including those without real talent are turning to music for a living. The net effect of this has been, in our view, a decline in the quality of the music. One must nonetheless recognize that today's young Congolese are better dancers and choreographers than their predecessors. Very many among them are "*Bawuta*" ("country folks"), or newcomers, unlike their predecessors who were born and raised in Kinshasa.

Dominant Themes

Many themes are identifiable in Congolese music. Five dominant themes are: (1) love, (2) male-female relationships, (3) politics and social life, (4) diatribe/satire, and (5) death and mourning.

Love. Whether one speaks or understands Lingala or not, a good listener of Congolese music consistently hears such words as: *motema na ngayi* ("my heart"); *bolingo na ngayi* ("my love"); *Cherie* ("Darling").[11] All these words express love. Through music, the artist unveils the romantic character of the people. Many old songs express pure love. For instance, in "Ndozi" (Dream), D'Oliveira says, "Last night (in my dream), I was talking with my darling. I felt like I was talking with an angel, showering me with blessings" ("*O mpimpa mbokene ye mama. Nkiena mono mbokene ye wanzio. Nsambu zame nkuenda baki*").[12] Under this theme one also learns about other aspects of love: jealousy, cheating, infidelity, love lost and regained, sexual promiscuity, and the like.

Male-Female Relationships. Many songs depict the images of men and women in the Congolese society. Since most musicians have been and are still men, their artistic productions have concentrated on women as mothers, lovers, and social beings. As a rule, Congolese men and women have the utmost respect for their mothers. The musician does reflect this attitude in his or her compositions. The picture, however, changes when they view the woman as a lover or a wife. Depending on the quality of the relationship, they portray the woman as a parasite, a junior partner (in a marital situation) or a cumbersome dependent family member. In urban settings, women, except for market/merchant women, did not work outside the home. Thus, they depended on men for support.

Both Fede Lawu and Luambo Makiadi (Franco) in a modern rendition of an old song from the Ntandu (a Kongo subgroup) show how a woman is less than a partner in a marital relationship. The language used is more than demeaning. They view the woman as a thing as related in this kikongo passage, "*Kio kileka kumanima, ikio kifinga ngudi munu*" ("That thing that sleeps behind my back, that thing dares to disrespect my mother"). Today, however, with the emergence of women artists like Mpongo Love, Mbilia Bel and Tshiala Mwana, they paint men, too, as evil, incompetent and irresponsible.[13]

By analyzing many songs, the student of culture and history may find a window of opportunity for penetrating further into the Congolese social fabric. Thus, listening to Luambo Makiadi's song titled "Mario," one learns about some fundamental changes that have taken place in the Congolese society as a direct result of political independence, including the emergence of nouveaux riches. Of course, some of these newly enriched persons are women. "Mario" is the story of a young man, well educated (at European universities). He is the lover of a woman who, according to Luambo, is as old as his mother. The woman takes care of Mario's needs, from clothing to housing. Despite this, the young man mistreats his benefactor/lover.

The proliferation of rich women, nicknamed *Bamama Benz* and *Bamama Cent Kilos*, is a new development. Bamama Benz (Mercedes Benz Ladies) and Bamama Cent Kilos (Hundred Kilogram Ladies) are pejorative nicknames for nouveaux riche women. These women used to drive large and expensive cars and to carry heavy trunks of banknotes for their business transactions at market place. They also tended to be overweight. Also, the class of men who depend on women for everything was unheard of and socially unacceptable in the past. Through the song, the artist criticizes the importation of European perversions into Congolese society. The Mario syndrome is not an isolated occurrence. Many young people live in similar relationships of dependence. Like Mario, most of them have attended European schools and universities. They abound in Kinshasa. The image they project in popular cynicism is that of "*petits poussins derriere la poule*" ("baby chicks behind a mother hen"). People refer to the woman in this kind of relationship as *mama mobokoli* ("mother caretaker").

Politics and Social Life. Even before independence, Congolese artists, particularly musicians, have shown a great interest in politics and social life. More often, they act as social critics. A title in this vein is "Ata Ndele," (Sooner or later). The full title is "Sooner or later the world will change." Once very popular in Kinshasa, "Ata Ndele" was composed and produced by Adou Eyenga in 1955, the year the young Belgian King Beaudouin visited the Congo. In that same year, the statutes recognizing the emerging Congolese elites, then called *évolués*, as a distinct social category were enacted. Many other signs of the winds of change blowing over Africa were noticeable in the Belgian Congo. In the words of the singer:

> Sooner or later the white man will be overthrown.
> Sooner or later the world will be purified.
> Sooner or later the world will be turned upside down.[14]

In the 1960s and 1970s the musicians targeted the politicians and the nouveaux riche. Rochereau, also known as Pascal Tabu Ley, in "Mokolo na kokufa," talks about the end of life from a rich man's and a poor man's eyes:

> The day I die, I the rich man,
> I will think about cars and trucks.
> I will think about the children I have sent away to Europe.
> The day I die, I the poor man
> I will think about Ida, the woman I married.
> I will think about the children I leave behind.[15]

Tabu Ley scored a huge success when his song "Zando ya Malonga" ("The happy/excellent market") came out around the same time. It is a diatribe against the new women's political and economic class.

They told me,
You refuse to buy in small quantities,
You buy things with your eyes closed,
You refuse to take your change.

This was the behavior of the nouveaux riche and parvenus in the years following independence. They had the money and they wanted everyone else to take note. They soon lost the respect of those they wished to impress (the masses) since everyone knew it was money stolen from the people.

However, Congolese musicians have always played this role of social critics. At times, they behaved like troubadours in service to politicians. Songs praising one political figure or another are too many to mention here. Under the guise of "Authenticity" (rebuilding African culture), they produced hundreds of songs to praise the accomplishments (real and imaginary) of the so called "Enlightened Guide," the late former president Mobutu. Before Authenticity those who were old enough in the 1960s will recall the song, *"Moise Tshombe, soki yo te na Congo nani?"* ("Moise Tshombe, if not you, who else for the Congo?"). Tshombe was very far from being a national hero, much less a savior. This brings us to our fourth theme: satire.

Satire/Diatribe. Producing a song to attack or vilify a rival or an enemy is common in Congolese culture. Franco mastered this style and used it more than any other musician. In "Course au Pouvoir" (Race to power), he chastizes a former partner whose career he had promoted, "Son, Son, stop singing about your father. Nobody will believe you because everybody knows me" (*Muana, O Muana, tika nionso ozali koyembela tata na yo. Bakondima yo te mpo bayebi ngayi*).

Death and Mourning. Death and mourning are a daily reality. In modern Congolese popular music, death is sometimes viewed as the great equalizer. No one is exempt, and, more important, all are treated the same. A passage from the song "Mabele" (The earth) declares, "On the day we die, all of us are wrapped up in the same white sheets" (*Mokolo tokokufaka, biso nionso tokendeke na draps ya pembe*). Songs about death can also be actual funeral orations. Tabu Ley, in "Kabasele in Memoriam," sings a tribute to his dead mentor Joseph Kabasele. He cites his accomplishments, praising Kabasele as the "father of modern music."[16]

Franco is the musician who has addressed this theme more often than any other. He uses this style to expose and chastise the despicable, but increasingly common, behavior of relatives who fight over the dead person's wealth and belongings before the remains are taken to their resting place.

Often, Franco decries sorcery (*kindoki*), which is a fundamental belief among the Bantu peoples, particularly the Kongo ethnic group. He wrote "Kimpa kisangameni" (A mystery is hanging up there) when his junior brother, Bavon-Marie, died. Bavon-Marie, exhorts the ancestors, the family elders and *Matunga* (literally, the Builder), the youngest of the clan elders, to watch over and protect the living members of the clan. The Kongo readily accept death as a natural and normal phenomenon, as God's will, only when it affects a very old person. Under any other circumstances (including terminal illnesses and accidents) the Kongo people look at a younger person's death as an evil act, the work of evil spirits and sorcerers. In this view, they seek the cause of the death in terms of who caused it and who is responsible, rather than what caused it.

NOTES

1. This chapter is the product of cooperative work between the author and Makidi Ku-Ntima, a political scientist at Paine College, Augusta, Georgia. The author wrote the section on traditional music and Ku-Ntima developed the section on modern music. Ku-Ntima's contribution is very much appreciated. However, the sole responsibility rests with the author.

2. Mufuta Kabemba, "Literature orale et authenticité (II)," *Revue JIWE 3* (June 1974): 68.

3. Situations discussed in this section about the Luba society are based on the author's research and life experiences in Luba villages.

4. Didier Demolin, "Music and Dance in Northeastern Zaire, Part I: The Social Organization of Mangbetu Music," in *African Reflections: Art from Northeastern Zaire*, ed. E. Schildkrout and C. A. Keim (Seattle: University of Washington Press, 1990), 207.

5. K.K.B. Fukiau, *Self-Healing Power and Therapy: Old Techniques from Africa* (New York: Vantage Press, 1999), 2.

6. Fukiau, *Self-Healing Power and Therapy*, 2–19, 23, 33.

7. Demolin, "Music and Dance in Northeastern Zaire," 197–204.

8. K.K.B. Fu-Kiau, *Mbongi: An African Traditional Political Institution* (Roxbury, MA: Omenana, 1985), 41.

9. This section was written by Makidi Ku-Ntima, who has extensive first-hand knowledge of Congolese music. He is also a personal acquaintance of many musicians and owns a large collection of recordings. Most of the songs—old and new—can be found at the archives of the Congolese National Radio and Television in Kinshasa.

10. The following unpublished manuscripts in French are among the few studies of Congolese music: Bwantsa Kafungu, "Congo en musique Léopldville" (Kinshasa, 1965); Lenoch (Michel) Malangi Bokelenge, "Essai de commentaire sur la musique

congolaise moderne" (Kinshasa, 1969); "Négritude, africanité et musique africaine" (Kinshasa, 1990); Kanga Matondo, "Musique zairoise moderne" (Kinshasa, 1972). The studies alone (individually) referenced are manuscripts of student field works at what was then the National University of Zaire, Kinshasa and Lubumbashi campuses.

11. Congolese musicians compose and sing primarily in Lingala, a Congolese vernacular language, which is spoken especially in Kinshasa, the capital, and the Upper Congo and Equator provinces.

12. The language in the song is Kikongo. D'Oliveira was a member of the Kongo ethnic group of Angolan origin but was born and raised in the former Belgian Congo.

13. This is from a popular song among the Bantandu, a Kongo sub-group. The musician Franco, using modern musical instruments, and with minimal change here and there, made it part of his repertoire.

14. Adou Eyenga, "Ata ndele mokili ekobaluka" (song lyrics, Kinshasa, 1955), in Isidore Ndaywel e Nziem, *Histoire Generale du Congo* (Paris: Duculot, 1999).

15. Tabu Ley, Rochereau, and African Fiesta National, "Mokolo nakokufa" (song lyrics, ca. 1967).

16. Mabele (the Earth) is the title of a song about death. Sam Manguana, the lead singer, is presumed to be the author. The song was produced by T.P. Ok. Jazz orchestra under the leadership of Luambo Makiadi/Franco.

9

Conclusion

IT IS A COMMON PRACTICE in Congolese humanity and social science literature, both scholarly and popular, to identify some customs and artifacts as traditional, others as modern. The practice has merit in that it forces the writer and his or her audience to keep in mind the fact that some customs and other cultural elements found in a particular region are traceable to that region's distant past whereas others are imports from other geographical spaces. The writings on ancestral traditions stress the contributions of various Congolese ethnic groups to the humanity's cultural heritage in various domains: political organization, religion, literature, art, family values and music and dance.

In the political field, the organizational structuring and operational principles of the bands, lineages and clans, chiefdoms, kingdoms and empires once found in various parts of the Congo provide abundant original models of participatory democracy. In religion, the belief in one creator who is the ultimate source of life and cause of death is universal. Other spirits (nature spirits, spirits of past heroes and ancestral spirits), the humans, the animal kingdom, the flora and the entire universe are his creations and derive their powers directly or indirectly from his. In literature, Congolese writers have revalorized ancestral traditions by recording, interpreting and translating literary materials pertaining to popular songs, riddles and enigmas, proverbs, animal stories and legends. In art, human motifs (statues, heads, faces, masks) dominate in sculpture, weaving, pottery and mural painting. The search for esthetics, including body adornment, is omnipresent as well.

In reference to family life, all Congolese societies hold marriage and procreation in high esteem. Motherhood is a supreme value. The conjugal family, monogamous (one man and one woman) or polygamous (one man and two or more women), is embedded in the extended family. The latter plays the role of the centralizing institution in the organization of social life. Respect for seniority and resource sharing are expected of everyone. By virtue of birth, legitimate birth particularly, the individual becomes a member of a hierarchy of descent groups in which he or she occupies a special position defining his or her rights and obligations toward other members.

Music and dance are omnipresent in Congolese people's lives. By and large, traditional music and dances are identified with either an ethnic grouping or a region. Everywhere, they accompany all human events: birth, initiation, marriage, chiefs' or kings' inauguration or funeral. Music and dance are present in royal court entertainment as well as in popular festivities. The drum, in various forms, is the number one musical instrument. It is a multiple-message carrier. Royal courts used it to communicate the sovereign's orders to the sub-chiefs under his authority. During entertainments, the main drummer sets the tone for the rest of the orchestra to follow; together, they send special messages to the dancers. The maraca, the thumb piano, the flute, the bell or double bell accompany the drum to various degrees. Each of these instruments is sometimes played alone depending on the nature of the event being celebrated in a particular cultural context.

Because of European imperialism, modernity for most part means Western style cultural imports which at first were imposed upon the Congolese people during the colonial period (1885–1960). With the passing of time, they were incorporated into the lives of the Congolese to various degrees of universality. Christianity, particularly Catholicism, is the most widespread religion in the Congo. Christianity spread European names throughout the country. At baptism, the Congolese were given European names glorified as Christian names or names of patron saints. Christian holidays (Palm Sunday, Easter, Pentecost, Day of the Dead, All Saints, Christmas) are celebrated with high devotion. Almost everywhere Christian churches are among the most imposing community buildings. Formal education is for the most part dispensed through state schools that are managed by Christian churches. Land expropriations and unpaid labor have outlived the colonial regime that introduced them. The market economy, a limited wage labor force and a widespread practice of paying substandard wages are other constants of the colonial legacy. Modern state, with its complex bureaucracy, is perhaps the most colossal import. Its inhumane brutalities have been reinstated, sometimes even exceeded, by the dictators of the post-independence era. Urban agglomerations, with their partially standardized residential lots and commercial zones, developed in response to the needs of the colonial administration and expatriate companies. The division of the city between luxurious urban districts reserved for the Europeans (la Ville) and lower quality quarters for the Africans (La Cité) is another transplanted practice. It is being replicated by the Congolese elite who replaced the Europeans in power.

Neither the Congolese traditions nor the European cultural imports exist in pure form today. Nor do they operate as mutually exclusive domains. In fact, each one has been tainted by influences from the other. Their interaction, mutual borrowing and mutual adjustment have given birth to an ambiguous category of hybrid practices. For instance, in religion, both in Christianity and in Congolese belief systems, doubting about the existence of God is an aberration, to say the least. To authentic Africans such as those who people the Congo, it is a blasphemy. The Christian commandment "thou shall not call the name of thy Lord God in vain" and the African practice of not addressing prayers to God in ordinary circumstances reinforce each other. Prophetic religions owe their popularity in the Congo today in large part to a quadruple identification: the sorcerer and the demon whose evil powers cause certain people to become sick; the practice of exorcism that cleanses the victim and brings about healing; the *nganga* (traditional priest) and the Christian prophet who administer the exorcism; and the spirit of a great ancestor figure and the Holy Ghost whose supernatural powers purge the sorcery or drive the demons out of the victimized individual and produce the healing.

In music and dance, the originality of the Congolese people is unmistakable. Nonetheless, the use of such modern instruments as the guitar, the trumpet and the saxophone in recording is not only transforming the quality of the music, but is also reaching a younger and more diversified audience. On the other hand, whereas modern Congolese music and dances find their roots outside of the Congolese cultural fabric, the creativity of the Congolese people has had such an imprint that even the least knowledgeable listener cannot fail to recognize the uniqueness of their rhythms and melodies. That Congolese musicians and dancers stand out in Africa is neither accidental or coincidental. They carry with them the cachet Kongo, Mbala or Luba, to name just a few, that inspires them.

The market economy and urbanism as a way of life, as introduced by the Europeans into the Congo, never provided the same quality services and other amenities for the Congolese masses as they did for the Europeans or the Congolese leaders who later replaced the Europeans in power positions.

The majority of the Congolese could make ends meet only by practicing some kind of petty business with high turnover. Such activities took place outside the controlled system hence their name of parallel activities. After independence the situation even aggravated as the infrastructures left behind by the Europeans fell into desuetude; the urban population exploded and paid employments shrank to near disappearance. Parallel activities became the standard. Buying and selling practices relative to parallel activities are not quite the same as in a typical capitalist system or a typical traditional system. They have their own logic and ethics. Their preponderance in daily life and their uniqueness owe them a new name: *The Informal Sector or The Informal Economy.* After independence the Congolese elite replaced the Europeans in La Ville with its large walled villas, paved streets and running water in every home. However, due to urban explosion, the carrying capacity both of La Ville and La Cite (where the majority of Congolese live), was exceeded. The squatting zones filled the gap. Here stand side by side the walled villas of the well-offs and the unfinished more modest houses of individuals with meager means who draw water from a "Patron's" pump for a fee (Patron: Boss, address term for a person in a authority position, or high socioeconomic status).

Many colonial policies were deliberately designed to destroy Congolese traditions. Customary chiefs and kings were the target of such policies. The colonial authorities destroyed them by abolishing the legitimate procedures by which they came to power and the traditional methods of governing, by balkanizing the kingdoms and the large chiefdoms and by substituting in-dependent minded and social conscious leaders by figureheads. Traditional initiation schools were sources of moral and social strengths. They too were targeted for destruction. In self-defense they turned into secret societies and, eventually, into revolt movements, which fact drew even harsher repressive measures on them. Consequently many stunted or disappeared completely. Before colonization figurative art had flourished in all corners of the Congo. Statues of ancestor figures and masks representing initiation or divination spirits were dominant motifs. Christian missionaries destroyed them literally in an effort to combat paganism. Europeans of all creeds and nationalities, including their American offspring, pillaged them systematically for their artistic, esthetic or commercial value. Because of these widespread acts of destruction, these cultural institutions and products have ceased to exist in the learning environment of most Congolese. Also, not even in absentia have they been placed into the curriculum of Congolese schools. Consequently most Congolese, including the educated ones, have not been exposed to them in any manner. Because of this loss also, many current accounts of traditional institutions and art, including sections of this book, are being written in past tense rather than present tense.

NOTE

This conclusion includes a contribution from Dr. Makidi Ku-Ntima.

Glossary

abacos Chinese style men's suit, imposed during the Mobutu dictatorship as national dress

bakulu most venerated ancestors who lived and departed as respected elders and noble members of the clan

Bankita special category of ancestors, includes the spirits of relatives who died violently

bawuta country folks, pejorative name for newcomers to the capital

bidia a starchy food made of cassava flour and a smaller quantity of corn flour

bilima nature spirits in Mongo tradition

bilungalunga green vegetable, sweet potato leaves

bisanji thumb pianos (singular: **tshisanji**)

bishishi non-edible caterpillars

bisimbi water spirits, living by creeks, springs and ponds

bitoto dish made of a mixture of several kinds of food

boubou men's shirt, West African style, generally known as **dashiki**

boyerie a smaller house for servants located behind the master's main house

bubawu a substance made out of certain wild leaves that fishermen scatter over the water to drug the fish and facilitate the catch

Bushoongs federation of 18 clans that founded the Kuba Kingdom

dashiki   men's shirt, West African style, also called **boubou** in the Congo

évolués   Congolese élite during the colonial period

fleaux du Zaire (les)   French for Zaire's scourges, also known as le mal zairois, Zaire's evil

fufu   a starchy food made from cassava flour

fumbwa   fish cooked in a special vegetable sauce

ifityoleko   riddle (in Bemba)

Jamaa   a movement within the Catholic Church in the Congo that encouraged infusion of African story-telling strategy into the teaching of Christianity

Kabitenda   month of white winged ants, October, also called **Kaswa Bitenda**

kamanyimanyi   smallest of the edible grasshoppers, also used as an ingredient in medicine

kamulangu   popular circle dance

kamundele   small pieces of barbecued goat or beef sold on skewers as shishkabob

kasala   epic song of the Luba

Kashipu-Nkenza   month of the developing dry season, June

Kashipushipu   month of the small drought, January, also called Tshiongo wa Minanga

Kaswa Banga   month in which the brown winged ants begin to swarm, November

Kaswa Bitenda   month of white winged ants, October, also called **Kabitenda**

kikwembe   long wrap, part of a typical Congolese woman's dress, worn from the waist down to the ankles

kindoki   sorcery

kipoyi   chair/stretcher for transporting authority figures

ku masa   (in Kongo worldview) an invisible location by the water where spiritual life continues after a person's death

kusawula   ceremonial house-to-house collection of goods for baby welcoming ceremonies

kusesa walk/run performed rhythmically by individuals transporting an authority figure to take their mind off the heavy burden on their shoulders

kwanga cassava bread, traditional starchy food of the Kongo people; consumed as a major staple food in several parts of the Congo

lengalenga a spinach-like green vegetable, also called **tshitekuteku** (singular) or **bitekuteku** (plural)

libaya name given to a woman's top when made from the same material as the bottom

likelele the most widespread variety of edible crickets

likelembe an organization whose members perform work or contribute money periodically for the benefit of each member in turns

likobe boneless game meat mixed with oil, onion and spices and baked in banana leaves

liputa the smaller wrap that Congolese women wear over a longer wrap rolled over at the waist to form a bumper

lituma dish made with baked plantains

loso rice, also called **losa** or **epunga**

Luabasnya-Nkasu month to distribute hoes for cultivation, April

Lumungulu the month of March

lunkamba dance accompanied with singing imitating the hauling of a heavy stone or tree attached to a long chain or rope

lupu wooden bowl that women use in fishing to scoop water from a pond

lutuku entertainment dance of young adults performed in the moonlight

lwishi the month of swarming insects, February

Lyangombe great spirit venerated by the Bashi and other peoples of the Great Lakes region

maboke highly peppered fresh fish baked in reed leaves or banana leaves

madesu beans

madesu ya bana a bribe (literally beans for the children)

mafundisho (Jamaa) teachings

maja a mu tshifuka dance executed in the waist, also called **maja a mu tshimono**

maja a mu tshimono   dance executed in the waist, also called **maja a mu tshifuka**

majina   dancing partner

makayabo   salted cod fish

makemba   plantains

malala   a variety of edible grasshoppers, also called mbedi

mal zairois (le)   French for Zaire's evil, also known as les fleaux du Zaire, Zaire's scourges

mamu   mother

manduwa   religious secret society to which the great spirit Lyangombe belonged

mankenene   red, non-flying edible ants that develop in mounds, called soldier ants in English

manseba   mother's brother, maternal uncle

matamba   cassava leaves, the most popular green vegetable in the Congo, also known as **kaleji** or **pondu**

matebo   spirits of relatives who lived undeserving lives on earth

mbala   sweet potatoes

mbenga   short for **mbenga wa tshiadi** (mbenga chest dance), version of the lutuku dance in which the couple bump into each other's chest, also **mbenga wa bana balela** (mbenga singles dance)

menga   Kongo term for blood

meshi   edible caterpillars

mintuntu   the most widespread variety of edible crickets, also called likelele

moyo   the principle of life, the essential element in the human as a spiritual being

mudibu   green vegetable, pumpkin leaves

Mudila-Ntongolo   the month of crying insects, September

mukaji   female

mulembwa   okra

Mulopwe Wa Bantu   a Hemba chief's title, meaning the people's chief

mulume   male

munyinyi   fresh meat

mushipu   dry season

muteta green vegetable, bitter leaf

mutu wa mbuji soup made of parts from goat head

mvul'a mbedi contracted form for **mvula wa mbedi**, first rainy season, September to December

mwambe chicken stew cooked in a sauce made out of dried cassava leaves and peanut paste

mwela machete

ndoki an individual who is endowed with supernatural powers through revelation or initiation, often translated as sorcerer or witch

ndozi dream

ndumba prostitute

ngabulira riddle or enigma (in Hunde)

nganda restaurants popular eateries in Kinshasa serving traditional foods from various regions of the Congo

ngoma wa ditumba skin drum

nitu Kongo term for the human body as a sacred reality

nkisi mystically empowered objects commonly called fetishes

nkongoloja muana curve of the arm where a mother rests her baby's neck while carrying the baby on her lap

nsawu baby welcoming ceremonies performed by Luba mothers

nshima starch made out of corn flour mixed with cassava flour, traditional food of the Luba of Kasai

nsonso malengela dance performed by dancers dressed in pleated-wraps

nsunza games youth evening games from Lower Congo described by the writer Batukezanga Zamenga

nteta ne meshi a stew of caterpillars cooked in a pumpkin seed sauce

pondu cassava leaves, the most popular green vegetable in the Congo, also called matamba or kaleji

tatu mukaji literally female father, father's sister, paternal aunt

Tshibungu Mukaji the cloudy month with mild cold, August

Tshibungu Mulume the cloudy month with harsh cold, July

Tshikala subchief in the Luba power hierarchy whose function was to provide hospitality for the chief and his entourage during chief's visits to the regions

tshikuna   planting, popular dance in which the dancer imitates with his right heel the movement of a farmer planting some seeds

tshimuku   a cake made by mixing mashed sweet potatoes with dry roasted peanuts

tshinkudimba   turning around in circle as pigeons do; cooperative work performed by a team for the members in turn; money contributions assembled by a team for its members in turn, also called **likelembe**

Tshiongo wa Minanga   Tshiongo Drought Month, January, also called **Kashipushipu**

Tshisanga   short form of **Tshisanga Nkasu**, the month for assembling and storing the hoes, May

Tshiswa Munene   the month of abundant brown winged ants, December

tshitekuteku   a spinach-like green vegetable, also called **bitekuteku** (plural) or **lengalenga**

tshivunga   skirt

tuleji   plural of **kaleji**, cassava leaves, often used as an alternative to **bitekuteku** in the generic sense of greens

tulombo   popular dance accompanied with xylophones

tupelepela   rituals that nurtured the 1931 Pende revolt in Bandundu

twishi   insects

ugali   a starchy food made of corn flour

vuvulu   the physical body

zones de squatting   squatting zones

Selected Bibliography

Adenoyi-Ojo, Onukalia. *Mbuti*. New York: Posen Publishing Group, 1996.

The African American Institute Performing Arts Program. *The National Dance Theatre of Zaire in Nkenge: An African Dance-Opera*. New York: African American Institute, 1981.

Amnesty International. *Human Rights Violations in Zaire*. London: Amnesty International Publications, 1980.

Balandier, Georges. *Daily Life in the Kingdom of the Kongo: From the Sixteenth to the Eighteenth Century*. Translated by Helen Weaver. London: Allen and Unwin, 1968.

Bemba, Sylvain, ed. *Theater and Politics: An International Anthology*. New York: Urban Repertory Theater, 1990.

Biebuyck, Daniel P. *Art from Zaire: 100 Masterworks from the National Collection*. New York: The African-American Institute, 1975.

———. *Hero and Chief: Epic Literature from the Banyanga Zaire Republic*. Berkeley: University of California Press, 1978.

———. *The Arts of Zaire*. Berkeley: University of California Press, 1985.

Brincard, Marie-Thérèse, ed. *The Art of Metal in Africa*. New York: The African American Institute, 1982.

Collins, Robert O., ed. "Central Africa." In *Central and South African History*. Princeton: Markus Wiener Publishers, 1990.

Cornet, Joseph. *Art from Zaire: 100 Masterworks from the National Collection*. Translation and Introduction by Irwin Hersey. New York: The African American Institute, 1975.

Davies, Carole Boyce, and Anne Adams Graves, eds. *Ngambika (Help Me to Balance this Load): Studies of Women in African Literature*. Trenton, NJ: Africa World Press, 1986.

Dembour, Marie-Bénédicte. *Recalling the Belgian Congo: Conversations and Introspection.* New York: Berghahn Books, 2000.

Devisch, René. "Pillage of Jesus: Healing Churches and the Villagization of Kinshasa." *Africa: Journal of the International African Institute* 66, no. 4 (1996), 555–585.

Droogers, A.F. *The Dangerous Journey: Symbolic Aspects of Boys' Initiation among the Wagenia of Kisangani, Zaire.* New York: Mouton, 1980.

Fabian, Johannes. *Jamaa: A Charismatic Movement in Katanga.* Evanston, IL: Northwestern University Press, 1971.

———. *Moments of Freedom: Anthropology and Popular Culture.* Charlottesville: University of Virginia Press, 1998.

Fu-Kiau, K. Kia Bunseki. *Mbongi: An African Traditional Political Institution.* Roxbury, MA: Omenana, 1985.

———. *Self-Healing Power and Therapy: Old Teachings from Africa.* New York: Vantage Press, 1991.

Higginson, John. *A Working Class in the Making: Belgian Colonial Labor Policy, Private Enterprise, and the African Mineworker, 1907–1951.* Madison: University of Wisconsin Press, 1989.

Hilliard, Constance B., ed. *Intellectual Traditions of Pre-Colonial Africa.* Boston: McGraw-Hill, 1998.

Hunt, Nancy Rose. *A Colonial Lexicon of Birth Ritual, Medicalization, and Mobility in the Congo.* Durham, NC: Duke University Press, 1999.

Jewsiewcki, Bogumil. "Popular Painting in Contemporary Katanga: Painters, Audiences, Buyers, and Sociological Contexts." In *A Congo Chronicle: Patrice Lumumba in Urban Art,* ed. B. Jewsiewcki, 13–28. New York: The Museum for African Art, 1999.

Jordan, Manuel, ed. *Chokwe! Art and Initiation among the Chokwe and Related Peoples.* New York: Prestel, 1998.

Kanza, Thomas. *The Rise and Fall of Patrice Lumumba: Conflict in the Congo.* Rochester, VT: Schenkman, 1994.

Kayongo-Male, Diane, and Philista Onyango. *The Sociology of the African Family.* New York: Longman, 1984.

Lopès, Henri. *Tribaliks: Contemporary Congolese Stories.* Translated by Andrea Leskes. Portsmouth, NH: Heinemann, 1987.

Lumumba, Patrice. *Congo, My Country.* Translated by Graham Heath. New York: Praeger, 1966.

MacGaffey, Wyatt. "Lineage Structure, Marriage and the Family amongst the Central Bantu." *Journal of African History* 24 (1983): 173–187.

———. *Modern Kongo Prophets: Religion in a Plural Society.* Bloomington: Indiana University Press, 1983.

Maquet, Jacques. *Civilizations of Africa.* New York: Oxford University Press, 1972.

Martin, Phyllis. *Leisure and Society in Colonial Brazzaville.* New York: Cambridge University Press, 1995.

Mbiti, John S. *African Religions and Philosophy*. 2nd ed. Portsmouth, NH: Heine-
    mann, 1990.

Miller, Thomas Ross, "Collecting Culture: Musical Instruments and Musical
    Change." In *African Reflections: Art from Northeastern Zaire*, ed. E. Schild-
    krout and C. A. Keim, 209–215. Washington, DC: American Museum of
    Natural History, 1990.

Mudimbe, V. Y. *Parables and Fables: Exegesis, Textuality, and Politics in Central
    Africa*. Madison: University of Wisconsin Press, 1991.

Mukenge, Tshilemalema. *Independence and the Spirit of Community*. Washington,
    DC: Institute for Independent Education, 1988.

The Museum of Primitive Art. *Traditional Art of the African Nations*. New York:
    University Publishers, 1961.

Nelson, Jack E. *Christian Missionizing and Social Transformation: A History of Conflict
    and Change in Eastern Zaire*. New York: Praeger, 1992.

Nyunda, ya Rubango. "Patrice Lumumba at the Crossroads of History and Myth."
    In *A Congo Chronicle: Patrice Lumumba in Urban Art*, ed. B. Jewsiewcki, 43–
    57. New York: The Museum for African Art, 1999.

Parrinder, Geoffrey. *African Mythology*. London: Paul Hamlyn, 1967.

Peek, Philip M., ed. *African Divination Systems: Ways of Knowing*. Bloomington:
    Indiana University Press, 1991.

Poynor, Robin. "The Eastern Congo Basin." In *A History of Art in Africa*, ed. Monica
    Blackmun Visonà, Robin Poynor, Herbert M. Cole, and Michael D. Harris,
    412–437. Upper Saddle River, NJ: Prentice-Hall, 2000.

————. "The Western Congo Basin." In *A History of Art in Africa*, ed. Monica
    Blackmun Visonà, Robin Poynor, Herbert M. Cole, and Michael D. Harris,
    366–411. Upper Saddle River, NJ: Prentice-Hall, 2000.

Ramsay, F. Jeffress. "Democratic Republic of the Congo (Congo Kinshasa: formerly
    Zaire)." In *Global Studies: Africa*, 81–87. 8th ed. Guilford, CT: Dushkin/
    McGraw-Hill, 1999.

Ray, Benjamin C. *African Religions: Symbol, Ritual, and Community*. 2nd ed. Upper
    Saddle River, NJ: Prentice-Hall, 2000.

Sangmpam, S.N. *Pseudocapitalism and the Overpoliticized State*. Brookfield, VT: Ash-
    gate, 1994.

Schatzberg, Michael G. *The Dialectics of Oppression in Zaire*. Bloomington: Indiana
    University Press, 1991.

Schildkrout, Enid, and Curtis A. Keim. *African Reflections: Art from Northeastern
    Zaire*. Seattle: University of Washington Press, 1990.

Scott, Bob F. *Historical Dictionary of the Democratic Republic of Congo (Zaire)*. Lan-
    ham, MD: Scarecrow Press, 1999.

Shillington, Kevin. *History of Africa*. Rev. ed. New York: St. Martin's Press, 1995.

Siy, Alexandra. *The Efe: People of the Ituri Rain Forest*. New York: Dillon Press,
    1993.

Tempels, Placide. *Bantu Philosophy*. Paris: Présence Africaine, 1959.

Thompson, Robert Farris. *The Four Moments of the Sun: Kongo Art in Two Worlds*. Washington, DC: National Gallery of Art, 1981.

Tshonda, Jean Omasombo. "Patrice Lumumba's Youth." In *A Congo Chronicle: Patrice Lumumba in Urban Art*, ed. B. Jewsiewcki, 29–41. New York: The Museum for African Art, 1999.

United Nations Educational, Scientific, and Cultural Organization (UNESCO). *Distinctive Characteristics and Common Features of African Cultural Areas South of the Sahara*. Introduction to African Culture Series no. 7. Paris: UNESCO, 1985.

Vansina, Jan. *Kingdoms of the Savanna*. Madison: University of Wisconsin Press, 1968.

———. "Kingdoms of the Savanna." In *Problems in African History: The Precolonial Centuries*, ed. Robert O. Collins, 115–120. New York: Markus Wiener Publishing, 1994.

Vass, Winifred Kellersberger. *The Bantu Speaking Heritage of the United States*. Los Angeles: University of California, Los Angeles, Center for Afro-American Studies, 1979.

Visonà, Monica Blackmun, Robin Poynor, Herbert M. Cole, and Michael D. Harris, eds. *A History of Art in Africa*. Upper Saddle River, NJ: Prentice-Hall, 2000.

Waife, Ronald S. *Traditional Methods of Birth Control in Zaire*. Pathpapers Series Number 4. The Pathfinder Fund, December 1978.

Williams, Chancellor. *The Destruction of Black Civilization: Great Issues of a Race from 4500 B.C. to 2000 A.D.* Chicago: Third World Press, 1987.

Yoder, John Charles. *The Kanyok of Zaire: An Institutional and Ideological History to 1895*. New York: Cambridge University Press, 1992.

Young, Crawford. *Politics in the Congo*. Princeton, NJ: Princeton University Press, 1965.

Index

About the Author

TSHILEMALEMA MUKENGE is Professor in the Department of African Studies at Morris Brown College in Atlanta, Georgia. He has published a major study on religion and family of the Luba of the Congo and continues research and writing on control policies, small business enterprises, and survival strategies in Congolese cities. His ongoing research activities also include the study of African influences on Afro-Brazilian culture and history.